S0-AHY-713

Corner House Publishers

SOCIAL SCIENCE REPRINTS

General Editor MAURICE FILLER

THE WOMEN

OF THE

AMERICAN REVOLUTION.

BY ELIZABETH F. ELLET.

IN THREE VOLUMES.

VOL III.

CORNER HOUSE PUBLISHERS
WILLIAMSTOWN, MASSACHUSETTS 01267
1980

E
206
E45

v 3

Entered according to Act of Congress in the year 1850, by

BAKER AND SCRIBNER,

In the Clerk's Office of the District Court for the Southern District of
New York.

REPRINTED 1980

BY

CORNER HOUSE PUBLISHERS

ISBN 0–87928–108–1

Printed in the United States of America

PREFACE.

IT can hardly be necessary to apologize for the appearance of a third volume of this work, in view of the favor with which the first have been received, and the general interest manifested in the subject. The materials for these new memoirs are derived altogether from private sources. It will be seen that I have occasionally added to sketches of the women, notices of brave men nearly related to them, whose services deserved mention, with anecdotes illustrative of the war or the state of the country. This has been done only where no account of the individual or of the incident is given in any published work. Many among the actors in that momentous drama, whose deeds should have been recorded, are scarcely mentioned by name in historical books, and no full history has ever been written of some parts of the Confederacy. It seemed, therefore, a duty to rescue from oblivion well authenticated facts which were likely to be of value to the future historian. For example—the battle at Williamson's, S. C., has been commonly spoken of as

Holyoke Community College Library

the *first* after the calm which succeeded the fall of Charleston; whereas it was preceded by the attack on the British and loyalists at Beckhamville, and by that at Mobley's Meeting-house. Nor are any particulars given in history of the surprise of General Sumter on Fishing Creek.

One of the neglected portions of our country is the upper part of South Carolina, where the Revolutionary struggle was more painful and destructive, owing to the divisions among the inhabitants, than in any other section. Those who charged me with partiality to this State in the first volumes, will perhaps be startled to see so much of the present occupied with sketches of one of its districts; for my own part, I wish only that I could have obtained as efficient assistance in the illustration of other States.

Soon after the publication of the former volumes, I was advised by Hon. Judge O'Neall to apply to DANIEL GREEN STINSON, Esq., of Chester District, S. C. for information respecting the women of the Catawba region. The application proved a most fortunate one. This gentleman is of Revolutionary parentage, being the son of William Stinson— a brave soldier—the adopted son of Daniel Green, and the son-in-law of Joseph Gaston. Tales of the war were the amusement of his childhood; his early associations were with survivors of that period, and in youth he frequented places where they were accustomed to meet and talk over their battles and adventures. In later years the Revolutionary pensioners of the neighborhood came to him as the magistrate, to get their papers drawn up; this brought them every six months to his house, and he not only extended liberal hospitality to the more destitute, but when they were no longer able to come to him, visited them and did their writing without charge. The task, therefore, of recording "the praises of the neglected and forgotten brave," was to him one of peculiar interest, and with unwearied assiduity he collected reliable accounts from various sources, with manuscript records of the day—comparing them with care, visiting aged persons in his vicinity and writing to those at a distance—and sent me from time to time the results ot his patriotic labors. To his generous exertions I am in debted for the entire materials of the Southern sketches from 'Katharine Steel' to 'Jane White'—eleven in number—enabling me to present a graphic picture of the war in that region, and such a picture of the condition and feeling of those times of bloody contest between neighbors and acquaintances, as can be found in no historical work. I take this opportunity of tendering him my inadequate tribute of thanks for his invaluable aid.

I have found advantage in appealing to the recollections of individuals, for suggesting the names of women whose influence was most prevalent and enduring in the communities where they lived. Isolated instances of heroism, interesting in themselves, may be recorded in journals; but no pen has done justice to the memory of many who by the impression of mind and character have nobly served their age, and whose influence is still felt and acknowledged. In almost every part of the country mention is naturally made of women unknown to history, yet well remembered in popular tradition as having been prominent. These will usually be found to have been representatives of classes, and as such it becomes doubly important to preserve a faithful record of them. As Mercy Warren and the intellectual group around her illustrate the higher order of women in Massachusetts, and Mary Slocumb is a marked type of the spirited dames of North Carolina, so in Katharine Steel, Nancy Green, Sarah McCalla, Sarah Buchanan, and others, are embodied the spirit and experience of a large portion of country.

I ought perhaps to give a reason for the omission of some details furnished for the first volumes. Traditions, however entertaining, should have no place in an authentic record, if they are unsupported by indisputable testimony, or if they are at variance with history or probability. No small portion of my labor has been in sifting truth from error, and if the scrutiny may be thought too rigid, excluding what might fairly have been admitted, it is better to err on the safe side. " Truth," says a distinguished correspondent, " is so noble and persuasive a quality in historical compositions, that no pains should be spared to preserve it from the least shadow or tint, which can impair its dignity or tarnish its beauty." In some cases contradictory statements were received from different sources, and the most cautious investigations were necessary to ascertain on which side lay the truth. Sometimes the total demolition of a pleasing story upon examination of authorities, gave warning to be distrustful. The following extract from a New Haven letter shows a case in point:

"I had heard, indeed, that Madam Wooster and Mrs Roger Sherman gave the Connecticut troops the first national flag ever used in this State, which flag was composed of their own sundry and several articles of dress; but I am sorry to say the story, though 'founded on fact,' was foundered by the facts which my learned researches brought to light. That they made a flag is certain, but it could not have been the first one; nor did they heroically rob their own persons to furnish it. I can assure you I was greatly disappointed, and almost resolved not to pry too curiously into the truth of interesting statements for the future. There would have been something so complimentary to your sex in the fact that the heroes of the Revolution placed themselves under 'petticoat government,' immediately after throwing off the English yoke, that I was unwilling to admit the evidence which overthrew the current tradition."

The fact, however, is established, that the two ladies above mentioned *did* make the flag displayed on occasion of the public rejoicing for the peace in New Haven.

" On learning this fact," says my correspondent, " I turned to President Stiles' Literary Diary, which is in manuscript, and fills between twenty and thirty volumes, confident that I should find something in relation to the matter. On turning to the proper date, the first thing which met my eye was a picture of the flag in the Doctor's best style of drawing, with the following description :—

" ' At sunrise the Continental flag displayed, being a grand silk flag presented by the ladies—cost one hundred and twenty dollars—the stripes red and white, with an azure field in the upper part, charged with thirteen stars. On the same field, and among the stars, were the arms of the United States, the field of which contained a ship and plough, and three sheaves of wheat; the crest, an eagle volant ; the supporters, two white horses. The arms were put on with paint and gilding. When displayed, it appeared well.'

" There is a tradition that this flag displayed at first, in all the pride of paint and gilding, the arms of Pennsylvania. A mistake which arose very naturally; as the ladies, turning in unsuspecting confidence to the Family Bible, which happened to be a Philadelphia edition, copied the arms from the title-page. The mistake was rectified, it is said, when Roger Sherman returned from Congress."

It may be proper to take this opportunity of answering one or two objections urged by persons whose opinions should command respect. One who has done much to illustrate American history, says : " Mrs. Slocumb could scarcely have said that Tarleton knew La Fayette was in North Carolina, since he did not go south of Virginia." To this it may be answered—the reply to Tarleton's inquiry if any part of the American army was in the neighborhood, in which Mrs. Slocumb gave the intimation, was plainly intended to mislead and alarm him ; her husband's life, as she well knew, depending on his conviction that the whigs who figured in the skirmish in the woods, were supported by a formidable force. It might thus happen that her language, designed to imply a sense of security on her part, and a warning of danger to the enemy, should express more than the facts warranted. The account of the incident was copied from notes taken of the matron's own narrative, by her friend and family physician.

In regard to Mrs. Motte, of South Carolina, the family tradition preserved among her descendants, contradicts the account of Lee, who states that a bow and arrows of inferior quality were provided for the purpose of conveying fire to the roof of the house, when she produced hers as better adapted for the purpose. Mrs. Motte, it is said, first suggested the idea of using a bow and arrows, when she presented hers to the American officer. Lee wrote much from memory, and it is very possible that he may have neglected to do justice to our noble-spirited heroine by giving due credit to her for the suggestion.

A British critic has charged me with having mentioned instances of cruelty among the royalists, without due notice of the forbearance and clemency frequently exercised. I am aware that it is difficult to avoid apparent partiality in narrating incidents received from descendants of the patriots, who, even if uninfluenced by any remains of political animosity, would naturally remember the noble acts and the sufferings of their ancestors, while forgetful of the provocations given, or the injuries inflicted, by individuals of their party. It must be confessed, too, that the very boldness of many among the women who took an active part, and the impunity with which they indulged in severe speeches to the royal officers, form a strong argument to show the humanity and respect with which they were generally treated. So far am I from being unwilling to do full justice to the other side, that I only regret my inability, from want of details promised, but not yet received, to portray in this volume as in the preceding ones, the devotion, self-sacrificing zeal, and courageous enterprize in the cause of the destitute and suffering, by which loyalist women softened the grim features of war, and lighted a period of darkness and distress.

E. F. E.

CONTENTS OF VOLUME III.

		PAGE
I.	ANNIS STOCKTON,	13
II.	LUCY KNOX,	35
III.	MARGARET WHETTEN,	52
	MRS. TODD,	63
IV.	BLANDINA BRUYN,	68
V.	ANNE FITZHUGH,	76
VI.	KATHARINE STEEL,	83
	MRS. BEARD,	87
	BARBARA McKENNY,	89
VII.	NANCY GREEN,	117
	MRS. MOTTE,	149
VIII.	ESTHER WALKER,	155
	MRS. GASTON,	162
IX.	MARY McCLURE,	175
	JANE MORROW,	195
X.	ISABELLA FERGUSON,	198
XI.	MARY JOHNSTON,	206
XII.	JANE BOYD,	216
	MRS. SIMPSON,	217

		PAGE
XIII.	Jane Gaston,	224
	Mrs. Strong,	226
	Margaret Elliot,	227
	Mrs. Haynes,	228
XIV.	Sarah McCalla,	239
	Mary Adair,	270
	Mary Nixon,	273
XV.	Mary Mills,	276
	Isabella Wylie,	284
XVI.	Jane White,	290
XVII.	Rebecca Pickens,	303
XVIII.	Sarah Buchanan,	310
XIX.	Nancy Van Alstine,	328
XX.	Eleanor Wilson,	347
XXI.	Margaret Moncrieffe,	357
XXII.	Mary Murray,	374
	Anecdotes,	376
	Mrs. Woodhull,	377
	Mrs. Smith,	378
	Mrs. Rapalje,	379
	Mary Knight,	382
	Mrs. Osborn,	383
	Miss Susan Livingston,	383
	Lady Stirling,	384
	Experience Bozarth,	385
	Elizabeth Ferguson,	386
	Letter of Mercy Warren,	387
	Appendix—Surprise of General Sumter,	390

WOMEN OF THE REVOLUTION.

I.

~~~~~~~~~~~~~~~~

ANNIS STOCKTON.

MRS. STOCKTON is entitled to a prominent place among the women who lived at the period of the Revolution, as the wife of one of the signers of the Declaration of Independence, and the mother-in-law of another. Her life, passed in the quiet of the domestic circle, and varied by few incidents, affords little material for the biographer, but the elevated character and superior endowments which adorned her high position gave her an extended influence, and renders her an interesting subject of notice. Her maiden name was Annis Boudinot. She was descended of a French family, her great-grandfather, Elias Boudinot, being a French Protestant who fled from his country after the revocation of the Edict of Nantes. The late Elias Boudinot, of Burlington, New Jersey, was her brother. The precise date of her birth cannot be ascertained, but it must have been some time in 1733.

From the period of her marriage she resided at Mr. Stockton's seat near Princeton. When he visited England in 1766, she refused to go with him, being unwilling to leave her children. He says in one of his unpublished letters—"I can never forget your refusing to accompany me in the various scenes of this delightful excursion, on their account. The answer you made me when I pressed you for your consent to go with me, still vibrates on my ear; that you could not see your way clear, nor think it your duty to go, as you had no particular call of Providence to venture both their parents in one bottom."

While she remained at home, occupied with maternal duties, her husband in his letters described what he saw and heard, his heart ever turning to her with an affection which seemed to "drag, at each remove, a lengthening chain"—and fondly looking forward to the hour of their reunion. These letters were copied by her in a manuscript volume for her daughter. They exhibit the writer in a very amiable light, as the tenderest of husbands and fathers, and indirectly throw light upon the character of her to whom he was so devotedly attached. In one, dated London, August 7th 1766, he writes—"Notwithstanding the great variety of amusing scenes in this country, I already feel that I shall be impatient for the time to arrive, when my business shall be done, and I again find myself within those delightful walls, where the voice of my dearest Emilia and her sweet babes, gives me the greatest earthly happiness."

Again, in November, he says: " Had you received a letter I wrote you from Dublin, and the one I wrote upon my return here, you would have laughed at those idle people at Philadelphia, who would persuade you that I would prefer the elegance of England to the sylvan shades of America. No! my dearest Emilia, the peaceful retreat which God has blessed me with at Princeton, you, and the sweet children you have brought me, are the sources from which I receive my highest earthly joys; joys which I prefer to the state of a prime minister, or a king upon the throne. I am entertained with the grandeur and variety of these kingdoms, as you wish me to be, and as you know I am curious, new objects are continually striking my attention and engaging my fancy; but

'One thought of *thee* puts all the pomp to flight,
Priests, tapers, temples, swim before my sight.' "

When the storm of civil war burst on the country, Richard Stockton had his full share of the peril, as well as the honor, awaiting those eminent men who had affixed their names to the Declaration. His beautiful residence at Princeton was directly in the route of the British army, on its triumphant march through New Jersey. Warned of the approach of the victorious invaders, he had barely time to remove his wife and family to a place of safety. His eldest son, Richard, then a boy twelve years of age, with an old family servant, remained in the house, while everything was left to the mercy of the enemy. The house was pillaged, the horses and stock were driven away, and the estate was laid waste. The furniture was converted into fire-wood ; the old wine, stored in the cellar, was drunk up, and the valuable library, with all the papers of Mr. Stockton, committed to the flames. The house became for some time the headquarters of the British general. The plate and other valuable articles belonging to the family had been packed in three boxes and buried in the woods, at some distance from the mansion. Through treachery—it is said— the place of concealment was discovered by the soldiers, and two of the boxes were disinterred and rifled of their rich contents. The remaining one escaped their search and was restored to the family. The daughter of Mrs. Stockton residing in Princeton, has in her possession several pieces of silver that were in this box, and are now, of course, highly valued. She has also two portraits—one of Mr. Stockton and the other of his wife, which were in the house when occupied by the British, and found among some rubbish after their departure. Both were pierced through with bayonets. Some years since, they were entirely restored by the modern process, and now occupy their honored place in Mrs. Field's house. The portrait of Mr. Stockton is a very fine one, and understood to have been painted by Copley.

When Mrs. Stockton heard of the destruction of her noble library, she is said to have remarked that there were two books in it which she particularly valued— the Bible and Young's Night Thoughts, and that if these had escaped the burning she would not grieve for the loss of the rest. Tradition relates that when she returned to her desolated house, those very books were the only ones left.

Mr. Stockton sought refuge for his family at the house of an old friend in the county of Monmouth. His retreat, however, was soon discovered by a party of refugee loyalists, who came at night, forcibly entered the house, and dragged him from his bed. Loading him with indignities, they hurried him to Amboy, and thence to New York, where he was thrown into a common gaol, and treated with the utmost barbarity. The sufferings, meanwhile, of his affectionate wife, unable to alleviate his distresses, were even more poignant than his own. Through the interposition of Congress he was at length released; but exposure to the rigorous weather, and inhuman treatment, had laid the foundation of disease from which he never recovered. It was now the part of her who had shared his brighter fortunes to cheer his declining days—under the embarrassments, too, of diminished resources—by her tenderness and devotion.

Mr. Stockton unconsciously portrays a most charming character in those passages of his letters that refer to his wife. Having been written without a thought that they would ever meet any other eye than hers, their testimony is the sincere voice of the heart. He calls her "one of the best of women," and his entire confidence in her is shown by laying open all his thoughts, purposes, and plans. Even his letters on business and public affairs he wishes seen by her. He writes: "I have left my letters to the Governor open, that you may see their contents. As soon as you peruse them, enclose the gazettes, seal the packet, and send them on immediately; don't let them lie by you an hour if you can help it." And on the 31st October, 1766 : " Let me tell you that all the grandeur and elegance that I have yet seen in these kingdoms, in different families where I have been received with great politeness, serves but to increase the pleasure I have for some years enjoyed in your society. I see not a sensible, obliging, tender wife, but the image of my dear Emilia is full in view. I see not a haughty, imperious dame, but I rejoice that the partner of my life is so much the opposite. But why need I talk so gallantly? You know my ideas long ago, as well as you would were I to write a volume upon this endearing topic."   *   *   " Kiss my dear, sweet children for me, and give rather the hardest squeeze to my only son, if you think it is right; if not, divide it equally without any partiality, but tell Dick I will bring him a laced hat, which seems to be his passion, and the little girls something pretty." It will be observed that the writer always gives his wife her favorite poetical name of Emilia. She called him her " Lucius."

Some further extracts from these letters may not be uninteresting. He asks—" Well, how does the farm go on—and how do your servants behave themselves? but the most important question is—how are *you* and the dear children? How is my dearest Dick? But lest you should again charge me with partiality, how is my sweetest Julia, Sukey, and Polly? Now the account is balanced. If it was not malapropos after writing about my little brats thus, I would tell you something about ministers of state; but though I know your children are by far the most pleasing theme to you, I will tell you that the great Commoner is degraded by a peerage, and has the title of Earl of Chatham. The people here are extremely disgusted with him for accepting it, and I know they will not like it better in America."*—"What abundant reason have I to bless God for his gracious protection through all the dangers I have passed, and for that great and uncommon degree of health which I now enjoy! Wherein my unthankful heart fails, my dear Emilia I know will not fail." * * "A few days ago I was introduced to General Conway, one of the Secretaries of State. He received me very politely, and asked me many important questions about America. I am happy that I have had nothing to ask of government, and, therefore, dare speak my sentiments without cringing. Wherever I can serve my native country, I leave no occasion untried. Dear America—thou sweet retreat from greatness and corruption! in thee I choose to live and die."

Another passage shows his attention to her commissions in the midst of business matters. "Your gown is at the dyers, but as it cannot be dyed without water-

* MS. Letter, August 7th, 1766.

ing, the ladies have persuaded me that a green will look badly watered, and therefore I have taken upon me to order it a pompadour, which pleases me and I hope will please you. I have bought Mrs. Franklin's and your table linen and sheeting in Ireland, and you may depend on my endeavoring to fulfil all your memorandums."

Mrs. Stockton's enthusiastic love of flowers is frequently alluded to by her husband. He writes from Westminster in the ensuing January : " I am making you a charming collection of bulbous roots, which shall be sent as soon as the prospect of freezing on your coast is over. The first of April, I believe, will be time enough for you to put them in your sweet little flower-garden, which you so fondly cultivate. Suppose, in the next place, I inform you that I design a ride to Twickenham the latter end of next month, principally to view Mr. Pope's gardens and grotto, which, I am told, remain nearly as he left them, and that I shall take with me a gentleman who draws well, to lay down an exact plan of the whole. In this I shall take great pleasure, because I know how it will please you. England is not the place for curious shells, therefore you must not expect much by me in that way ; but I shall bring you a piece of Roman brick, which I knocked off the top of Dover Castle, which is said to have been built before the birth of Christ. I have also got for your collection a piece of wood which I cut off the effigy of Archbishop Peckham, buried in the Cathedral of Canterbury more than five hundred years ago; likewise a piece from the king's coronation chair, and several other things of the same kind, which, merely as antiquities, may deserve a place in *your* grotto. Again, if I tell you that I go about once a week to the theatrical entertainments of Covent-Garden and Drury-Lane, you will suppose me sufficiently diverted in that way." * * "Last Wednesday, the merchants trading to North America had a general meeting with respect to the paper currency—which I have been dinning in their ears for six weeks past—when they sent for Dr. Franklin and me, for a full information respecting that important point, and I flatter myself, that they have got so engaged in the matter, from the prospect of losing their own debts, that they will make an united application to Parliament for the repeal of the late act prohibiting future emissions in America. They have appointed a committee of thirty-two merchants to meet next Wednesday, when Dr. Franklin and I are again desired to attend, and for my own part I shall not fail to exert every nerve in a matter which I deem of such mighty importance to my own country."

In the same letter is related his introduction to the Marquis of Rockingham. Announcing his intention to go to Scotland for the purpose of inducing Dr. Witherspoon to accept the Presidency of the College of New Jersey, he writes, Feb. 9th, 1767: "I purpose to keep an exact and circumstantial account of my tour to Scotland, which will be a second volume for your perusal. The first will contain the most interesting things I have viewed in this part of Britain and Ireland. I have taken this pains to refresh my own memory when I shall have to satisfy your inquiring mind respecting everything I have seen or heard; for I know you will not be put off with superficial answers. Public affairs here are but in a bad way; the people still continue to abuse Lord Chatham, and he seems desirous to keep from the scene of action, and therefore is nursing the gout at Bath. His enemies say it is only a political gout, which attacks him at his own command. Mr. Grenville and his party cannot brook the repeal of the Stamp Act, and cannot keep from venting their rancor against America in the House of Commons upon every occasion. Mr. Charles Townsend, the Chancellor of the Exchequer, informed the House last week, that he was preparing a scheme to lay before them for raising money from the Colonies, urged the necessity of sending more troops there, and the propriety and justice of their supporting them. *I exceedingly fear that we shall get together by the ears, and God only knows what is to be the issue!*"

Notices of political matters are thus mingled with references to his wife's delicate taste for flowers and shell-work, as if he knew she took an interest in the former subject for his sake, as he in the latter for hers. In a letter dated Feb. 2d, he says, " I send you herewith a little box of flower-seeds, and the roots that will do at this season. They are the best

collection I could procure, and I have been very much
provoked at the seedsman I employed, who disappointed me in the fall, because he said his best had
not arrived from Holland, and now assures me that
nothing but anemonies and ranunculus will do to
move, as the others are all in the ground, and would
perish if they should be taken up and sent over the
sea. I hope these, which are the best of their kind,
will please you for the present; but I really believe
you have as fine tulips and hyacinths in your little
garden, as almost any in England ; yet I shall order
some of the finest to be sent next July, so as to be
set out in the fall. The sensitive plant is a great
curiosity ; it will stir upon touching as if it was possessed of animal life. You had best sow the seeds in
distinct beds. Some seeds which I know you have I
send, because the seedsman says they are of very
various and beautiful colors.

" I have dined with Mr. Neat several times. Miss
Neat is exceedingly obliged for the shells you sent
her. She has made some curious flowers out of them.
She and her mamma are both engaged to find out for
me the best cement for sticking shells in the large
way, which I know will be needful for you when
you begin your grotto. You see I do not omit attending to your commands. I told you in my last that I
intended a visit to Twickenham, to see Mr. Pope's
house, gardens, and grotto, for your direction. This I
shall execute if it please God. Your friend, Lord
Adam Gordon, only returned from Scotland a few

weeks ago. He was so obliging as to call immediately at my lodgings, and sent me an invitation
to dine with him a few days after. He inquired very
particularly after you and your dear little boy. A
few days ago I had the last meeting with the merchants, &c." * * "Your verses directed to me,
gave me great pleasure. They are elegant, and exceedingly amuse me ; your impromptu epitaph upon
the old deacon, as he used to call himself, instead of
sexton, is so good of its kind, that I think you may
now venture to write one upon a bishop. If I could
be vexed with you I would, for your apologising for
your writing so much about your children and domestic matters. These are the subjects that most
delight me, and the length of your letters gives them
the highest relish." * * " I must tell you now
that I was so much the man of fashion as to go to
court the Queen's birth-night. The assembly which
attended the ball in the evening was the most brilliant which has ever appeared on the like occasion, it
is said. The Duke of York and the Princess of Bruns-
wick opened the ball with a minuet. The Duke of
Gloucester and the Princess Louisa succeeded to
them ; the Duke of Cumberland and the Duchess
of Bolton, (the lady who was to have married the
late General Wolf;) the nobility and gentry then followed in order as their names were down. The affability of the King and Queen, in talking to every
gentleman and lady within their reach, the magnifi-
cence of the foreign ambassadors and their ladies, and

the dress of the English nobility and gentry who attended, were all very entertaining. Here I saw all your Duchesses of Ancaster, Hamilton, etc., so famous for their beauty. But here I have done with this subject, for I had rather ramble with you along the rivulets of Morven or Redhill, and see the rural sports of the chaste little frogs, than again be at a birth-night ball." It is pleasant to notice the serenity of mind, and enjoyment of all things surrounding him, evinced in these letters, in contrast with the trials of his later years.

Mrs. Stockton was a woman of highly cultivated mind and refined literary taste. She wrote with great facility, and there is reason to believe that she possessed no ordinary poetical talents. She left a large collection of poems, many of which are said by those who have been permitted to read the manuscripts, to have considerable merit. But her country had no opportunity of enrolling her name among its distinguished female poets ; for she seems to have had a morbid aversion to the idea of publishing the effusions of her fancy. Her youngest daughter received the volume into which she had copied her poems, with the strictest injunction that its contents should never be given to the world. This resolution could have been owing to no lack of praise, for her friends often allude to her poetry with much admiration. Mrs Ferguson, in a manuscript volume of poems extant, refers to her in some lines beginning—

" Here flow the good Emilia's strains
    In Morven's rural bowers ;"

and in an explanatory note speaks of her as the writer
of many very pleasing verses appearing under the
signature of Emilia, and of some beautiful pastoral
dialogues illustrating the progress of the war. Her
husband writes in one of his letters from London :
" If, after this reaches you, there be time to send me
the piece you wrote on the erection of the college,
and two or three of those other pieces which you
know I most admired, I will thank you for them. I
fully intended bringing them with me, but they were
forgotten. I shall like much to have them to spell
over for my amusement on my passage home."

Among her poetical epistles is one addressed to Col.
Schuyler upon his return to New Jersey after a two
years' captivity in Canada ; another poem celebrates
the death of Gen. Warren at Bunker Hill, and another was written after the fall of Gen. Montgomery.
The deeds of Washington also inspired her pen. She
sent him an address after the battles of Trenton and
Princeton, and a pastoral celebrating the surrender of
Lord Cornwallis and the British army. How highly
Washington estimated the merit of these complimentary effusions, and how much pleasure the perusal
afforded him, may be seen from his letters of acknowledgment. His playful manner of disclaiming her
praise, and replying to her pleasant fancies, exhibits
the Father of his country in a new light, and as the

letters have never been published, I insert them as literary curiosities:

"*Philadelphia, July* 22, 1782.

"MADAM—Your favor of the 17th, conveying to me your Pastoral on the subject of Lord Cornwallis's capture, has given me great satisfaction. Had you known the pleasure it would have communicated, I flatter myself your diffidence would not have delayed it to this time.

"Amidst all the compliments which have been made on this occasion, be assured, Madam, that the agreeable manner, and the very pleasing sentiments in which yours is conveyed, have affected my mind with the most lively sensations of joy and satisfaction.

"This address from a person of your refined taste and elegance of expression, affords a pleasure beyond my powers of utterance, and I have only to lament that the hero of your pastoral is not more deserving of your pen; but the circumstance shall be placed among the happiest events of my life.

"I have the honor to be, Madam,
"Your most obedient and respectful servant,
"G. WASHINGTON.
"Mrs. Stockton."

"*Rocky Hill, Sept.* 2, 1783.

"You apply to me, my dear Madam, for absolution, as though I was your father confessor, and as though you had committed a crime, great in itself, yet of the venial class. You have reason good; for I find myself strangely disposed to be a very indulgent ghostly adviser on this occasion, and notwithstanding 'you are the most offending soul alive,' (that is, if it is a crime to write elegant poetry,) yet, if you will come and dine with me on Thursday, and go through the proper course of penitence which shall be prescribed, I will strive hard to assist you in expiating these poetical trespasses on this side of purgatory. Nay more, if it rests with me to direct your future lucubrations, I shall certainly urge you to a repetition of the same conduct, on purpose to show what an admirable knack you have at confession and reformation; and so, without more hesitation, I shall venture to recommend the muse not to be restrained by ill-grounded timidity, but to go on and prosper.

"You see, Madam, when once the woman has tempted us, and we have tasted the forbidden fruit, there is no such thing as checking our appetite, whatever the consequences may be. You will, I dare say, recognize our being the genuine descendants of those who are reported to be our great progenitors.

"Before I come to the more serious conclusion of my letter, I must beg leave to say a word or two about these fine things you have been telling in such harmonious and beautiful numbers. Fiction is, to be sure, the very life and soul of poetry. All poets and poetesses have been indulged in the free and indisputable use of it, time out of mind; and to oblige

you to make such an excellent poem, on such a subject, without any materials but those of simple reality, would be as cruel as the edict of Pharoah,
which compelled the children of Israel to manufacture
bricks without the necessary ingredients.

"Thus are you sheltered under the authority of
prescription; and I will not dare to charge you with
an intentional breach of the rules of the Decalogue in
giving so bright a coloring to the services I have been
enabled to render my country, though I am not conscious of deserving anything more at your hands than
what the purest and most disinterested friendship has
a right to claim; actuated by which, you will permit
me to thank you in the most affectionate manner, for
the kind wishes you have so happily expressed for me
and the partner of all my domestic enjoyments. Be
assured, we can never forget our friend at Morven,
and that I am, my dear Madam, with every sentiment
of friendship and esteem,

"Your most obedient and obliged servant,

"G. WASHINGTON.

"Mrs. Stockton."

Some months afterwards, in acknowledging a pastoral on Peace, General Washington writes: "It
would be a pity, indeed, my dear Madam, if the muses
should be restrained in you; it is only to be regretted
that the hero of your poetical talents is not more deserving their lays. I cannot, however, from motives
of false delicacy, (because I happen to be the principal

character in your Pastoral,) withhold my encomium on the performance. For I think the easy, simple, and beautiful strains with which the dialogue is supported, do great justice to your genius, and will not only secure Lucinda and Aminta from wits and critics, but draw from them, however unwillingly, their highest plaudits, if they can relish the praises that are given as highly·as they must admire the manner of bestowing them."

Mr. Stockton did not live to see the independence for which he had done and suffered so much, finally established. The commencement of the disease which terminated his life, was in an affection of his lip. He carefully concealed his sufferings from his wife for some time ; but early in December, 1778, wrote to her from Philadelphia that he had submitted to an operation, from which he hoped relief. Mrs. Stockton received this letter about eight o'clock in the evening, and was so affected with its contents that by the dawn of day she was several miles on her way to Philadelphia. Her husband's surprise to see her appeared to agitate him more than the operation had done. She gives account of this illness in some notes written for her daughter Abby.

"Your dear father rode on a very cold and windy day to Somerset Court. When he returned I observed that his lip was cracked just at the parting, it was so much chapped. The winter was cold, and he went a good deal out, and it did not speedily get well. He seemed a little alarmed at it, and would frequently mention it to me, but I persuaded him not to think of it, as I was assured it would get well as soon as the weather became warm. But very early one morning, he got up and told me not to expect him to breakfast, as he intended riding out a few miles on some business he had with a gentleman in the neighborhood. On his way he met Dr. Jones in the road, going to New York, and as he was uneasy that his lip did not heal, he stopped him and desired he would look at it. He told him that he did not think it was much, but he might send for him at Dr. Rush's, on his way to Gloucester Court, which was to be the next week, and he would advise him what to do. What was done, the foregoing letter informs you. But the sequel was this fatal stroke to me. Dr. Jones put him upon so strict a regimen in order to heal his lip after so large a piece was cut out, that Dr. Rush frequently remonstrated with him, and told me the consequence of so total a change in the diet of a person of fifty years of age who had lived well; that it would probably produce a scrofulous tumor in his neck that might be more dangerous than his lip would ever have been. You may readily suppose with what energy I strove to persuade your dear father to listen to Dr. Rush's advice, take a little wine in his water, and alter the general abstemiousness of his living. But all was in vain, Dr. Jones being accounted the best surgeon on the continent.

" For near six weeks he observed the same strictness in his diet, when, soon after, the prediction of Dr.

Rush was verified by the appearance of a tumor about
the size of a marble. Many gentlemen of the faculty
said if he would suffer them to make an incision
across the skin it would turn out; but he declined it,
and wrote to Dr. Jones, who was up the North River,
describing it to him. He returned for answer that
it was only a kernel occasioned by the healing of
the lip, and would disappear of itself, but that he
should return to Philadelphia in a month and would
call on him. It was three months before he returned,
and all that time the tumor was growing at an ama-
zing rate, which obliged your papa to go to Philadelphia and have another operation performed by Dr.
Bond. But it was too late. It had fixed itself on the
main artery and could not possibly be all extracted.
As soon as the wound would heal so that you might
cover the orifice with your finger, the acrimonious
matter at the bottom would cause the edge to grow
hard, and it would break down again to the same
size it was when first cut."

The cancer could not be extirpated, and the patient's
lingering sufferings were so great that he could not
enjoy the smallest repose but by the help of anodynes.
He died at Morven, his residence in Princeton, Feb.
28th, 1781. The subject of the funeral discourse by
the Rev. Dr. Smith, was selected by the afflicted
widow; "I have seen an end of all perfection;
but thy commandment is exceeding broad." "A
subject," said the preacher, "that hath been familiar
to her thoughts, during this long and painful illness,

which she hath nursed and alleviated with an assiduity and tenderness which is truly a model of conjugal affection." She looked on this calamity with a mind enlightened by religion. A few impromptu verses she wrote while watching one anxious night, though they cannot be given as a specimen of her poetic abilities, will be felt by all who have known the bitter anguish of watching the slow decline of a beloved friend.

Sleep, balmy sleep, has closed the eyes of all
    But me—ah me! no respite can I gain;
Though darkness reigns o'er this terrestrial ball,
    Not one soft slumber cheats this vital pain.

All day in secret sighs I've poured my soul;
    My downy pillow, used to scenes of grief,
Beholds me now in floods of sorrow roll,
    Without the power to yield his pains relief;

While through the silence of this gloomy night
    My aching heart reverb'rates every groan,
And watching by that glimmering taper's light,
    I make each sigh, each mortal pang my own.

But why should I implore sleep's friendly aid?
    O'er me her poppies shed no ease impart;
But dreams of dear *departing joys* invade,
    And rack with fears my sad prophetic heart.

Oh! could I take the fate to him assigned,
    And leave the helpless family their head!
How pleased, how peaceful to my lot resigned,
    I'd quit the nurse's station for the bed!

Oh death! thou canker worm of human joy!
    Thou cruel foe to sweet domestic peace,

2*

HE soon shall come, who shall thy shafts destroy,
And cause thy dreadful ravages to cease.

Yes, the Redeemer comes to wipe the tears,
The briny tears from every weeping eye,
And death, and sin, and doubts, and gloomy fears
Shall all be lost in endless victory.

It was Mrs. Stockton's custom to write annually an elegiac poem on the death of her husband, whom she survived many years. For some time before her death she resided at Whitehill, in Burlington County, the residence of Robert Field, who had married her youngest daughter, Abby. Here she died February 6th, 1801. Her closing days were calm and peaceful, and she met the approach of death with Christian faith and joy. Just before she breathed her last, she repeated in a clear, firm voice the psalm of Watts beginning,

"Lord, I am thine; but thou wilt prove etc."

She left two sons—Richard and Lucius Horatio—who became eminent in the profession of the law. Of her four daughters, Julia married Dr. Benjamin Rush, and lived to an advanced age; Susan was married to Alexander Cuthbert, of Canada, and Mary, to the Rev. Dr. Andrew Hunter.

II.

LUCY KNOX.

In preparing the brief notice of Mrs. Knox contained in Volume First, I was not so fortunate as to receive information from any of her surviving relatives. The account gathered from tradition was felt to be an inadequate tribute to one so high in station and character. I have since been favored by her daughter with one more satisfactory. In offering this to the reader, I shall endeavor to avoid repeating what has been already recorded.

Lucy Flucker was the daughter of Thomas Flucker, Secretary of the Province of Massachusetts under the royal government. Her first acquaintance with him who was afterwards her husband, and their courtship, had not a little of romance, and has lately formed the groundwork of a newspaper tale published in Boston, the heroine being represented as the daughter of a baronet, while the name of Henry Knox is given to the hero. It is not to be questioned that there existed such a difference, in point of station, between the young people, as rendered the idea of their marriage a wild vision. The social position of Lucy's father, who had long been high in office, was an elevated one; his family was prominent among the aristocracy of the land, at a time when distinctions in society were strongly marked, and clung to as a test of loyalty to the government. The idea that a daughter of this family should favor the pretensions of one inferior to her, was not to be tolerated; still less that she should look upon a lover branded with the name of " rebel." Henry Knox moved in a sphere comparatively humble. Bereaved of his father while yet a boy, his energies had early been called into action by the pressure of necessity; he labored to supply the wants of an excellent mother, to whom he was devoted, and a young brother, to whom he supplied the place of a father as long as life continued. At this period he kept one of the few large book-stores of which Boston could boast. Miss Flucker was a young lady of literary taste, and it was natural that she should frequently visit the book-store, where she was not long in discovering that the fine figure she had so much admired in military costume, was not the only or chief recommendation to her favor possessed by young Knox. His well-stored and intelligent mind, his warm heart and engaging manners, were soon appreciated by her, and the favorable impression produced by his captivating exterior was confirmed and strengthened. She found, too, that his views and feelings on most subjects coincided with her own. Education and associations had established some points of difference; but the bonds of sympathy between them were strong, for nature had created them. On the great and absorbing question which then agitated the public mind, and in which every member of the community felt a deep interest, the two between whom the sentiment of regard was fast ripening into love, soon learned to think and feel alike. It is fair to suppose that the opinions of the young officer influenced those of the maiden at least so far as to induce a candid examination into the merits of the question,—the result of which was, that with all the ardor of her enthusiastic nature, she espoused the cause of her oppressed country, and thenceforward identified herself with all its interests.

The change could not remain unknown to the parents and friends of our heroine, who grieved sincerely over what they termed her "apostacy," and used both arguments and entreaties to dissuade her from a course which they believed must be destructive to all her worldly prospects. They had earnestly desired that she would favor the addresses of a British officer named George, whose attentions had been assiduous, and whom they regarded as a suitor far more worthy of her choice. With the most flattering prospects, and the certainty of pleasing all her relatives on the one hand, Lucy saw on the other a lot of obscurity, perhaps of poverty, with separation from all her youthful heart held dear. The storm was gathering darkly in the political horizon; the time had arrived when her decision was to be made, and she cast her all upon the die that was to decide the nation's fate. Her father believed she had consigned herself to an unworthy

destiny, and predicted that she would suffer in the
troubles that were to come, while her sisters were
enjoying the luxury and station she had unwisely
renounced.   How dimly did they discern the future!
The proud loyalists who had borne honors conferred by
the British government, were compelled to fly from
their country, forfeiting the wealth they deemed secure,
or inadequately compensated for the sacrifice after
long delay : the poor and self-denying patriots, who
gave up affluence and ease for their country's sake,
stand eminent in the light of her triumph, crowned
with undying fame!

The separation from her nearest and dearest relatives involved in the choice of Mrs. Knox, caused her
intense grief and a severe struggle, but the path of
duty was plain before her, and she bore the trial with
firmness, indulging the hope that when the unhappy
contest was over, they would again be united.   Mr.
Flucker decided to remove with his family from the
country, until what he deemed a hopeless rebellion
should be crushed.   The duties of Gen. Knox keeping him near the Commander-in-chief, his wife was
much in the society of Mrs. Washington.   She was
even more constantly in camp with the army, and
always located as near as possible to the scene of
action, that she might receive the earliest intelligence,
and be at hand should any accident render her presence necessary.   This was undoubtedly the most-
anxious and eventful period of her life.   An ever-
varying scene was it truly, of trouble and triumph,

disaster and rejoicing; many were its privations and trials, yet a certain wild pleasure was not wanting in the changeful camp life, when the mental faculties were kept in full play, and expectation was continually excited as to what the morrow, or the succeeding hour, would bring forth. Mrs. Knox often remarked that she *lived* more in one year at this period of intense excitement, than in a dozen of ordinary life. Painful and trying as were many scenes through which patriotic wives were called to pass, there were times when a brief repose was granted from the toils and terrors of grim war, and care was cast aside for the moment. General and Mrs. Knox were both of a sanguine and cheerful temperament, and felt strong confidence that all would eventually be well. The beneficial influence of Mrs. Knox in the camp, the deference shown to her superiority of intellect, and the courage, faith, and self-devotion with which she encountered hardships and perils, have been already mentioned. During the siege of Yorktown, she remained with Mrs. Washington at Mount Vernon, having with her her eldest son, then an infant. Often in after years did she describe to her children the agitating suspense of that momentous period, the alternations of hope and fear they experienced, and the trembling that seized them on the arrival of the daily express. In the deep anguish Mrs. Washington was called to bear while the joy and gratitude of millions proclaimed her husband the savior of his country, she had the affectionate sympathy of her friend—

fated to have her own heart wrung too often by similar afflictions.

After the establishment of peace, General and Mrs. Knox returned to Boston, the place of their nativity, and so long their beloved home. Of this return she was accustomed to speak as one of the most painfully interesting periods of her life. The changes produced by the lapse of a few years were striking indeed ; the whole aspect of society was altered, and while the outward appearance of the city was the same, few improvements having been made, the friends of their youth, with a few scattered exceptions, had given place to strangers, in whom they could feel no interest. The melancholy change brought to mind the truth expressed by the poet—

"Our very wishes give us not our wish."

But grateful for the happy termination of the contest, they had no disposition to indulge in useless regrets. Among those whom the events of the Revolution had brought forward in society, they found many agreeable acquaintances, and some worthy of esteem and affection. A remark made by a cousin of Mrs. Knox—a single lady, whose pride of family had survived the shock of a change of government, and who could not be persuaded to associate with those she regarded as the parvenues of the day—that "the scum had all risen to the top," is illustrative of the feeling prevalent among many who were loth to become republicans in practice. Mrs. Knox was little influenced by this feeling; perhaps her connection with one who owed his elevation to merit rather than birth, was sufficient to convince her of the real superiority of nature's nobility to that conferred by accident or fortune. She became much attached to some of her new Boston acquaintances, and parted from them with regret when, after a year of comparative quiet, her husband was again summoned to active duties, and took charge of the war department under the old confederation. On their removal to New York, then the seat of government, they found the community disposed to welcome the commencement of a new era with festivity. The sympathy of Mrs. Knox with the general confidence and joy was enhanced by a personal feeling. Her intimacy with Mrs. Washington, to whom she had become warmly attached during her visit at Mount Vernon, was renewed, and as they occupied adjacent houses in Broadway, constant opportunities occurred of enjoying the society so much prized. A sincere and lasting friendship was thus cemented between two persons who were, in some respects, widely dissimilar.

The removal of the seat of government from New York to Philadelphia, was the signal for much hilarity among the citizens of the latter place. Their triumph over a rival city being attributed to the exertions and influence of the Hon. Robert Morris, some of the New Yorkers took their revenge by lampooning this leader in an unpopular movement, and caricatures were circulated, representing the wealthy financier in

the act of carrying off the whole body of Congress on
his back, the words, " Stick to it, Bobby," being in-
scribed underneath. . The Philadelphians, on the other
hand, were eager to show hospitality to the new
comers. Entertainments of every description were
the order of the day, and the prominent fashionables
were emulous in gaiety. An acknowledged leader
of the *ton* was Mrs. Bingham, daughter to one of the
first merchants of the city. She had but recently
returned from France, and her loveliness and accomplishments drew around her the *élite* of the city, and
rendered her house a most attractive place of resort.
It was her ambition to give a new tone to society,
and to introduce customs more congenial to the at-
mosphere of Paris, than the simplicity of a young
republic. One of these customs, for instance, was
that of having the visitor's name taken at the door by
a servant, and passed to others on the different land-
ings of the stairs, till it reached the door of the reception room, where it was announced in a loud voice
to call the attention of the lady of the house. This
custom, which never prevailed extensively, occasioned
many amusing blunders, one of which happened in
the case of a distinguished person, afterwards President of the United States. He gave his name as
requested at the door, but was surprised to hear it
reverberated in different tones, and could only suppose
the calling meant to expedite his movements. " Coming!" he exclaimed ; and again, " Coming, coming !"

till at length, quite out of patience, he called out, "Coming, as soon as I can get my great coat off!"

The position of Gen. Knox at this time, and probably the inclinations of his wife, rendered her a leader in these gay circles, and their house was the favorite resort, not only of the fashionable, but the intellectual and cultivated. Her talents for the management of life at the *court*, as some called it, were of great service to Mrs. Washington, who, retiring and domestic in her habits, relied on the guidance of her friend. It was not long after this period that Philadelphia received an accession of visitors, driven to this land by the French Revolution. Among these were many of the French nobility, hurled from affluence to poverty, and compelled to convert those accomplishments which had adorned their days of luxury into a means of subsistence. Sympathy and kindness were abundantly shown them by the citizens, and in many cases substantial aid. The house of Gen. Knox, where the first characters of the day were entertained, was open, and his hospitalities freely tendered to these unfortunate persons, and some of them were among his most cherished guests. In one of these—the Duc de Liancourt—both he and Mrs. Knox became warmly interested; and he afterwards passed several seasons with them in Maine. Their daughter remembers having heard him, while there, exclaim one day, after a fit of deep musing, "I have three dukedoms on my head"—beating his head with violence—"and not one coat to my back!" This was literally true, and he was presented by the General with a suit of clothes, of which he was actually in need. More fortunate, however, than most of his countrymen, he was afterwards restored to favor and fortune, and died in the possession of great wealth. Another visitor, both in Philadelphia and Maine, was the celebrated Talleyrand. It is mentioned as indicative of his well-known character, that he affected ignorance of the English language, and too great stupidity to acquire it, for the purpose, as a gentleman who knew him assured Mrs. Knox, of observing the unguarded conversation of individuals who were not aware that he understood them.

La Fayette visited them in Boston the year following the war. At one time he officiated as godfather to the son of Mrs. Knox under circumstances somewhat peculiar—he being a Roman Catholic, General Greene, the other sponsor, of Quaker parentage, the mother an Episcopalian, and the father a Presbyterian.

After eleven years service in the war office, General Knox decided on retirement from public life. His private affairs demanded attention, and the expenses inevitably attendant on his situation, and the maintenance of his establishment, with his munificent hospitality, were enough to impair a private fortune. His wife's views coincided with his own, and she felt that it had become her duty to quit scenes in many respects so congenial to her habits and inclinations. She shared her husband's trials in resisting the solicitations of his beloved chief to remain until the close of his own public career, and in parting with him and Mrs. Washington. She had other friends besides these endeared ones, whom it cost her a pang to leave ; but though in the prime of life, the idea of retirement was not distasteful to her, for she had already tasted the bitter cup of affliction. A lovely boy, eight years of age, was suddenly taken from her, being thrown into convulsions from perfect health, by a stroke of the sun, which proved fatal after a succession of fits. He was a child of unusual depth and purity of character, and his loss was severely felt by both his parents ; yet, while grief disposed the bereaved mother to avoid general society, the sad dispensation showed her that amidst much frivolity and insincerity in the gay world about her, were some warm and kind and true hearts, ready to feel for the sufferings of others. The affectionate sympathy of the President and Mrs. Washington was especially grateful, and from others she received proofs of cordial interest. General Hamilton was deeply affected at the funeral, where he walked as chief mourner with the daughter of Mrs. Knox, who felt herself unable to attend.

It was in the spring of 1795, that she and the General took their final leave of Philadelphia, to enter upon a new life. Mrs. Knox, as the only one of her family entitled to inherit property in this country, owned one fifth of a large tract of land in the District of Maine, originally the property of her grandfather, General Waldo, and called the Waldo Patent.

From another branch of the family General Knox purchased a tract of equal extent, and determined to establish on this noble estate a new home, which should be a suitable abode for his wife and family, and an attraction to that portion of country, at that time little known. At Thomaston, at the head of St. George's river, he built a splendid mansion, a palace in its dimensions, and called a chateau by French visitors. This he furnished with all the taste of modern luxury, built outhouses of every description, and set in motion various branches of industry—relying on the gradual rise of the property to repay the vast amount of expenditure. Montpelier, for that was the name given to the place, was indeed a princely abode, and a delightful retreat for the soldier and the scholar—for the indulgence of literary tastes and the companionship of friends. Mrs. Knox was never more entirely pleased with her situation ; but her anticipations of retirement were far from being realized. The hospitality of her husband was unbounded ; everything was provided that could contribute to the amusement or entertainment of the guests, and among the crowd of visitors were often entire strangers, whose visits were sometimes protracted beyond reason.

Louis Philippe and his two younger brothers, the Duc de Montpensier, and Count de Beaujolois, were frequent visitors at the house of General Knox in Boston, where the family then passed their winters. Mrs. Thatcher—the lady to whom I am so much indebted —says that "personal privations affected those young men little in comparison with anxiety for the fate of their mother and sister, who were still in the power of the French Jacobins. Never shall I forget the delight expressed in their countenances, when, coming one day to dine at my father's, they tore the tricolored cockades, which they had hitherto worn, from their hats, and trampled them under their feet—saying that they had just learned the escape of these beloved relatives into Spain, and no longer felt disposed to keep terms with the wretches who then bore sway in their beloved land."

The second summer of their residence in Maine, a party from Philadelphia, consisting of Mr. and Mrs. Bingham, their two daughters, Miss Willing, the sister of Mrs. Bingham, who was afterwards engaged to Louis Philippe during his residence in this country— the Viscount de Troailles—the brother-in-law of La Fayette and one of the most polished nobles of the French court—Mr. Richards, an English gentleman— and Mr. Baring, afterwards Lord Ashburton, passed six weeks at Montpelier, during which time the gentlemen made extensive excursions through the adjacent country. Messrs. Bingham and Baring were induced to purchase a million of acres on the Kennebec, and a tract somewhat smaller east of the Waldo Patent.

While this gay party remained, the wilds of Maine were enlivened by the most brilliant of the society of the capital. Such intelligent companionship proved a solace to the depressed spirits of Mrs. Knox; for again she had been called to mourn the loss of her children, two of whom, seized with the scarlet fever, had in one day been consigned to the tomb. These repeated bereavements were the great trial of her life. It was the will of God to take from her nine out of twelve children, and the anguish she endured, as one by one those she so loved were withdrawn, showed that her heart was feelingly alive to the most tender and sacred claims of domestic affection. In these severe trials she could lean on the sympathy and support of her best earthly friend, who, equally strong in his affections, was able sooner to rise above the pressure of sorrow, and to say with heartfelt submission, "It is the Lord; let Him do what seemeth to Him good." "I have heard my mother say," writes her daughter, "while bending over the bed of a darling dying child, 'Bitter as is this cup, the time may come when I may look back upon this as a period of happiness!' And so indeed it proved; for when the hour arrived that took from her the prop and stay on which she had so long leaned, then she realized that all previous trials were merged in this *one* great affliction."

The sad event that closed the brilliant career of General Knox, almost overwhelmed the wife whose whole existence had been so devoted to him. Though she struggled painfully for resignation, her energies were crushed by the unexpected blow, nor did her mind ever fully recover its tone. Often, after the first agony had passed, did she express the difficulty she found in feeling interest in anything; the charm was gone from life, which henceforward was rather endured than enjoyed. Yet gratefully did she acknowledge the blessings spared, and clung with strong affection to her few surviving children, finding her sweetest solace in their love. Her youngest daughter, whose delicate health had in her early years rendered her an object of peculiar solicitude, was, although married, fortunately still her mother's companion, and had the privilege of soothing her sorrows, and ministering to her comfort by the thousand nameless attentions prompted by affection, and so grateful to the stricken heart. The remaining days of Mrs. Knox were chiefly spent in the retirement then most congenial to her feelings, and in the spot endeared to her by so many interesting associations and remembrances of past happiness. The beauty that surrounded her was in a measure the creation of him she mourned, his taste and skill having done much to improve its natural advantages. His tomb was within view of the house, and it was a melancholy satisfaction to imagine that his spirit lingered near.

During the eighteen years of her widowhood, Mrs. Knox continued hospitably to receive her friends, but found her chief pleasure in the exercise of benevolence. So many affecting proofs of the uncertain tenure of earthly blessings had taught her to look beyond the passing scene, and to seek to lay up treasure in Heaven. Her fondness for reading was the solace of many a sad hour, and her sight was never impaired so as to require the aid of glasses. Her death took place on the twentieth of June, 1824, at the age of sixty-eight. She is described as having been, even at that age, a remarkably fine-looking woman, with brilliant black eyes and blooming complexion. Her style of dress, which was somewhat peculiar, and her dignified manners, gave her an appearance of being taller than she really was. It is a subject of regret with her family that no portrait of her remains that does her any justice. The one taken of General Knox, in the last year of his life, by the celebrated Stuart—said to be a perfect likeness—is now suspended in Faneuil Hall. The same artist had made considerable progress in one of Mrs. Knox; but one day while working at it, became suddenly dissatisfied with what he had done, and rubbed it out. He was, as is well known, much governed by impulse, and could not be prevailed on to renew the attempt.

Those who speak of Mrs. Knox, either from recollection or tradition, concur in the testimony that she was "a remarkable woman." It cannot be doubted that she possessed a mind of a high and powerful cast, with such qualities of character as make a deep and abiding impression, and that her influence on all with whom she came into contact was very decided. The deference mingled with the friendly regard of General and Mrs. Washington, and the homage paid to her intellectual superiority by many persons of judgment and talent, show this influence to have been great and well founded; in general society it was commanding, and gave a tone to the manners of the time. It can

hardly be wondered at, that among those who could
not properly appreciate such a character, injustice
should have been done to her; that dignity should
have been called haughtiness, and the independence
of a high and calm spirit represented as unfeminine
boldness. Those who had the best opportunities of
knowing her intimately, assure us that there was
nothing masculine or bold in her appearance or deportment, although she may at times have seemed distant
and haughty to visitors who presumed too much on
her hospitality, and abrupt to those to whom her perfect sincerity of character would not permit her to
show favor. That she had a heart as well as a mind
—a heart full of warm sensibility—all who knew her
could testify. The strength of her domestic attach-
ments, her devotion to husband and children, for whom
she was ready, in the noon of life, to give up the
delights of society in the metropolis—the keenness of
her suffering in those bereavements

"That woke the nerve where agonies are born,"

show that all the deep and tender feelings which belong
to feminine nature were hers in an eminent degree. In
the busiest scenes of her eventful life, the claims of
maternal duty were never forgotten; and the love and
reverence of the children who survive her are the best
evidence of the excellence of her who was the guide
of their early years.

III.

MARGARET WHETTEN.

MARGARET TODD was born in the year 1736, in New
York, and married William Whetten, a native of
Devonshire, England. He had emigrated to this
country when a boy, without his parents, before the
French war, and after having commanded vessels
trading with the West Indies, settled in New York as
a merchant. At the commencement of the Revolution he was the owner of several vessels, which he
sold, investing the greater part of the proceeds in the
paper issues of the state government and Congress.
When the British ship Asia fired upon the city, August 23d, 1776, he took the alarm like many of the
inhabitants, and removed with his family to New
Rochelle. Here, so far from finding a refuge from the
perils of war, they soon discovered themselves to be
in a situation of even greater danger. After the battle
of Long Island, and the occupation of New York by
the British, the American forces, contending the
ground from one post to another, were for some time
stationed within a few miles of the village, near which
the troops of Lord Howe were posted. The residence

of Capt. Whetten was thus midway between the hostile lines, and during the movement of the two armies towards White Plains, devastation and famine marked the whole region of country through which they passed. Whetten was a zealous patriot, though prevented by infirm health from taking any active part; yet he was often constrained tó entertain loyalists as well as whigs. The alternate visits of friends and foes, talking of the news of the day, or sitting down to the table spread by the liberal providence of Mrs. Whetten, gave rise occasionally to singular encounters.

The Hessians, who had joined the British at New Rochelle, were the peculiar terror of the defenceless people, stories of their ferocity being circulated by both parties. Mrs. Whetten was perhaps the first to discover that such rumors might be exaggerated and that these mercenaries were sometimes less to be dreaded than soldiers speaking the English language. Observing one day that black colors were suddenly hoisted in an adjacent field, she asked a British officer who chanced to come in, what it meant. "Heaven help you, madam," was the reply; "a Hessian camp is to be set up there." It turned out better than was anticipated. A good feeling was speedily established between her and the Hessians, who came almost daily to the house; for her acquaintance with the low Dutch dialect then familiarly spoken in many families in New York, enabled her to converse readily with them. In consequence of this partiality her house was exempted from depredations to which many of her neighbors were subjected, and she was sometimes enabled to save their property from destruction. She often corrected the errors of these foreigners respecting the country. Hearing one of them boast that the next day they would be in Philadelphia, she informed him that two rivers were to be crossed, and a long journey accomplished, before they could reach that city.

Among other interesting recollections of those days is that of a mother of her acquaintance, who melted all the pewter she had into bullets for her two sons, whom she sent from her hearth-stone to fight in the armies of their country. As she stood in the door to bid them farewell, one of the young men turned back, saying he had no gun. She urged him to go on, fearing naught, and trusting in God's protection, for he would find a gun to spare in the army. When she had lost sight of both, she wiped from her eyes the streaming tears, and went back into the house to pray for her devoted ones.

The village of New Rochelle suffered by incursions of the enemy from the commencement of the war. At one time when it was laid waste, the house of Capt. Whetten escaped destruction, being protected by a guard set by the Hessian general, at that time quartered in it. Mrs. Whetten, however, not trusting entirely to the enemy's favor, had sent away several articles of value for concealment. A family near them, compelled to fly and leave a dying father in their house, entreated her to take care of the helpless invalid, and if possible, save their property from the rapacious soldiers. The sacred trust was accepted and fulfilled, but she was not able to protect all the articles left by the fugitives; an iron chest that stood in the piazza was plundered while the old man was expiring, and while her cares and those of her daughters were in requisition for him. The following evening, Mrs. Whetten requested her daughters to go some distance to the place where her store had been deposited, for clean sheets to furnish a bed for the Hessian officer. The young girls objected, expressing their opinion— for they supposed that the officer, who was present, could not understand English—that what they had was good enough for their unwelcome guest. The discussion, after being continued some time, was ended by the officer's saying—to the no small consternation of the ladies—" Do not trouble yourself, Madam; straw is a good enough bed for a soldier." It may be conjectured that there was no further delay in procuring the sheets.

But the family was not always so much favored as to be exempted from aggression. On one occasion, when English soldiers came to the house to demand if any rebels were harbored there, the Hessians broke into the cellar and carried off a cider cask. At another time, after having plundered the house of Mrs. Todd, heaped her china together and broken it in one crash, they came to Mrs. Whetten's to finish their work. The ruffians snatched a handkerchief from the neck of her daughter Margaret, for the purpose of tying up various articles they had found about the house. The young girl was crying with indignation and fright, when an officer, who just then entered, asked what was the matter. " The Hessians are plundering us," was the answer. "And what are you?" demanded the officer. " We are whigs," replied the girl, but terrified at his fierce scowl and angry exclamation, she corrected herself, saying, " I am so confused, I knew not what I said, sir ; we are friends to government." This little ruse saved the house from spoliation ; the officer called off his men, who had taken as yet but little, and the family was left in peace. On another occasion, when the soldiers were robbing the house, a British officer interposed, beating off his men with his own sword.

One day, returning from their grandmother's, two of the daughters of Mrs. Whetten were witnesses to a hostile encounter. Meeting an American captain of their acquaintance, they invited him home to dinner. They were watched by a redcoat in the adjoining field, who presently leaped the fence and advanced towards the captain. Both fired, and then closed in a struggle. In a few moments several other British came up; some whigs who were cooking provisions in an orchard near at hand, hastened to join the fray, and a skirmish took place in presence of the frightened girls, who were glad, as soon as they could, to escape to the shelter of their home.

One night, after the family had retired, Mrs. Whetten was awakened by a noise without, and called her husband, supposing some of the Americans had come to the village for provisions. The captain rose, and going to open the door was assailed by oaths and cries from British soldiers demanding entrance. To the question, "Are you king's man or rebel?" he replied, "I am a friend to humanity." The intruders spread themselves through the house to seize whatever plunder they might find. Several came into the chamber of Mrs. Whetten, who was keeping guard over her infant lying asleep on a pillow. They rudely snatched the pillow, throwing off the child on the floor, and demanded money. The mother had put her purse in one of her pockets and hid it under the bolster. One of the robbers snatched a pocket from under the pillow, which she strove to get away from him. Her husband begged her to give it up, as it would certainly be wrested from her; she answered that she would not; but presently perceiving the man had not taken the pocket containing her purse, and that the one in his possession held only her snuff box, she relinquished it after some further show of resistance. The soldier bore away his prize, while she took care to secrete her treasure. Meanwhile one of her daughters, who had some money in charge, fled from the house towards a neighbor's, fancying herself pursued by the enemy, though it was only her invalid father who was hastening to protect her from danger. She reached the neighbor's door perfectly bewildered with fright, and when her father came up was beating against it and calling for admittance, in her agitation using the soldiers' language that rung in her ears—" Open, you d—d rebels, or we'll blow you to pieces!" etc.

The scarcity of provisions caused great suffering among the inhabitants of the village, supplies that might reach the continental troops being intercepted by the enemy. The little the people had was often taken from them. At one time Gen. Agnew sent word to Mrs. Whetten that she could have some milk, as he had been lucky enough to procure a cow. His offer to share the advantage with his neighbors did not long avail them; by the next morning nothing was left of the cow but the head and skin,—the Hessians having landed and left the usual tokens of their presence. One of their female neighbors, leaving the village with a wagon loaded with different articles, met on the road a party of British soldiers whom she took for Americans. When questioned, she answered that she was carrying off her property to save it from British depredation. Her wagon was immediately seized and driven down to the river, while she was left to rue her unguarded speech.

During the action at White Plains, Mrs. Whetten and her daughters heard the firing, and awaited the result with deep anxiety, praying earnestly for the success of their countrymen. At one time, when the news was discouraging, and suspense was at its height, one of the daughters observed, despondingly, " Our people will be defeated and slaughtered !" " Not so !" exclaimed her sister Sarah—afterwards Mrs. Brevoort—" the sword of the Lord and of Washington !"

The difficulty of procuring provisions at New Rochelle at length compelled the Whettens to return to New York. The captain's health was declining rapidly, and he died a short time after the removal of his family. Its care in the midst of danger and disaster now devolved upon the widow, who proved herself equal to the charge. It has been mentioned that nearly all their property was in paper money, which Capt. Whetten had estimated as more valuable than gold, saving it as a sure provision for his family, while he paid all current expenses in specie. When the currency depreciated, Mrs. Whetten was often urged to exchange her paper for hard money, or to purchase land with it, but steadily refused. " I will never," she said, "undervalue the currency established by Congress !" The consequence of this disinterested patriotism was the loss of all ; but the high-spirited matron never regretted the sacrifice which she imagined could not have been avoided without casting a slight upon the honor of her country.

For some time the family could not obtain possession of their own house ; but through the friendly offices of Andrew Elliot, collector of the port of New York under the crown, they were at length permitted to occupy it. This house stood in Cliff street, adjoining the rear of St. George's Chapel. A full account of their experience during their residence in the city for the succeeding years of the war, would present a graphic picture of the state of the times. Mrs. Whetten bore her part without shrinking, both in action and endurance. Her benevolent feelings prompted her to do good to all, but especially the oppressed whigs, for whom her house was always an asylum. The British were sometimes quartered upon her, and she was required to board many of the prisoners, who had reason to remember her generous kindness. Once, when some of her countrymen, having dined with her, asked what compensation was due—she replied, " Nothing, if you all eat heartily ;" and such was the spirit of her dealings with them. She made it her daily business to prepare food for the American soldiers, and sent it regularly to the prisons, as well as mush to the hospitals, using thus all the Indian meal she could obtain. She went sometimes with her daughters to see the prisoners, and encouraged them by cheerful conversation. Occasionally they visited that modern Bastile, the Provost, where the marshal—the notorious Conyngham—would now and then show his displeasure by kicking over the baskets of food they brought, and beating the unfortunate prisoners with his keys. Sometimes he received them with a surly courtesy, making himself amends, however, by indulging in boastful language. Miss Margaret Whetten once went with a female friend to see a woman imprisoned here, and heard Conyngham brag of having dug up in a church yard at New Rochelle various buried articles, which happened to be the property of the friend who accompanied her. The Provost stood in the Park, and the northeast apartment on the second floor, appropriated for officers or persons of distinction, was used for the reception of visitors. It was called " Congress Hall," and the black fellow in attendance went by the name of " Washington." Mrs. Whetten and her daughters continually provided not only provisions, but clothes for the use of the captive soldiers, not heeding the surliness of their gaolers or the risk of indignity to themselves. Conyngham told a gentleman that these ladies were " the d—dest rebels in New York," but so true to the prisoners, he could not often refuse to let them come. Sometimes they went to a guard house close to the old sugar house, which adjoined the Middle Dutch Church in Nassau street, and the sergeant permitted them to sit at the window while the prisoners came into the yard below and talked with them. The prisoners taken on Long Island were here confined, and almost starved. How many desponding hearts were comforted by such ministering visits, and the examples of constancy and heroism exhibited by these generous women !

Not satisfied with such daily ministrations, Mrs. Whetten often had provisions conveyed to the unfortunate inmates of the prison ships. A boat was usually sent to receive the supplies, and it is said the prisoners were sometimes permitted to speak with the ladies. Nor did our heroine hesitate to risk her own safety by receiving persons suspected of serving the American cause. Several of her descendants remember a story of her having assisted in the escape of a spy. When a party of soldiers was sent to her house to arrest the suspected person, having notice of their approach, she had just time to slip a dressing-gown and night-cap upon her guest, place him in a large easy chair, and put a bowl of gruel into his hands. When the guard came, she showed them the seeming invalid, and they left him, intending to return and take him as soon as he should be sufficiently recovered to accompany them. The officer was reprimanded, and immediately ordered back ; but by that time the object of suspicion had disappeared.—Capt. Hunter, who often came with a flag to the city, was in the habit of sending and receiving communications through Mrs. Whetten's family. On one occasion he was ordered to remain three or four days at her house, but finally permitted to depart.

It was not long before Mrs. Whetten learned that she was suspected of harboring spies, and feeling some uneasiness, she was advised to address a letter to the British commander, soliciting his protection. She went herself to deliver it at his quarters, and her absence till late in the afternoon greatly alarmed her daughters, who could suppose nothing else but that she had been arrested and sent to the Provost. She had only been detained by waiting for the aid-de-camp who had promised to favor her, to find an opportunity of presenting her letter. The dread of being persecuted as obnoxious, was no small part of their trials, for they knew how others had been treated under such circumstances. Some of the royalists once finding a military suit in a trunk belonging to one of their neighbors,—their rage at the discovery was vented in the hearing of Mrs. Whetten's household. At another house where a British officer was billeted, he chose to take with him a female favorite, whose presence and caprices the lady was compelled to endure. Once having ventured to strike her lap-dog, she received from the virago not only a violent scolding, but a quantity of liniment thrown in her face.

Mrs. Todd, the mother of Mrs. Whetten, who accompanied her in her removal to the city, had been obliged for a time to take up her residence in a cooper's shop. A member of Congress with whom she was acquainted requested her to occupy a house belonging to him; but her removal thither seemed to give offence. A party of soldiers came the same night, plundered the house of several articles, and then seating themselves at the table, ordered supper. After drinking their punch, they would toss the cups and glasses they had emptied to the ceiling, breaking them to pieces. They would not permit the terrified women to leave the room, but compelled them to witness their brutal revelry. On their demand that the mistress of the house should give them a toast, she replied, "Why, we *eat* toast!" with so much simplicity that supposing her really ignorant of their meaning, they did not insist further. Her ingenuity in thus avoiding the necessity of pledging her enemies, was equalled by that of a tory lady, who once asked some whigs to join her in a toast, and gave—"the first two words of David's third —" her guests not being aware, till they had leisure to look into the Psalms, that they had drunk the health of " Lord Howe."

Some of the British soldiers showed much courtesy to Mrs. Whetten and her daughters. Once, when they expressed uneasiness at having a quarter-guard stationed opposite, they were assured that so far from being subjected to annoyance, they would be safer than before, and might leave their windows open by night as well as day. After the close of the war, one of this guard, passing the window, stopped to pay his compliments to one of the daughters. His hair was plaited on the top of his head in the usual fashion, and as he removed his high-pointed cap, he made bold to beg " Miss Peggy's" acceptance of his comb. The young lady declined the offered token of remembrance, but promised not to forget the polite guardsman.

Early in August, 1778, a ship lying not far from the Long Island shore, having a large quantity of gunpowder on board, was struck by lightning and exploded. The shock was like an earthquake, causing great alarm, and several houses were injured ; St. George's Chapel, next door to Mrs. Whetten's, was violently shaken, some of its glass being shattered and the scuttles blown off

The time approached which was to end these dangers and sufferings. It was announced that New York was speedily to be evacuated by the British. The rejoicing of patriotic families who had lived so long in the midst of enemies, was of course great at the cheering prospect. One dame who lived near Mrs.

Whetten's was rather premature in her joyful demonstrations. Hearing the news flying from mouth to mouth, and seeing preparations for the departure of the royal troops, she imagined that her countrymen had already taken possession, and forthwith hoisted in full view from the top of her house a flag bearing the thirteen stars. Not long after this feat, the family of Mrs. Whetten was startled by the report of a neighbor, who came running to inform her that the provost marshal, Conyngham, at the head of a party of soldiers, was marching towards her house. That was not, however, his destination : he was in pursuit of the woman who had dared to insult His Majesty by hoisting the flag. The woman, meanwhile, hearing of his approach, locked her doors, and when the soldiers came to get possession of the flag, not only refused them admission, but stood and berated them with all the force of her tongue, joined by a number of boys, who were glad of an opportunity to insult the British. Conyngham judged it most prudent to draw off his men, and retire from the shower of abuse, which at another time would probably have been returned with a shower of bullets.

The house of Mrs. Whetten, called during the war " Rebel Headquarters," was the first in New York to which the news of peace was brought. A French gentleman—a prisoner—who boarded with her, received from the French ambassador at Philadelphia a letter containing the earliest account. After the establishment of peace, the services of Mrs. Whetten to the American cause did not fail to receive thankful acknowledgment, and a letter was written to her by General Washington, expressing his warm gratitude on behalf of the country. He also desired leave to breakfast with her, and during the meal, while conversing about the scenes through which she and her family had passed, he rose twice to thank her for the kindness she had shown the prisoners at such risk to herself, and the substantial aid she had rendered.

Mrs. Whetten was remarkable, like many other matrons of Revolutionary times, for quickness of repartee and a rather pungent humor. Once in conversation with a British officer, the news of a signal victory gained by the Americans having just arrived, she asked with much archness—" And did my countrymen run again this time ?"—" Ay, in truth, madam,"—was the candid reply : "they did run ;. but it was after us." Some time after peace, being in the stage on the road to Hartford, she chanced to find herself in company with two Englishmen not remarkable for comeliness, who took pleasure in abusing everything American. She observed quietly, that in one respect her country appeared to have the advantage ; " we beat you," she said, " in handsome men." The Englishmen were good natured enough to join in the laugh this remark created among the passengers, and were afterwards so much pleased with the lively conversation of their travelling companion, that they were sorry to part with her at her place of destination.

Mrs. Whetten continued to live in New York till her

death, which took place in March, 1809. Her eldest daughter, Sarah, married Henry Brevoort. During the occupation of New York by the British, the relations of this gentleman with Mr. Elliot, who was highly esteemed by both parties for his integrity of character and urbanity of manners, had been very friendly—Mr. Elliot's house adjoining his country-seat. This friendship was more lasting than the war. The son of Mr. Brevoort, on a visit to England many years afterwards, received a letter from Lady Cathcart, the daughter of Mr. Elliot, enquiring if he were related to the Brevoort who had been her father's friend, and his answer was followed by a pressing invitation to visit her. Margaret, the second daughter, married Capt. Dean—whose romantic adventures have been made the subject of a pleasing tale by Miss Sedgwick. The naval career of Capt. John Whetten, who was for twenty years President of the New York Marine Society, was a remarkable one. He often spoke of his excellent mother, whose pious counsels had such influence to restrain from vice and incite to virtue in the vicissitudes of his roving life. The fact is a curious one, that living to the age of eighty-two, and wandering in distant parts of the earth, his last resting place, in the family vault in the churchyard of St. George's chapel, was within half a cable's length of the spot where he was born.

IV.

~~~~~~~~

BLANDINA BRUYN.

MANY are yet living in whose hearts is cherished the memory of Mrs. Bruyn, while the tradition of her virtues is familiar to the inhabitants of the neighborhood where she resided. Her days were chiefly passed in the seclusion of the family circle, remote from the show and bustle of public life, but her high social position, and attention to the duties of a widely-extended and generous hospitality, brought her into contact with many of the leading minds of the period, and her exemplary discharge of the continual requirements of charity and benevolence, made her known as the protector of the unfortunate, looked up to with reverent and grateful regard by all who experienced her bounty.

Her father, Petrus Edmundus Elmendorf, was descended from the earliest settlers of Hurley, a small town on the bank of the Esopus, about three miles from Kingston, in Ulster County, New York. She was born at Kingston, then called Esopus, August 8th, 1753. Losing her father when very young, she was left entirely to the care of her mother, Mary Elmen-

dorf, a lady whose noble character, energy, and benevolent exertions in the cause of the destitute and
suffering, rendered her name widely known at that
period, not only throughout a large portion of New
York, but in the adjoining provinces of New Jersey
and Pennsylvania. She was the Mrs. Elmendorf who,
it is said, studied medicine that she might be qualified, while the men of the neighborhood were generally absent in the defence of their country, and the
physicians especially were in requisition in the army,
to practise the healing art among the poor families in
the country around her. She appears not only to
have possessed a mind of superior order, but the
advantages of cultivation. From this intellectual
and accomplished parent the daughter received her
early instruction, with the best means of education
which, in that day, it was possible to enjoy. She
was placed for some time under the care of Miss
Blanche Beyeau, a teacher celebrated at that period,
and had the advantage of being at a boarding-school
in the city of New York. However limited may have
been the range of mere accomplishments then taught, it
does not appear that the more substantial and useful
acquirements were neglected; Blandina learned to
write and speak, with ease and correctness, the English, Dutch, and French languages, in each of which
she had numerous correspondents at a later period
of her life. These attainments must have caused her
to be regarded as a learned lady at a time when even
the privilege of a common country school was enjoyed

by few, and so many of the daughters of the wealthy
gained their only instruction from books at home.

Miss Elmendorf's youth passed in quiet occupations
and amusements, till a short time before the rupture
between Great Britain and the American Colonies.
She then formed a matrimonial engagenent with
Jacobus S. Bruyn, afterwards colonel in the American
army, whose services to his country brought upon him
the hardships of a long captivity. The tranquil happiness to which the young lovers looked forward was
destined not yet to be their portion—the duties of
Col. Bruyn calling him to Quebec, and afterwards to
other places.

In the early part of October, 1777, the British
General, Sir Henry Clinton, with the small force that
could be spared from an important post left under his
command, made an attack upon Forts Clinton and
Montgomery. These forts were separated by a stream
that came from the mountain, communicating by a
bridge with each other. The British commander saw
that his only prospect of securing them was by a
coup de main in their then unguarded state, allowing
no time for the arrival of succor. Sir James Wallace
moved up to Peekskill Neck, to mask the only communication the Americans had across the river on
that side of the Highlands. The attack on both forts
succeeded at the same time, and Col. Bruyn, one of
the officers engaged in the defence of Fort Montgomery, was taken prisoner.

The sad separation from her affianced husband, the

severest trial Miss Elmendorf had hitherto been called to undergo, was but the beginning of sorrows. The capture of Fort Montgomery was immediately succeeded by the burning of Esopus. This town, it will be remembered, was one of the earliest Dutch settlements in New York—said to be the third place settled, and commenced about 1618. It is beautifully situated on the fertile flats elevated above Esopus Creek. The Catskill Mountains are seen in the distance. It had been in former times the scene of battle and violence. In 1663, the Indians of that region, who had been for some time discontented with their Dutch neighbors, made an attack on the village, but were compelled to flee to the mountains by troops sent from New Amsterdam by Gov. Stuyvesant. A British account of the burning of this place is quoted in the postscript of a letter written by Sir William Howe to Lord George Germain. He calls the affair "a very spirited piece of service." The report says, in the words of Major-General Vaughan—" Esopus being a nursery for almost every villain in the country, I judged it necessary to proceed to that town. On our approach they were drawn up with cannon, which we took and drove them out of the place. On our entering the town, they fired from the houses, which induced me to reduce the place to ashes, which I accordingly did, not leaving a house. We found a considerable quantity of stores of all kinds, which shared the same fate." The American account states that one house was spared at the burning—that of

Mrs. Hammersly, who was acquainted with some of the British officers, and for that reason was favored with their protection.

" Thus, by the wantonness of power," says the Connecticut Journal, Oct. 27, 1777, " the third town in the state for size, elegance, and wealth, is reduced to a heap of rubbish; the once happy inhabitants, who are chiefly of Dutch descent, are obliged to solicit shelter among strangers, and those who possessed lately elegant and convenient dwellings, obliged to take up with such huts as they find can defend them from the cold blasts of approaching winter." But a faint idea can be formed from description of what was endured by the helpless inhabitants. An invasion at night, and the conflagration of the entire town, at a season when the cold must have been severely felt— the distress caused by the destruction of so many homes, and the anguish of those who knew not the fate of their beloved ones—form a scene whose horrors can scarcely be compassed by the most vivid imagination. At this particular period, marked by the reverses that overspread with such gloom the prospects of the country, and the dreary picture of Valley Forge, there was hardly a ray of hope to cheer the most sanguine, or lighten the pressure of calamity. In this melancholy state of public affairs, individual misfortune was felt not the less keenly. The fate of Miss Elmendorf seemed linked with that of her suffering country. By the destruction of her native town her mother's family was broken up, and the members for some time dispersed. Her own time was divided, after this, between Hurley, Albany, and Raritan in New Jersey, as duty called for her presence in either place, or as Providence directed her movements. Many incidents, both of an amusing and distressing character, which occurred during her journeys, were remembered by her, and related afterwards to her children. An interesting light would have been thrown upon the manners and life of that day by detailed accounts ; but for lack of a record, much that might have given expression and coloring to the outline pictures of history, is lost beyond recovery.

Col. Bruyn was kept for some time in close confinement in a prison ship, where he could have no communication with his betrothed. The horrors of these abodes of suffering, despair, and death, have been often described. He was afterwards so fortunate as to obtain release, being transferred to Long Island on his parole. Yet he was still for three years doomed to endure the weariness of captivity, and to witness the struggles of his country for freedom without being able to take part in the contest. During this long and painful separation, the faithful affection of his fair and gentle mistress remained unchanged.

The season of disaster and trial was succeeded by brighter times, and in the spring of 1782 the lovers were restored to each other and united in marriage. After the close of the war, and until their death, they continued to reside at Kingston. The various perils and calamities to which Mrs. Bruyn, during her youth, had been exposed, both from Indian and British depredation, as well as the aid she frequently afforded to the patriots, connected her name with incidents of the Revolution. In spirit and feeling she was a true and worthy daughter of the heroic age of the Republic.

Her house was always distinguished, far and near, as the seat of liberal hospitality, and she was universally beloved by her acquaintances. Modest and retiring in her manners, and disposed to shrink from, rather than court the public gaze, the energy of her nature showed itself constantly active in deeds of charity and kindness. It was her delight to minister to the sick, to relieve the wants of the poor, and to succor distress everywhere as far as her ability extended. Liberal without ostentation, attentive to every duty, and forming the happiness of her household, she was emphatically one of those whose children, in the words of Scripture, rise up and call her blessed. The assemblage of virtues in her character would have been incomplete without the crown of piety, and that, unaffected and unobtrusive, but fervent and cheerful, was her own.

In writing the memoirs of so many women distinguished at that period, I have been struck by the fact that almost all were noted for piety. The spirit that exhibited itself in acts of humanity, courage, magnanimity, and patriotism, was a deeply religious one. May we not, with reason, deem this one important source of the strength that gave success to the American cause ? ·Who can tell how much availed the prayers of those righteous women !

Mrs. Bruyn died in 1832, in the seventy-ninth year of her age. Her sight and hearing had been considerably affected for some time previous, but both were wonderfully restored a little before her death. Almost to the last remained unimpaired her cheerfulness and vivacity, and her faculty of entering with interest into the feelings of those with whom she conversed—a faculty of " companionship for all ages." Her son resides at Kingston, and some of her relatives in New York.

V.

~~~~~~~~~~

ANNE FITZHUGH.

ANNE FRISBY, the daughter of Peregrine Frisby,
of Cecil County, in Maryland, was born Sept. 5th,
1727. Her first husband was John Rousby, and
their only daughter married John Plater. On the
7th Jan., 1759, Mrs. Rousby was united to Wm. Fitzhugh, colonel in the British service. He won considerable distinction in his military career, and his
services in the West India expedition. At the commencement of difficulties between the colonies and the
mother country he was living on his half pay. The
large estate, highly improved, on which he resided, lay
at the mouth of the Patuxent River, in Maryland, and
he had in operation extensive manufactories of different kinds. When discontent ripened into rebellion,
though he was advanced in years, in feeble health,
and had almost entirely lost his sight, neither the
infirmities of age, nor any advantage to be derived
from adhesion to the government, prevented his taking
an open and active part with the patriots. On account
of his influence in the community, he was offered a
continuance of his half pay if he would remain neu-

tral, but he at once declined the offer, resigned his commission, and declared for the land that gave him birth. Unable himself to bear arms, he furnished his two sons—Peregrine and William—for the army, and dismissed them with his command to be true to the interests of their country. These were both officers, and served with distinction under the continental standard. Their father took his seat in the Executive Council of Maryland, giving his vote and influence to the debates, till the political opinions of that body were no longer wavering. Not only thus did he render service, but he was seen and heard at every public meeting, going from place to place through the country, haranguing the people in stump speeches, and devoting all his energies to the task of rousing them to fight for their own rights.

This active zeal for American freedom of course did not fail to render the venerable patriot obnoxious. He was often apprised of danger from British enmity, but no risk could deter him from the performance of duty. At one time, when he had disregarded a warning from some unknown hand, Mrs. Fitzhugh was surprised in his absence by news of the near approach of a party of British soldiers. She instantly decided on her course in the emergency, and collected the slaves, whom she furnished with such arms as could be found. Then taking a quantity of cartridges in her apron, she led the way out to meet the enemy, resolved that they should have at least a round of shots by way of welcome. Finding preparations for resistance where they probably expected none, the party retired from the grounds without doing any damage.

At another time when they received information of a design on the enemy's part to attack the house that night, take the colonel prisoner, carry off what plunder could be found, and lay waste the premises, Col. Fitzhugh was dissuaded by his anxious family from making any attempt at defence. Perhaps thinking that, meeting no opposition, they would be content with plunder, he reluctantly consented to leave the place with his household. The next morning nothing remained of the mansion but a heap of smoking ruins. The family then removed to Upper Marlboro', about fifty miles up the river, where they continued to reside till the close of the war.

In the fall before peace was declared, a detachment of British soldiers having landed on the shore of the Patuxent, marched to the house of Col. Fitzhugh. It was about midnight when he and his wife were roused from sleep by a loud knocking at the door. The colonel raised a window and called out to know who was there. The reply was, "Friends." He asked, "Friends to whom?" "Friends to King George!" was shouted in answer, with a peremptory order to open the door. Knowing well that remonstrance or resistance would be useless, and that delay would but irritate the intruders to acts of violence, the colonel assured them that his wife—he being blind—would immediately descend and admit them Mrs. Fitzhugh did not hesitate, though not smal was her dismay and terror when, parting the curtains for an instant she saw the courtyard filled with armed men The night was cloudy, and a drizzling rain was falling, but by the faint moonlight their bayonets could be distinctly seen. Hastily lighting a candle, and putting on her slippers, she went down stairs, stopping only for a moment to give her sons, who happened to be in the house, their pistols, and warn them that they must lose no time in making their escape. They left the house by the back door as their mother with difficulty turned the ponderous key which secured the front. The intruders instantly rushed in, touching her night dress with their bayonets as she turned to leave the door. She walked calmly before them into the parlor, and addressing the officer, said she hoped they intended to do the inmates of the house no harm. He replied that they did not, but he must see Col. Fitzhugh at once ; then, his attention being suddenly attracted by some articles of military dress, he demanded quickly, " What officers have you in the house, Madam ?" " There is no one here but our own family," answered Mrs. Fitzhugh. The men spoke together in a low voice, and then the question was repeated, to which the same reply was given with perfect calmness. She noticed a smile on the countenance of the officer as he said, " We must take these, Madam," pointing to the cap, holsters, etc. It is proper to mention that nothing else was touched in the house, although the supper table, with plate upon it, was standing as it had been left at night, and the side-board contained several other articles.

Mrs. Fitzhugh, in obedience to the order that her husband should come down, went to assist him in dressing, and returned with him, unmindful, in her anxiety for him, that she had taken no time to dress herself. The officer informed him that he was his prisoner, and must go with them to New York, then in possession of the British. Col. Fitzhugh replied that his age and want of sight made it scarce worth their while to take him, as he could neither do harm nor service, being unable, indeed, to take care of himself. Such arguments, however, availed nothing, and he was hurried off immediately, the captors, it is likely, fearing a surprise. Mrs. Fitzhugh had made no preparations for a journey, but had too much decision of character and courage to hesitate a moment. Walking up to her husband, she took his arm, and when the officer endeavored to persuade her to remain, saying she would suffer from exposure, she answered that Col. Fitzhugh was not able to take care of himself, and that even if he were, she would not be separated from him. The officer then took down a cloak and threw it over her shoulders. With only this slight protection from the cold and rain, she left the house with the rest. Their boat lay off about half a mile, and going to the shore they had to walk through the mud, the ground being soaked with rain, but the matron's resolute spirit did not fail her. An alarm was caused by the discharge of a gun, which the soldiers

took to be the signal of a gathering in the neighborhood. They had already reached the boat, when they
consented to permit Col. Fitzhugh to remain on his
parole, which was hastily written out, and leaving
the prisoner on shore, they pushed off as rapidly as
possible.

On their return to the nouse, the colonel and Mrs.
Fitzhugh were much surprised to find all the negroes
gone, except one little girl who had hid herself in the
garret. They had evidently been taken or persuaded
to go off in their absence, and there was ground for
the suspicion that the enemy's real object had been to
obtain possession of the slaves without any resistance
that might alarm the neighbors. Many of these missing ones returned to their master of their own accord,
the fair promises made to allure them from his service
not having been kept.

Miss Plater, the granddaughter of Mrs. Fitzhugh,
displayed much courage upon this occasion. After
her grandparents had left the house in charge of the
soldiers, one or two of the men came back to obtain
some fire, and in carrying it from the room, let some
fall on the carpet. The young girl started forward,
put her foot upon it, and asked if they meant to fire
the house; then speaking of the outrage upon the old
gentleman, expressed herself with so much dignity
and feeling, that the hearts even of those rough soldiers were touched, and they answered kindly, that
the house should stand, and no harm come to her.
They then asked for wine, which she ordered to be set

4*

before them. They would not drink, however, fearing it might be poisoned, till she had tasted each bottle, and insisted on her doing so. This young lady was afterwards the wife of Col. Forrest.

Capt. Peregrine Fitzhugh, one of the sons already mentioned, who was for some time aid to General Washington, married Miss Elizabeth Chew, of Maryland, and removed in 1799 to Sodus Bay, on Lake Ontario, where he spent the remainder of his days. His venerable widow still resides at Sodus Point, in the midst of her children and descendants, by whom, and a large circle of acquaintance, she is equally revered and beloved. She is one of the earliest and most highly esteemed friends of the writer of these memoirs. Col. William Fitzhugh married Miss Anno Hughes of Maryland, and removed to the vicinity of Geneseo, Livingston County, in the western part of New York.

VI.

KATHARINE STEEL.[*]

THIS heroine was of a stamp rarely seen or described in recent times. It needed a primitive country, as well as unusual hardships and perils, to develop such lofty, yet unambitious heroism, such sagacity mingled with homely simplicity, such a spirit of patience, constancy and self-sacrifice, without an aspiration for praise, or a thought of reward. In one prominent character of that period we may see a type of many who lived and labored like her, unappreciated by those around them, unknown in the annals of their land, unconscious themselves of the influence they exercised, or the value of their freely-rendered services. The memory of these stout-hearted, high-souled matrons is well nigh swept from the earth; but here and there recollections survive by which we may learn how noble was the race that nursed the nation's infancy.

It might be a subject for discussion, whether the

* Most of the details of this memoir were received by Mr. Stinson from the daughter of Capt. Steel. Some incidents were related to her by her maternal grandmother, Mrs. Beard, who lived more than a century. I have already acknowledged my great obligations to Mr. Stinson in this and the succeeding Southern sketches.

matrons of the Revolutionary era were intrinsically
superior to those of the present day in the strength of
spirit that qualified for enterprise and endurance, or
whether the same circumstances would now create
such heroines.   An English critic, noticing the "Women of the American Revolution," thinks that the
mere housewife, or the toy of luxury would hardly, on
the outbreak of a storm, start up ready armed with
self-command and self-sacrifice; that there could be
no making a "Sidney's sister, Pembroke's mother," out
of such by the force of circumstances.   However it
may be, it cannot be denied that the women of our
country's early day were framed of admirable stuff, as
well as trained to strength in the school of hardship,
and that their influence on the age was very decided.

Katharine Fisher was a native of Pennsylvania.
When about twenty years old she was married to
Thomas Steel, of the same State.   Both belonged to
the race called the Pennsylvania Irish, so many of
whom emigrated to Carolina about the middle of the
century.   Katharine had this destination in view at
the time of her marriage, and being of a mirthful disposition, as well as romantic and fond of adventure,
she looked upon it as quite a matter of frolic to lead
the life of a pioneer on the borders of the wilderness.
The young pair made their removal to South Carolina
some time in 1745, to the upper, or what is called the
granite region of the State.   Their first acquaintance
in the country resided upon the eastern side of the
river called Catawba, after the tribe of Indians who

were located on its banks. He was a Scotchman named Daniel McDonald, one of the same people with themselves, and had lived some fifteen or twenty years in his present home among the Indians, in entire seclusion from any of the white race. The Catawbas were gentle in disposition, and lived in friendship with the settlers; McDonald probably reaped some advantage from their protection, for he was the first pioneer into that district of country, had amassed considerable wealth, and reared a large family of sons and daughters. The new comers into the wild crossed the river near his house, and fixed their residence close to Fishing Creek, about a mile from the Catawba. It was not long before the young wife began to understand what was to be the life of pioneers. She was too light-hearted, however, to be discouraged by hardships, and with the good humor which is the best philosophy, endeavored to find food for merriment in the various inconveniences they had to encounter. She spared not her own strength, not shrinking from her share of labor in the field or the woods; she also learned in a short time the use of the rifle, and became an excellent shot.

They were not long solitary; the two currents of emigration, from Charleston and the sea coast on the one side, and Pennsylvania and Virginia on the other, meeting in this neighborhood, in the course of a few years several other families came to settle near them. John Gaston had taken up his abode a mile or so up Fishing Creek, on the west side, and other dwellings

rose at intervals in different directions. These families visited each other, going up and down the creek in
canoes. In time, it became necessary to unite in
their defence against the hostile Indians—the Cherokees giving them much trouble. The place owned by
Mr. Steel was fortified as a block-house, to which the
inhabitants could betake themselves when danger
threatened. These block-houses were scattered over
the country at convenient distances for the unprotected
settlers. One at Landsford, near the spring, commanded the river and a large extent of country, and
was called Taylor's Fort, while the first-mentioned was
named Steel's Fort, after the proprietor. While the
men were out fighting the Cherokees, or engaged in
providing for the defence and maintenance of their
families, the women were in the habit of resorting on
any alarm to this place of refuge. Mrs. Steel was
chief and ruler among them, not merely by her right
of ownership, or her superior firmness and courage,
but by virtue of her hearty kindness and good humor.
She was acknowledged master of the Fort, and was
called familiarly, "Katy of the Fort." Possessing
great influence, she could at once calm the fears of
the women who had quitted their homes at the dead
hours of night to flee thither; they felt in fact a sense
of security in her presence. She taught the young
girls the use of the rifle, a useful accomplishment in
those days, when no one knew what hour she might
be compelled to wield that deadly weapon, relying on
her skill in its use to save herself or her children from

the hands of bloody savages. For weeks together the females would occupy the fort in the absence of their husbands or fathers. Their place of public worship, the attendance on which was never willingly neglected, was the Waxhaw meeting-house, in after years the scene of so much suffering and such disinterested benevolence.

Some thrilling incidents of peril and female prowess are related of this period, the settlers near the frontier being peculiarly exposed to Indian ravages. Late one night the alarm was given that the Indians were just upon them, and the helpless inhabitants of the neighborhood fled to the fort for protection. One young woman—Mrs. Beard—who had married an old man, bade her husband carry the child, while she bore the rifle, in readiness to use it for their defence. A young girl who lived with them was unwilling to quit the house without taking some of her clothes; she must "get on her blue skirt" at least. Mrs. Beard seized and dragged her from the house, exclaiming, "Very fine you would look, to be sure, with your blue skirt on and your scalp off!" At another time, on a Sabbath day, while the people were listening to the preaching at Waxhaw church, an alarm came that the Indians were close at hand. The congregation was immediately scattered, and the women fled to the block-house, where they remained several days, while the men were out scouring the country in every direction. This proved a false alarm. At other times the news of danger came so suddenly that the startled families

were not able to make their way to the forts. The
only resource in such emergencies was to hide in the
woods or swamps nearest at hand, and wait till the
foe was gone ; and not unfrequently the women had to
remain all night in the canebrakes without covering
or shelter. Mrs. Beard, relating her own experience,
said : " On one occasion I indulged the impious wish
that my children were dead ! I lay one night alone
in a thick canebrake with my two little ones. I had
them both at the breast, the elder as well as the babe,
to keep them from crying ; I was quaking with fear
that they would cry, and the Indians would find us
out. In the morning, as soon as it was light enough
to see——there lay a large rattlesnake within a few
feet of me !" The mother's repinings were turned to
thankfulness for the wonderful preservation of her
children. The child of which she was then pregnant
was marked with a rattlesnake ; she was Mary Beard
—the late Mrs. Sweet, of Charleston.

In a few years the little settlement had spread over
the rich lands on Fishing and Rocky Creeks, the
dwellings being gathered into clusters, of which there
were some three or four within a short distance of
each other. Not a great way from Steel's and Taylor's Forts was another settlement consisting of a few
families, among which were those of William McKenny
and his brother James. These lived near Fishing
Creek. In the summer of 1761, sixteen Indians, with
some squaws of the Cherokee tribe, took up their
abode for several weeks near what is called Simpson's

Shoals, for the purpose of hunting and fishing during
the hot months. In August, the two McKennys being
absent on a journey to Camden, William's wife, Bar-
bara, was left alone with several young children. One
day she saw the Indian women running towards her
house in great haste, followed by the men. She had
no time to offer resistance; the squaws seized her and
the children, pulled them into the house, and shoved
them behind the door, where they immediately placed
themselves on guard, pushing back the Indians as fast
as they tried to force their way in, and uttering the
most fearful outcries. Mrs. KcKenny concluded it was
their intention to kill her, and expected her fate every
moment. The assistance rendered by the squaws,
whether given out of compassion for a lonely mother,
or in·return for kindness shown them,—proved effectual for her protection till the arrival of one of the chiefs,
who drew his long knife and drove off the savages.
The mother, apprehending another attack, went to some
of her neighbors and entreated them to come and stay
with her. Robert Brown and Joanna his wife, Sarah
Ferguson, her daughter Sarah and two sons, and a
young man named Michael Melbury, came in compliance with her request, and took up their quarters in
the house. The next morning Mrs. McKenny ventured out alone to milk her cows. It had been her
practice heretofore to take some of the children with
her, and she could not explain why she went alone this
time, though she was not free from apprehension; it
seemed to be so by a special ordering of Providence.

While she was milking, the Indians crept towards her on their hands and knees; she heard not their approach, nor knew anything till they seized her. Sensible at once of all the horror of her situation, she made no effort to escape, but promised to go quietly with them. They then set off towards the house, holding her fast by the arm. She had the presence of mind to walk as far off as possible from the Indian who held her, expecting Melbury to fire as they approached her dwelling. As they came up, he fired, wounding the one who held Mrs. McKenny; she broke from his hold and ran, and another Indian pursued and seized her. At this moment she was just at her own door, which John Ferguson imprudently opening that she might enter, the Indians without shot him dead as he presented himself. His mother ran to him and received another shot in her thigh, of which she died in a few days. Melbury, who saw that all their lives depended on prompt action, dragged them from the door, fastened it, and repairing to the loft, prepared for a vigorous defence. There were in all five guns; Sarah Ferguson loaded for him, while he kept up a continual fire, aiming at the Indians wherever one could be seen. Determined to effect their object of forcing an entrance, some of the savages came very near the house, keeping under cover of an outhouse in which Brown and his wife had taken refuge, not being able on the alarm, to get into the house. They had crept into a corner and were crouched there close to the boarding. One of the Indians, coming up, leaned against the outside, separated from them only by a few boards, the crevices between which probably enabled them to see him. Mrs. Brown proposed to take a sword that lay by them and run the savage through the body, but her husband refused; he expected death, he said, every moment, and did not wish to go out of the world having his hands crimsoned with the blood of any fellow creature. "Let me die in peace," were his words, "with all the world." Joanna, though in the same peril, could not respond to the charitable feeling. " If I am to die," she said, " I should like first to send some of the redskins on the journey. But we are not so sure we have to die ; don't you hear the crack of Melbury's rifle? He holds the house. I warrant you, that red-skin looked awfully scared as he leaned against the corner here. We could have done it in a moment."

Mrs. McKenny, meanwhile, having failed to get into her house, had been again seized by the Indians, and desperately regardless of her own safety, was doing all in her power to help her besieged friends. She would knock the priming out of the guns carried by the savages, and when they presented them to fire would throw them up, so that the discharge might prove harmless. She was often heard to say, afterwards, that all fear had left her, and she thought only of those within the building, for she expected for herself neither deliverance nor mercy. Melbury continued to fire whenever one of the enemy appeared ; they kept themselves, however, concealed, for the most part, behind trees or the outhouse. Several were wounded by his cool and well-directed shots, and at length, tired of the contest, the Indians retreated, carrying Mrs. McKenny with them. She now resisted with all her strength, preferring instant death to the more terrible fate of a captive in the hands of the fierce Cherokees. Her refusal to go forward irritated her captors, and when they had dragged her about half a mile, near a rock upon the plantation now occupied by John Culp, she received a second blow with the tomahawk which stretched her insensible upon the ground. When after some time consciousness returned, she found herself lying upon the rock, to which she had been dragged from the spot where she fell. She was stripped naked, and her scalp had been taken off. By degrees the knowledge of her condition, and the desire of obtaining help came upon her. She lifted up her head, and looking around, saw the wretches who had so cruelly mangled her, pulling ears of corn from a field near, to roast for their meal. She laid her head quickly down again, well knowing that if they saw her alive, they would not be slack in coming to finish the work of death. Thus she lay motionless till all was silent, and she found they were gone ; then with great pain and difficulty she dragged herself back to the house. It may be imagined with what feelings the unfortunate woman was received by her friends and children, and how she met the bereaved mother wounded unto death, who had suffered for her attempt to save others   One of the blows received by Mrs. McKenny had made a deep wound in her back; the others were upon her head. When her wounds had been dressed as well as was practicable, Melbury and the others assisted her to a bed. Brown and his brave wife having then joined the little garrison, preparations were made for defence in case of another attack; the guns were all loaded and placed ready for use, and committing the house to the care of the Browns, Melbury sallied forth, rifle in hand, and took to the woods. He made his way directly, and as quickly as possible, to Taylor's Fort at Landsford. The men there, informed of what had happened, immediately set about preparations for pursuing the treacherous Indians who had thus violated the implied good faith of neighbors by assailing an unprotected woman. The next morning a number of them, well armed, started for the Indian encampment at the shoals. The Cherokees were gone; but the indignant pursuers took up the trail, which they followed as far as Broad River. Here they saw the Indians on the other side, but did not judge it expedient to pursue them further, or provoke an encounter.

In the meantime William McKenny had reason for uneasiness in his absence from home; for he knew that the Indians had been at the shoals some time, nor was the deceitful and cruel character of the tribe unknown to him. He was accustomed long afterwards to tell of the warning conveyed to him while on his road to Camden; two nights in succession he dreamed of losing his hat, and looking upon this as an omen of evil, became so uncomfortable that he could proceed no

at the sight of familiar faces, was more than reward enough for their deliverers. They had no parents to welcome their return, but their uncle, Hugh McDaniel, received them. Such incidents were in those times of common occurrence, but this encounter was the last, the Cherokees venturing on no more incursions. Mrs. Steel had about this period some friends who lived on the Yadkin in North Carolina, ninety miles from her home. When she wished to visit them she was accustomed to take her child, a year old, twelve miles distance, to the house of Robert Brown, the nearest neighbor she had in the direction of the Yadkin. Leaving the infant in their care, she would proceed alone, on horseback, making her way through the Catawba Nation, and travelling through a wild country which might be called uninhabited, for so sparse was the population that from Camden to the Catawba Nation—a distance of sixty miles, there were but four houses of white settlers. She was unsurpassed in the qualities of a horsewoman, nor was she impeded by trifling inconveniences or dangers. She probably gave each of the four settlers a call as she passed to visit her friends, and on her return, though tradition preserves no instance of her needing their assistance or hospitality. A hardy race must the wives of the pioneers have been!

In 1763, Thomas Steel, with James Hemphill and Stephen White, left home on a trading expedition, taking with them packhorses, loaded with articles suited for traffic with the Indians. They were absent a year or more, going through the far west to the

Mississippi, where they took canoes and went down the river to New Orleans. On their way homeward they were taken by some Indians, who stripped them of everything, even their clothes; but they escaped with their lives, and succeeded in getting back into the French settlements. White was a blacksmith, and worked at his business to procure clothes and food for himself and his companions. Having been thus refitted for the journey, they set out once again, travelling through the primitive forest. One morning, when they were about to resume their journey, Steel had chanced to walk out of sight. The others waited for his return, and after some time heard a gun discharged at a distance. They quitted their place of encampment to go in search of him; but their search was fruitless, nor did their missing companion ever come back. They supposed he had been killed when they heard the shot, and that his body was either carried off by the murderer or so concealed in the woods that no search availed to find it. Certain of his death, they pursued their way home, bearing the sad news to his family. Mrs. Steel was now left alone with a family—three daughters and two sons—and she devoted all her energies to their careful training, instructing them in all things useful, and teaching them to labor not merely for their own benefit, but the good of the community. The sterling principles she instilled into their minds produced their fruit in the actions of after years, when trials even more severe than any she had undergone in early life, fell to her lot and theirs.

Before the year 1780 she had given her daughters in marriage—Margaret to William Wylie ; Mary to Robert Archer; Nancy to Thomas Bell ; she living with John, now grown to manhood, and the youngest child, Thomas. She divided the land belonging to her deceased husband equally among the children—giving to each of the daughters a valuable plantation. The lands on the Creek—the finest then and even at this day in the district, she divided between John and Thomas. It is worthy of note, that her eldest son, although by the law of primogeniture entitled to claim all the lands, confirmed his mother's acts, and contentedly received only the portion she assigned him in the distribution. The early recollections of this young man went back to the time of danger from Indian incursion, and it was natural he should be imbued with strong veneration for the high-spirited mother with whom he had so often been in the midst of peril, sustained by her firmness, encouraged by her boldness, and accustomed to be cheered by her in every despondency or privation. Always meriting her popular name, "witty Katy of the Fort," she would laugh away the fears of her timid companions, when she could not reason them into bravery. Her influence over her children, therefore, was not to be wondered at—strengthened as it was by habit and affection when left to her sole care.

The home of Mrs. Steel was at no great distance from that of John Gaston, whose family she and her children often visited, going in canoes up and down

the stream. She was in the habit of sending for the
newspaper, by which she learned from time to time
what was going on during the first years of the war.
In their friendly meetings, she and the old Justice
would read for one another the news of battles lost and
won at the North, and converse on the subjects then
absorbing the general attention. The sons of Gaston
were the companions of her son, and when there was
a call for men, John Steel was foremost in proffering
his services. He was at the head of the company from
Chester despatched against the Cherokee Indians in
the Snow campaign of 1775. At the battle of Fort
Moultrie, on Sullivan's Island, he was also engaged,
with seven of the sons of Justice Gaston. At the siege
of Savannah, he took part in the charge made under
the command of Count Pulaski, and was with the
troops hovering around to annoy the British army
during the siege of Charleston. After the fall of that
city, when news came of the horrible butchery of Buford's men by Tarleton at the Waxhaws, he was
among those assembled at the house of John Gaston,
appealing solemnly to the God of battles, and pledging
their oath that they would never accept British protection, nor lay down the arms they had taken up
while there remained an enemy in the land. How
must his mother have exulted in the knowledge
that her first-born displayed a spirit worthy of her,
and did such honor to her lessoning !

On that memorable morning, when the devoted little
band went forth from Justice Gaston's to make the

attack upon the British, on the spot where Beckhamville now stands,* Katharine Steel called upon her
younger son, the only child remaining with her, and
then about seventeen, to go out with the rest. "You
must go now," she said to him, "and fight the battles
of our country with John. It must never be said the
old Squire's boys have done more for the liberty of
their country than the Widow Steel's!"

"It was a solemn morning," would John Steel say
afterwards in telling of it. "Some of those who had
come to join us over night, had gone off and left
us, deeming it too perilous an enterprise for a handful of men to attack two hundred—many of them
British soldiers. We had sworn solemnly before high
heaven, and our resolution was like the law of the
Medes and Persians—not to be altered. As we started
off, there came up eight men from Sandy River, who
had been travelling all night. This was a bright spot
—like the sun coming out from under a cloud! We
felt that our men were true men."

Capt. Steel—who has been called "the Murat of
Catawba River"—was in every engagement during the
summer of 1780. He commanded a company of
mounted rangers, and at the taking of Carey Fort performed feats that drew the attention of Gen. Sumter
to the brave young officer. During the retreat with
the stores and prisoners captured from the British, he
acted as a scout. The retreat was continued during
the nights of August 16th and 17th, and at eleven

* See memoir of Esther Walker.

o'clock on the morning of the 18th, Sumter's army
was posted in the stronghold of Fishing Creek, two
miles from its junction with the Catawba, where a
bend in stream and river leaves a ridge of elevated
ground between them from which both can be seen.
In front and rear of this space deep ravines run from
the river and the creek, leaving a narrow strip along
which the road passes, while below, the road left the
ridge and entered a valley opening to the creek with
steep hills on either side. In this position, certainly
well chosen for its natural advantages, the army was
encamped, fearing no enemy's approach. The particulars of the memorable surprise that here took place,
are not recorded in history. Mr. Stinson, whose residence is near the spot, has collected them from survivors of that day. (See Appendix.)

Gen. Sumter had stripped off his coat and boots, for
he was in need of repose, and was lying fast asleep
under his marquée. None of his men perceived the
approach of the British; the first intimation given of
their presence was a general fire from Tarleton's dragoons, instantly followed by a bold charge into the
midst of the camp. With the assault, resistance, and
endeavors to escape, the wildest confusion of course
ensued. In the moment of alarm Steel's first thought
was for the General. With admirable presence of
mind, and thoughtless of his own safety, he ran
directly to the marquée, caught Sumter in his arms,
and had carried him out through the back part of the
tent before he was fully awake. He had also seized

the portmanteau in which, as he knew, valuable public papers were carried, and brought it along with him. He bore the General to a horse ready saddled, and hastily assisted him to mount, bareheaded as he was ; his rangers were already mounted and clustering around him, and under their protection Steel brought him through a shower of bullets, while in all directions around them the soldiers were running, as many as could catch horses mounting and making off. The British, knowing their chief prize was eluding their grasp, hotly pursued Capt. Steel; but whenever the dragoons came too near he would order his rangers to wheel their horses about suddenly and fire upon them. As the foremost fell, their horses running loose were caught and mounted by the flying soldiers, and this proving a losing business, they soon abandoned the pursuit and returned to the disordered camp. One characteristic incident deserves mention. James Harbinson (the late Capt. Harbinson), one of Steel's company, and at that time a noble-looking youth of eighteen, rode up by the side of Sumter, took off his hat, and with a gesture of graceful courtesy presented it to the General, tying a handkerchief around his own head.

It cannot be ascertained how far Steel conducted General Sumter, or if he proceeded with him all the way to Charlotte. It was not long, however, before he was sent back by his order, with a force of some fifteen men, one of his objects being to find, if possible, the valise containing the public papers, which had been dropped by the man to whose care he entrusted it shortly after they left the camp. It was supposed to have been lost somewhere in the woods, not more than a mile from the place of the surprise. Every foot of the ground was familiar to Steel, for it was the home of his childhood. He was also commissioned to collect men wherever he could find them, and send them to join Sumter, who intended to rally his forces at Charlotte. On this mission he was traversing the country day and night. When he reached the place of the late disaster, he learned that the valise had been found by one of the tories from the Wateree, and carried to Hogfork, on Wateree Creek. Thither he proceeded and obtained it—none of the papers having been taken out. On his way back he chanced to meet the wife of one of his acquaintances, and stopped to bid her tell her husband that all patriots were summoned to meet their General at Charlotte, and that he must come and join him the next morning at Neely's on Fishing Creek, whence he could go on with his party. Steel was not aware that the man to whom he sent this message had turned loyalist. The woman, of course, immediately carried the news to her husband, who set out to collect tories for the purpose of intercepting Capt. Steel, travelling all night through the neighborhood, for the attack was to be at Neely's on the following morning.

Meanwhile the brave captain, suspecting no treachery, reached his home late that night, and once more embraced the excellent mother who had trained him

to his present career of duty. Early the next morning he set off for Neely's, about four miles distant,
Mrs. Steel accompanying him on horseback. Proud
was she that the gallant son riding by her side had
risked his life in the country's service, and by his
courageous efforts saved his General from being captured in the late attack; proud also of his bold
recovery of the papers, and his energetic appeal to his
countrymen to arm themselves and rally round the
standard of liberty. Her heart swelled with exultation, as she saw men on all sides responding to the
call, and if some anxiety for the safety of her children
and neighbors mingled with her patriotic joy, she had
before her eyes the battles of Rocky Mount and Hanging Rock, and had good hope that they would return
to victory. No motives of ambition mingled with her
enthusiasm, nor did the services of her son receive any
reward save the consciousness of having nobly performed his duty. His name and his brave deeds,
which should have been remembered and recorded
with others in the Revolution, have been honored only
in the section of country where he lived, and among the
descendants of those who were his companions.

When the party arrived at Neely's, Mrs. Neely and
some of her daughters immediately busied themselves
in preparing breakfast. The horses were hitched to
trees in the yard, and two other daughters of the
landlady went out into the cornfield to keep watch.
All was silent for some time ; at length a man named
Andrew Lockart left 'the premises, followed by David

McCance, a young lad, to get his horse from the pasture. While going through the field, he saw a body of tories, in two divisions, approaching through the standing corn. The leader, whom he recognized as Coonrod Huntsucker, one of his near neighbors and a noted loyalist, waved his hand at him in token that he should keep silence. Lockart paid no heed to the signal, but halloed with all his might to give the alarm at the house. Thereupon another of the advancing party,—one David Ferguson of Wateree,—snapped his gun at him; Lockart then taking deliberate aim at the leader, fired and cut off his bridle reins, crippling one of his fingers, and stopping not to see the effect, turned and fled precipitately. In his flight he fell into a deep gully, which probably saved him, for the tories' shots passed over him as he lay still. Coonrod's horse in the meantime taking fright, ran away with him before he could recover his control of the bridle. This accident in all likelihood saved the party at the house. From the hollow where he lay, not venturing to move, Lockart heard firing at the house with the shouts of the tories, crying " Well done, Scoggins !" &c. When he found they were out of the way, he came out from his concealment, as far as the stream called Rocky Branch. Hearing steps approach, he took up a large stone to throw at the supposed foe ; but it proved to be only the boy David McCance, who narrowly escaped being killed by the missile. While the two stood there, they saw the whole body of tories going off, evidently disappointed of their expected prey ; and sure

5*

of their friends' escape, both lost no time in catching their horses, and started at their utmost speed for Charlotte, not knowing but that a reinforcement of loyalists might suddenly arrive.

At the time of the alarm, Mrs. Steel was engaged in combing the captain's hair. He boasted a remarkably fine head of hair; it was very long and of raven blackness, and was usually worn tied in a queue behind. John's important services to the whig cause, employing him almost night and day, had of late left him little leisure for attention to his locks; they had been long uncombed, and probably showed very plainly the neglect they had experienced. The personal appearance of her son was a matter of pride to the matron, only less than her delight in his gallant conduct; she loved to see him look well, for he was a fairer image of herself. With her features he inherited her high qualities of mind and heart; he regarded her with reverence as well as affection, and never once in his life had disobeyed her. She had instilled into him the principles which guided herself; she had breathed into him her own romantic and unconquerable spirit. It was a common remark at the time and afterwards, that any one who might chance to overhear the conversation between the mother and son, not knowing who they were, might suppose from its tone and tenor that two young men were discoursing upon some animating theme. The disasters that from time to time had overtaken the American arms, could not discourage their hopes, nor subdue their ardor. *" We are in the right*," Mrs. Steel would repeat, and that knowledge was the source of confidence and comfort through every trial

To retu ——while thus occupied, they heard the sharp crack of the rifle, followed immediately by Lockart's warning shouts, and the screams of the young girls who had been stationed in the field. In a moment after, several guns were fired in quick succession, and the girls were seen running towards the house, while the two divisions of the enemy, at no great distance behind them, could be perceived advancing through the standing corn. Not an instant was to be lost ; yet such was the effect of sudden surprise on the brave men who, only two days before, had been taken unawares on Fishing Creek, that they seemed utterly at a loss what to do. Mrs. Steel alone retained perfect self-possession. Starting up, she called to the men, " You must fight !" but directly after, seeing the confusion that prevailed, she shouted an order for them to " clear themselves" as fast as possible. She urged her son to mount his horse at once, and save the public papers in his charge, while she pulled down the bars to let out him and his men. John was quick in all his movements, and it may easily be conceived that no time was now wasted. First in the saddle, he spurred his noble horse towards the bars, which he cleared at a bound—his mother having had no time yet to let them down—and galloped off. He was followed by James Harbinson, and the greater number of his men, for whom Mrs. Steel removed the bars as

fast as she could ; several, however, were slower in
getting off, and paid the penalty of their delay, being
now exposed to the fire of the advancing tories. About
fifty guns were discharged at the bars, and two of the
whigs—William Anderson and James Barber—fell
dead from their horses, bearing Mrs. Steel under them
to the ground. Another received wounds of which
he expired in a few days, and three others,
also severely wou·.ded, succeeded in making their
way to the house of McFadden, one of the neighbors. Robert McFadden, who could not get his horse,
in leaping the bars had part of his foot shot off; Samuel McCance, riding at full speed up the lane, received
a shot in the hip, and John Lockart's hunting-shirt
filling with the wind as he rode, was riddled through
and through with bullets that missed his body. Capt.
Steel, determined to cut his way through the assail-
ants, rode foremost up the lane at full speed, his long
hair, unfastened, streaming in the wind, his rifle in
one hand, held high above his head in defiance of the
foe. He was closely followed by those of his company
who had escaped. The tories made no attempt to
stop them ; but startled by the fury of their onset on
their own party, gave way precipitately and scattered
from the road, though they might have overpowered
them by numbers ; nor were they able to rally till the
fugitives were beyond their reach. The whigs who were
taken prisoners were carried to Camden ; one or two
died in the gaol there, while others languished for
seven months, suffering incredible cruelties.

How was it meanwhile with the matron, as she struggled to release herself from the weight of the dead bodies, rising from the ground covered with the blood of the slain, her dress pierced in different places with bullet holes! Her first thought was for " John and the papers." When she heard they were safe, she burst into an exclamation of thankfulness, and as she was fortunately unhurt, turned her attention to the relief of others. The tories, meanwhile, enraged at their disappointment, and ascribing their failure to the energetic aid of Mrs. Steel, with one accord turned their course to her house. This they burned to the ground, and destroyed her property of every description, wherever they could find anything belonging to her. This vindictive outrage was the strongest testimony they could give of their estimate of the importance of her services to her friends.

The captain often related this adventure, and said that when flying along the lane with his hair streaming, he thought of Absalom, and vowed, if he escaped his fate while passing under the trees, to sacrifice the hair which had brought him into such peril. This resolve was carried into effect; for the Misses Hemphill afterwards at his request cut it off. James Harbinson, who also wore his hair in a queue, lost it by a singular chance: it was cut off by a rifle ball as he leaped the bars. The vow he then made was different from the captain's; for he resolved to wear it long while he lived, in defiance of British or tories, and religiously kept his resolution for more than half a century. It is still

remembered that at a large Fourth of July celebra-
tion, this aged soldier appeared with his hair, then as
white as cotton, tied up in a queue, and that he
enlivened the festival with song after song and story
after story of the Revolution.   His voice was remarkably sweet and powerful, and he was a tall, strongly-
built, and noble-looking old man, whose ripened age
had redeemed the promise of his youth.   He lived to
see the national prosperity his stripling arm had
helped to win, his death taking place about 1840.

Captain Steel and those who escaped with him made
their way that night to Charlotte.   Andrew Lockart
and his young companion became separated accidentally, and lay during the night in a thicket near the
Nation Ford, neither knowing that the other was close
in his neighborhood till the next morning, when they
discovered each other, and went on together.   Steel
continued to act a distinguished part in the partisan
service, was at Charlotte when Cornwallis advanced
upon the place, and also at King's Mountain.   He was
afterwards with Col. Lacey when, after leaving
Fishdam Ford, Sumter, aware of Tarleton's approach,
made a hasty retreat, and took up his position at
Blackstock's, near Tyger River.   On the retreat, Sumter ordered his servant to dismount, gave the horse to
Sergeant Rowan, and desired him to go back with Mr.
Hannah, of York, to watch the enemy's movements.
The two ere long discovered that two officers of Tarleton's kept in advance of the main body.   Rowan
offered his canteen of whiskey to Hannah, and took a

long draught himself, for he had much faith in that
sort of inspiration; he then proposed to "take a nigh
cut and wait upon those two gentlemen." As the
doomed officers came near the ambush, both were shot
by the concealed whigs. Rowan rode back and
secured the sword of his victim, and they brought Sumter information of the near approach of Tarleton's cavalry. On this report the General prepared for immediate action. The encounter, with its result, is detailed
in history; the Americans had the advantage, but
Sumter received a severe wound, and was carried on
a litter the same night into North Carolina. Capt.
Steel returned home in November, and by the aid of
his faithful rangers reduced the neighborhood to order,
organizing the militia, bringing some of the tories to
trial and execution for murder, driving others of the
worst from the country, and pardoning less culpable
offenders who promised reformation. The condition
of the times demanded such summary measures;
a fatal disease threatened destruction to the body
of the state, and it needed a sharp weapon and
an unshrinking hand to eradicate it. Steel was
encouraged in all he did by the counsels and approbation of his mother. She rejoiced in seeing the friends
of liberty rally once more to recover the State, and exulted not a little when Morgan's and Davison's troops
crossed the river near her residence.* In every matter relating to the war she took a special interest. The

* A record of all these military movements, is extant in a manuscript written by George Wade, who at the time furnished the

story of Col. Washington's log cannon, she thought one of the best jokes she had ever heard. Early in December, 1780, this colonel, who had penetrated with a small force to the neighborhood of Camden, appeared in hostile array before the house of Col. Rugely, who had taken a commission in the British militia. He had surrounded his house with a stockade fort, and kept there one hundred and twelve men, who were under his command. Washington's cannon was a pine log, one end of which was stuck in the ground, while the other, elevated a few feet by its branches, was presented. The imagination of the garrison converting the harmless timber into a piece of artillery completely equipped with the apparatus of destruction—they immediately surrendered.

An anecdote of one of the "fighting men" of the neighborhood is illustrative. After the whigs had begun to re-establish themselves on the soil, John Gaston the younger, having returned home, heard from Andrew Lockart the particulars of the affair at Neely's, and the shout of the tories—" Hurra for Scoggins!" Resolved to visit the offence with summary punishment, he took his rifle, mounted his horse, and rode at full speed to Scoggins' house, which stood near the river, just below the spot where Sumter had been surprised. Scoggins saw him galloping that way in fiery haste, and conscious of his deserts for having

American troops with corn and other provisions. He and the McDonalds were the wealthiest planters on the Catawba, and their fine lands along the river produced large supplies of corn.

conspired to entrap and murder his neighbors, was in no small trepidation. As Gaston neared the house, he fired at him, but missed his aim. Gaston dashed on to the door, driving back Scoggins, cocked his weapon, presented it and fired, but also missed, the man dodging at the instant, and his own eyes being somewhat blinded with the smoke. Scoggins seized the opportunity to dart past his assailant, who, flourishing his empty gun, rushed after the fugitive, pursuing him along the river, and up and down the high hill at Cloud's fishtraps. The race continued for more than an hour, till Scoggins finally made his escape, either the anger or the strength of his pursuer being exhausted. No further attempt was made to punish him, for the fright and race for his life were considered as entitling him to immunity.

John Steel continued in active service, and was engaged in every battle during the campaign of 1781. In the spring following, he was married to Margaret Beard, Esther Gaston and Alexander Walker officiating as bridesmaid and groomsman. Thomas Steel, the younger brother, afterwards married the sister of Margaret. John was accustomed jocularly to apologise for the interruption in his military career, by protesting he had deferred to his bride's wish to have the marriage hastened; he was willing to please her at inconvenience to himself, but being absent only on a furlough, was obliged to leave her directly and return to the camp. He laid his commands on the affianced lovers Esther and Alexander, that they should not be

wedded till he finally came home ; threatening punishment if they disobeyed his injunction. They chose,
however, to be guided by their own judgment in so
important a step, and as John's return was delayed till
he had seen the British fleet leave his native shore, he
found his friends comfortably settled in their new
abode. He, for his part, had thoroughly enjoyed the
soldier's life ; he was at home in the camp, and the
ever fresh and varied excitement, with continual
change of scene, suited his adventurous spirit. It is
not a little remarkable that he was never wounded in
all his battles, though he never shrunk from perilous
enterprise, always exposing himself among the foremost. His home was upon the old plantation,
where his family grew up around him. The produce
of his lands supplied his wants, and he never showed
any desire to accumulate wealth. His disposition was
amiable, and he seemed not to remember injuries he
had received during the war, though others did not
always show an equal readiness to forgive him. As
an illustration of his placable nature, his daughter,
Mrs. Jane Thompson, mentioned a singular fact—that
she never learned from her father who had been whig
or tory among their neighbors. On one occasion when
they were at a religious meeting, she noticed a man
with his hand bound up, and asking her father what
was the matter, was answered simply that it had been
hurt. She learned from others that the man's
hand had been wounded while he served with
the loyalists, and that afterwards turning patriot he

was ashamed of his former conduct and unwilling that it should be mentioned. This generosity on Steel's part will appear the more worthy of commendation when we consider the state of feeling then prevalent between opposite parties, throughout the country.

When peace returned to the country and order once more prevailed, Mrs. Steel's zealous efforts were not wanting to heal breaches among the neighbors, and remove obstacles to a good understanding. Her eldest son the pride of her heart, was aided by her, when the necessity for strong measures ceased, in holding out the hand of fellowship to the erring, reclaiming the depraved, and restraining the vindictive ferocity of her younger son and her sons-in-law. All she could influence were disposed to the exercise of a conciliatory spirit, and to forgetfulness of past wrongs. It was no trifling part of woman's mission to reconcile the discordant elements left by the disorganizing ravages of civil war, and to build up a new and promising state of society. Mrs. Steel showed no less of the truly heroic in her character in her labors after the establishment of peace, than in the darkest hour of the actual struggle. Her days were ended at the old fort in 1785. She was surrounded by her children, all of whom were married. Her eldest son, who had fought so many battles, was killed in 1812, by a fall from his horse. Even at an advanced age he was one of the best riders in the country, and it is said he had scarce a rival in this martial accomplishment, in the American army. When making a charge, his massive eyebrows drawn down, his teeth set, and his whole aspect denoting iron determination, he was said to look like a commissioned demon of destruction. Yet in the social circle he showed himself one of the most jovial spirits in the world. His hair, which in youth had been such an ornament, at the time of his death had the same glossy blackness, and his fine countenance and powerful frame betokened no diminution of strength. All the survivors of the Revolution in the region where he lived spoke with warm admiration of Capt. Steel, and among their descendants his memory is venerated as one of the bravest of the brave, and a benefactor to his native land. The mother to whom he owed so much, retained to the last of life the sprightliness and sweetness of disposition that had distinguished her in youth. She was always ready to enter into the lively conversation of those around her, and could laugh and jest with the merriest; while all the tenderness of the woman, as well as an indomitable courage, marked her character. Her personal appearance was striking and attractive, and her face bore the impress of the spirit that shone forth in so many noble actions.

The descendants of the Steel family, with those of Mrs. Steel's sons-in-law, have removed to the west, and are scattered through different States. The only one remaining in South Carolina is Mrs. Jane Thompson, before mentioned as the daughter of Capt Steel.

VII.

NANCY GREEN.

An interesting glimpse into the life and character of
the Scotch-Irish patriots of South Carolina at the period of the Revolution, is afforded in the history of
Mrs. Green. She was the daughter of Robert Ste-
phenson, (commonly called Stinson) a native of
Scotland, and was born in the county of Antrim, Ireland, in 1750. The family was reared in the strictest
tenets of the covenanting faith, in the parish of Ballymoney, under the pastoral care of the Rev. William
Martin, who about the year 1773 emigrated to America
and took up his abode on the banks of Rocky Creek, a
branch of Catawba River, in the county, now district
of Chester, South Carolina. Many of his congregation quitted their country with him, following their
pastor under the impulse of the same desire—of
" freedom to worship God." Among these emigrants
were James, William and Elizabeth Stinson and their
brother-in-law, William Anderson, who had married
Nancy Stinson shortly before the sailing of the ship.
Her wedded life thus commenced with a voluntary re-
nunciation of home and the society of her early friends,

to seek a new country—encountering unforeseen privations and difficulties. They were accompanied by an orphan girl—Lizzy Craig—a niece of Anderson, and his only relative who came to America. At this time bounty lands were bestowed by the government as inducements to emigration. Those who received such warrants, on their arrival took care to fix their location as near as possible to a central point, where it was their intention to build a meeting-house. The spirit was that of the ancient patriarchs, who, wherever they went, first built an altar unto the Lord. The spot selected for this purpose was the dividing ridge between Great and Little Rocky Creek. Here, in the summer of 1773, the pious covenanters might be seen from day to day, felling trees and clearing a space of ground, on which they reared a large log meeting-house, many of them living in tents at home, till a place was provided in which they could assemble for religious service.

The land selected by William Anderson lay about two miles to the east, half a mile from what is now Rossville, near Great Rocky Creek. On a small elevation near the road leading to McDonald's Ferry, stood his tent, until the meeting house was completed. He then went to work for himself, and built a log cabin, clearing around it a patch of ground in which he planted Indian corn. He was ignorant of the manner of cultivating this grain, but the first settlers, or "country-borns," were ever ready to offer assistance, and took pains to instruct the Irish emigrants in its

culture. The wants of a small family were supplied
with small crops, for corn was then only used for making bread, the woods affording abundant supplies of
grass, cane and wild pea vines, to serve their horses
and cattle for provender the year round. The streams
abounded in shad and various other fish in their season, and the trusty rifle that hung on the rack over
the door, was never brought back without having performed its duty in slaying the deer, the bear, or whatever small game might be sought in the forest. Often
have the old men who lived at that day spoken of the
abundance that prevailed, and the ease with which
money could be made; a good hunter, when he chose
making five dollars a day in deer skins and hams,
while if generous he might give away the remainder
of venison to the poor. The hams and skins were
sent to Charleston and exchanged for powder, lead,
and other necessary articles. The wealth of these
primitive planters consisted in stock, their labors in
tilling the earth, felling the woods and fencing their
fields, while they were disturbed by none of the wants
or cares created by a more advanced state of civiliza-
tion. Such was the condition of the Covenanters who
had left their native Ireland for the religious liberty
found in these wilds. During seven years after their
settlement in the woods, the Andersons enjoyed a life
in which nothing of earthly comfort was wanting.
Year after year the little patch of corn was enlarged,
till it became a field of respectable dimensions, ten
acres being then considered a good clearing for a farm.

Their stock, small in the beginning, had increased to a numerous herd of cattle. William was now a man of substance, well to do in the world, able to assist others, and now and then to show his kind feeling towards a countryman or old acquaintance by the present of a cow. Not only had their basket and store been blessed, but their dwelling was gladdened by the voice of infancy. Of their three children the first-born—Mary—was able to read and repeat the catechism to the minister; Robert could read the Bible, and little William was just able to walk. Every Sabbath morning the parents, in their Sunday clothes, with their neatly-dressed and well-behaved little ones, might be seen at the log church, their pocket Bibles containing the old Psalms, in their hands. Turning over the leaves, they would follow the preacher in all the passages of Scripture cited by him, as he commented on his text. Thus their simple, trustful piety caused the wilderness to rejoice.

But this happiness could not be lasting. The rumor of war had gone over the land; it was heard even in this remote section, and these refugees who had found peace could not but sympathise with their oppressed brethren. The desolation that ravaged the North, ere long took its way southward. The attack on Sullivan's Island startled many who had fancied themselves in security. Some persons from the Catawba region were at the scene of strife, and brought a report to those remaining at home, while several did their part by going out against the Cherokee Indians; yet so far

this pleasant neighborhood had been spared, and
seemed likely to continue exempt from the miseries of
civil war ; its families were unmolested, and the pure
ordinances of the gospel were regularly administered,
with none to make them afraid. This immunity was
of short duration. John McClure, of Fishing Creek,
coming home, brought intelligence of the surrender of
Charleston, and his own defeat at Monk's Corner.
Still worse was the news from across the river—of the
inhuman massacre of Buford's command by Tarleton's
corps, at the Waxhaws. This event gave a more san-
guinary character to the war. Directly after this appalling announcement, spread the rumor that a strong
party of British was posted at Rocky Mount, that the
people of Wateree were flocking to take protection, and
profess themselves loyal subjects of King George, and
that the conquerors were sending forces in every direction to reduce the province to submission. Such was
the aspect of affairs up to a certain Sabbath in June
1780.

On the morning of this memorable Sabbath—the
picture is drawn in no hues of fiction—the different
paths leading to the log meeting-house were unusually
thronged. The old country folk were dressed with
their usual neatness, especially the women, whose
braw garments, brought from Ireland, were carefully
preserved, not merely from thrift, but as a memorial
of the green isle of their birth. They wore fur hats
with narrow rims and large feathers—their hair neatly
braided,—hanging over their shoulders, or fastened by

the black ribbon bound around their heads. The
handsome dress of silk or chintz—a mixture of wool
and flax—or of Irish calico, fitted each wearer with
marvellous neatness, and the collar or ruffles of linen
white as snow, with the high-heeled shoes, completed
their holiday attire. It was always a mystery to the
dames who had spent their lives, or many years in the
country, how the gowns of the late comers could be
made to fit so admirably, their own, in spite of every
effort, showing a sad deficiency in this respect. The
secret of the difference probably lay in the circumstance that the females from the old country wore
stays well fortified with whalebone. The men, on
their part, appeared not less adorned in their coats of
fine broadcloth, with their breeches, large knee buckles
of pure silver, and hose of various colors. They wore
shoes fastened with a large strap secured with a
buckle, or white topped boots, leaving exposed three
or four inches of the hose from the knee downward.
It must be acknowledged that this people, so strict in
their religious opinions, were somewhat remarkable in
their fondness for dress. They considered it highly
irreverent to appear at church not clad in their best
attire, and though when engaged in labor during the
week they conformed to the custom of their neighbors,
wearing the coarse homespun of their own manufacture,
on the Sabbath it was touching to see how much of
decent pride there was in the exhibition of the fine
clothes brought from beyond seas. As years rolled on,
many of the dresses and coats began to show marks

of decay ; but careful repairing preserved the hoarded garments linked with such endeared associations, and only a few who had married with the " country-borns" had made any alteration in them. This peculiarity in dress gave the congregation assembled to worship in that rude sanctuary, a strange and motley appearance—European finery being contrasted with the homespun gowns, hunting-shirts and moccasins of the country people. It was always insisted on as a point of duty among the Covenanters, that children should be brought to church with their parents. The little ones sat between the elders, that they might be kept quiet during divine service, and be ready at the appointed hour for the catechism. The strict deportment and piety of this people had already done much to change the customs formerly prevalent ; men and women who used to hunt or fish on the Sabbath now went regularly to meeting, and some notorious ones, whose misconduct had been a nuisance to the community left the neighborhood. The Strouds, Kitchens and Morrises, formerly regarded as the Philistines of the land were regular in their attendance upon divine worship.

On this particular day, the whole neighborhood seemed to have turned out, and every face wore an expression of anxiety. Groups of men might be seen gathered together under shade trees in every direction, talking in loud and earnest tones ; some laying down plans for the assent of their friends; some pale with alarm, listening to others telling the news, and some, transported with indignation, stamping the ground and gesticulating vehemently as they spoke.   Everywhere the women mingled with the different groups, and appeared to take an active part in what was going on. At eleven o'clock precisely, the venerable form of Martin, the preacher, came in sight.   He was about sixty years of age, and had a high reputation for learning and eloquence.   He was a large and powerful man, with a voice which it is said might have been heard at the distance of half a mile.   As he walked from the place where he had hitched his horse, towards the stand, it being customary, when the congregation was too large to be accommodated in the meeting-house, to have the service in the open air, the loud and angry words of the speakers must have reached his ears. The voices ceased as he approached, and the congregation was soon seated in silence upon the logs around the stand.

When he arose to speak, every eye was fixed upon him.   Those who had been most noisy expected a reproof for their desecration of the Sabbath, for their faithful pastor was never known to fail of rebuking those whose deportment was unsuited to the solemnity of the day.   But at this time he too seemed absorbed with the subject that agitated every bosom.   " My hearers," he said, in his broad Scotch-Irish dialect— " talk and angry words will do no good. *We must fight !*   As your pastor—in preparing a discourse suited to this time of trial—I have sought for all light, examined the Scriptures and other helps in ancient and modern history, and have considered especially the controversy between the United Colonies and the mother country. Sorely have our countrymen been dealt with, till forced to the declaration of their independence—and the pledge of their lives and sacred honor to support it. Our forefathers in Scotland made a similar one, and maintained that declaration with their lives; it is now our turn, brethren, to maintain this at all hazards." After the prayer and singing of the Psalms—he calmly opened his discourse. He cited many passages from Scripture to show that a people may lawfully resist wicked rulers; pointed to historical examples of princes trampling on the people's rights; painted in vivid colors the rise and progress of the reformation—the triumph of truth over the misrule and darkness of ages—and finally applied the subject by fairly stating the merits of the Revolutionary controversy. Giving a brief sketch of the events of the war from the first shedding of blood at Lexington, and warming with the subject as he went on, his address became eloquent with the fiery energy of a Demosthenes. In a voice like thunder, frequently striking with his clenched fist the clapboard pulpit, he appealed to the excited concourse, exhorting them to fight valiantly in defence of their liberties. As he dwelt on the recent horrid tragedy—the butchery of Buford's men, cut down by the British dragoons while crying for mercy —his indignation reached its height. Stretching out his hand towards Waxhaw—" Go see," he cried— " the tender mercies of Great Britain ! In that church

you may find men, though still alive, hacked out of
the very semblance of humanity : some deprived of
their arms—mutilated trunks : some with one arm or
leg, and some with both legs cut off. Is not this cruelty
a parallel to the history of our Scottish fathers, driven
from their conventicles, hunted like wild beasts ?
Behold the godly youth, James Nesbit—chased for
days by the British for the crime of being seen on his
knees upon the Sabbath morning !" etc. To this
stirring sermon the whole assembly responded. Hands
were clenched and teeth set in the intensity of feeling ;
every uplifted face expressed the same determination,
and even the women were filled with the spirit that
threatened vengeance on the invaders. During the
interval of divine worship they went about professing
their resolution to do their part in the approaching
contest; to plough the fields and gather the crops in
the absence of the men—aye, to fight themselves,
rather than submit. In the afternoon the subject was
resumed and discussed with renewed energy—while
the appeals of the preacher were answered by even
more energetic demonstrations of feeling. When the
worship was concluded, and the congregation separating to return homeward, the manly form of Ben Land
was seen walking among the people, shaking hands
with every neighbor and whispering in his ear the
summons to the next day's work.

As the minister quitted the stand, William Stroud
stepped up to him. This man, with his sons, was
noted for strength and bravery. They were so tall in

stature, that like Saul, they overlooked the rest of the congregation. He doubted not, he said, that Mr. Martin had heard of his " whipping the pets." "I rather think," he continued, " some people will be a little on their guard how they go to Rocky Mount for 'tection papers! Yesterday I was down at old deaf Lot's still-house; who do you think was there? John and Dick Featherston! John said he had been to Rocky Mount to see the fine fellows, and they were so good to him, to give him 'tection. Do, John, tell me what that is, I asked. He said it was a paper, and whoever had one was safe; not a horse, cow or hog would the British take from him without paying two prices for it. So, John, says I, I know now who told the British about James Stinson's large stock of cows, which they drove off yesterday, knocking down Mrs. Stinson for putting up old Brindle in the horse stable, so as to keep one cow to give milk for the children! Now, John, as you have British 'tection, I will give you Whig 'tection! With that I knocked him down; Dick came running up; I just gave him a kick in front; he doubled up; John got up and ran for it, and Dick begged like a whipped boy. I told him he might carry the news that 'tection paper men should be whipped and have their cows taken from them to pay James Stinson for his. I think this is what you call the law of Moses! and as for these Britishers, if I don't make old Nelly ring in their ears and be *dad* to them! Excuse me for swearing this time, if you please. Now, Mr. Minister, here is old Bill—that is two: then here

is young Will, Tom, Jack, Hamp, Erby, Ransom, and
Hardy ; and there are some girls, you know, and the
baby, little Anzel.   I have heard you say children are
a crown to old men who sit at the gate."   The manner in which this characteristic speech was delivered,
may be imagined.   Martin showed his acceptance of
the proffered aid by taking William's hand, and introducing him to Capt. Land.

On his way home from meeting William Anderson
was unusually silent, as if some weighty matter engaged all his thoughts.   Mrs. Anderson spoke first—
after she too had been reflecting.   " I think, William,
little Lizzy and I can finish the crop, and gather it in
if need be, as well as take care of the stock."   "I am
glad of that, Nancy," was the reply.   " I was silent,
for I did na ken how to let you know it, but to-mor-
row morning I leave home.   The way is now clear ;
the word of God approves, and it shall ne'er be said
that the Covenanters, the followers of the reformers of
Scotland, would na lend a helpin' hand to the renewal
of the Covenant in the land of America !   Now, Nancy,
Capt. Land will be out before day, giving notice that
up at the cross road hard by, he will drill the men
who are willing to fight ; this was agreed upon as I
left."   Their conversation through the day was in the
same strain.   As they rose from dinner, Mrs. Anderson said, " William, were you out at kirk in Ballymoney on that Sabbath when Mary Martin, our minister's first wife, lay a corpse in his house ?   No one
thought he could attend to preaching in his sore dis-

tress; but precisely at the striking of the hour he was
seen walking down the long aisle to the pulpit. I
never shall forget the sermon! there was not a dry
eye in the whole congregation; old men and women
fairly cried aloud. I thought of that, to-day, when
after sermon old Stroud went up to him as if he had
been one of the elders. Did you see the man of God
clap Stroud on the back as if he were going to see
him have a fair boxing match? Our minister is a
wonderful man; he can persuade people to almost anything." William Anderson looked up quietly and
asked, " Did he persuade you to marry him, Nancy,
when he went to your father's a courting?"

" Na, indeed, William; I could na think of an old
man when I had you fairly in my net. But I did
him a good turn in letting him know that Jenny
Cherry was setting her cap for him, and sure enough
he took my advice, and they were married. You
know they called their first child for me—Nancy—a
little older than our Mary."

That Sunday evening wore away, and early on the
Monday morning the plough stood still in the furrow,
and the best horse, saddled and bridled, was at the
door. Mrs. Anderson had been up since a little after
midnight, making hoe cakes on the hoe, and corn
dodger in the oven, and while the cooking of meats
was going on, busily plying the needle, running up
sacks and bags to hold provision for man and horse on
a long journey. Good " Ball," accustomed to range
for his food, when not at liberty could not do without

6*

a few ears of corn.   As soon as he had taken his breakfast, William Anderson, bidding his wife farewell,
mounted and rode off.   In about two hours she heard
the firing of horsemen's pistols in the direction of the
muster-ground, and soon William made his appearance,
riding as fast as the horse could carry him.   Passing
around the house, he took the path to the spring, rode
down the stream from the spring and crossed the creek
at the cowford.   Some British dragoons who had been
in close pursuit, failing to overtake him, gave vent to
their rage by plundering the house of the most valuable articles of furniture, and insulting Mrs. Anderson
with gross and indecent language.   Their visit brought
the small pox ; and the poor mother's attention was
soon too entirely absorbed by the sufferings of her
children to leave time for distress on other accounts.
The brief glimpse she had of her husband as he fled
was probably the last ; it is not known that he ever
again came home, though he was not killed till two
months after.   She had only the assistance of Lizzy
in nursing the three little ones, and was often compelled to leave them, to plough the cornfield and finish
working the crop.   Thus the sufferers had not proper
attention, and it went hard with poor little Willie.
For a long time the mother despaired of his life, and
when he did at last recover, how altered was the beautiful boy whose fresh blooming face had been her delight!   This child was the late Col. William Anderson
of Chester District.

Before the return of the next Sabbath, Mrs. Ander-

son's stock had been driven off by the enemy, and the
log meeting-house was burned to the ground.   Stripped now of almost everything within doors and without, she had no resource but to roast the ears of green
corn, or dry the corn in the milk, and grate it on a
rough stone into coarse meal, of which she made mush
for herself and the sick children.   Meanwhile her husband joined the forces of Sumter under Capt. John
Steel, at Clem's Branch, on the east side of Catawba
River.   He was in the battle at Williamson's, at
Rocky Mount, Hanging Rock, and Carey's Fort on the
Wateree.   He was shot by the tories in the attack on
Steel's party at ʻNeely's, mentioned in the preceding
memoir.   In the confusion his body and Barber's were
left·unburied during the day ; but at night Mr. Culp
and one of his negroes dug a grave and interred them
by the bars where they fell.   Such was the end of a
brave man, whose name deserves honor from his adopted State.

Mrs. Anderson was now a widow in peculiar circumstances of desolation.   Her brothers James and William
were in the camp : the whigs had retired to North
Carolina, and the neighborhood was in consequence
left to the depredations of the tories.   In two months
great changes had taken place within the circuit of
three miles : in this limited neighborhood were five
newly made widows—Mrs. Anderson—Mrs. Land—
Mrs. Boyd—Mrs. James Barber and Mrs. Joseph
Barber.   Joseph had been taken at Fishing Creek,
and carried to Camden gaol, where he died, probably

of starvation. Young William Stroud was taken by
the British, and hung on the road—it is said by
Tarleton's orders—for the crime of fighting the battles
of his country when they chose to consider him a
British subject. His body hung upon the tree three
weeks during the month of August, a placard forbid-
ding his burial being fastened to it—and the loyalists
passing on the road daily to Rocky Mount. At last a
few friends bold enough to risk the vengeance threatened, came at night, and digging a hole in the earth
under the suspended corpse, climbed the tree, cut the
rope, and let it fall into the grave.* This happened
about half a mile below Green's meeting-house. A
strip of red clay about fifteen feet long—the only
patch of that color on the road, marked the last resting place of one who, in the short space of two months
had killed more soldiers of the royal army than probably any one else during the whole war. It was not
surprising that when taken, he should be punished so
barbarously for the purpose of striking terror into
others.

The season for harvest now approached, and the
wives of absent whigs, and the widows of those who
were slain, were obliged to cut and gather in the corn
for the use of their families. But what certainty had
they—exposed to cruel marauders—that they would
ever have a bushel of the grain for bread? It was
truly a dismal prospect, for in the state of the country

* Other accounts state that Stroud was buried by his sister. It
was Capt. Dickson, of York District, who cut him down.

they had little to expect but nakedness and starvation.

At the proper season Mrs. Anderson pulled her flax, watered and put it through the break, then scuttled it with the hand-scuttle, and hackled it on the coarse and fine hackle. Day after day, and at night too, the humming of her busy little wheel might he heard as she spun the flax. She had now no stock to attend to except the old sorrel mare and colt. The corn, when gathered, was put for safe keeping into the crib of Samuel Ferguson, one of her neighbors, and other articles, which she thought might be taken from her on some marauding visit of the tories, she gave into the charge of his excellent wife Isabella. These precautions were taken in view of her own approaching confinement, which took place in the winter. The child—a boy—called James Barber, after the unfortunate man who met his death at Neely's at the same moment with her husband, died in infancy of the scarlet fever.

From time to time some whigs of the neighborhood venturing to visit their homes, would call to inquire after her, and assist her by doing little turns of service, such as cutting wood, and the like ; but a great part of the fuel she used, she gathered herself, and carried it home on her shoulders, or with the help of Lizzy. Her brother, William Stinson, had removed, some years before the war, to the vicinity of King's Mountain. He served in Capt. Barber's company, and was engaged in the battle of King's Mountain. He paid

several visits to his sister, generally accompanied by
Ben Rowan, a hero whose history has all the interest
of a romance, and whose motto through life was,
" Never shrink from danger." Mrs. Anderson was encouraged by both, and assured that should she be maltreated, the offender would not escape the punishment
Rowan was in the habit of inflicting upon tories who
had distressed whig women. The food on which Mrs.
Anderson and her children subsisted during the winter
was chiefly bread, though occasionally a little meat
was brought to her by patrolling whigs. In February—
when in a southern climate the winter begins to soften
into spring—she contrived to build up the rock dam
at the place used for a fish trap, spending the whole of
several days, while at work, in the water up to her
knees. When the fish began to run, she went every
morning with Lizzy to the trap, and carried home
what had been taken. Some days she made several
traps, and the gain was proportionate. These fish she
dried in the wooden chimney, hanging them all the
way up, and thus supplied herself with provisions
against a time of need. Often has she been heard to
say that her life at this period was not an unhappy
one, though she suffered many privations. Incessant
occupation kept her thoughts from dwelling on past
sorrows, or anticipating distress, and her trust was
placed in Him who has said to the faithful, " I will
never leave thee nor forsake thee." She still mourned
for the brave man who had found a patriot's grave, but
resigned herself to the decree of Providence, endeavor-

ing to fill his place in the care of her helpless children. About the time she began preparations for putting in a new crop of corn, an occurrence took place which brought about an event having much influence on her future life.

One morning in April, 1781, long before the dawn of day, she was startled by hearing the sound of a huntsman's horn, on the road leading towards the spot where the meeting-house had stood. She thought she recognized the sound of Littleton Esbel's horn, and was not mistaken. Esbel was a mighty hunter in those days. He had no scruples about taking horses, and was always in possession of a good one ; he was, moreover, fond of good liquor, and always carried a canteen of whiskey with him. Withal, he was a good soldier, had been much in camp, fought valiantly, and was esteemed an active and intelligent fellow. He often boasted of successful cunning, and was heard to say "any fool could take a horse, but it took a wise man to keep him." On this occasion it happened that several other men, not so well mounted as himself, were in his company. As they rode, the merry hunter, in the exhilaration of spirits elevated by more than moderate draughts from the canteen, continually blew his horn. It chanced that a troop of British dragoons, from one of the royal posts below, were out that day, and hearing the continued blowing of the horn, they were induced to suppose there might be a general mustering of the rebels. They set off, accordingly, in the direction of the sound, and before Esbel had the least intimation of their approach, the tramp of their horses showed they were within a short distance. He saw at once the danger of his situation, but with the quickness of lightning bethought himself how to remedy the difficulty. At once he commenced in a very loud tone giving the usual military orders to prepare for action, while in a lower voice he bade his party clear out instantly and be off on peril of their lives. The stratagem succeeded to admiration; the dragoons halted, hearing the orders, and formed a line to face the expected attack, preparing to meet the enemy as well as they could. As soon as Esbel saw that his men were out of danger, putting spurs to his horse, he made for the road about a hundred and fifty yards to the left of the British, giving them a discharge of his rifle as he passed. The fire caused them to look in that direction, and seeing but a single foe, they started in pursuit. This was just what Esbel desired; he was out of reach of pistol-shot, and knew well that he rode the swiftest horse in the country, having picked him out for his speed with a view to some such accident. "Butterfly," as he called him, had won more whiskey by his racing than would have sufficed to buy half the ponies in the land. He had no fear, therefore, of being overtaken, and had a mind for some sport with his pursuers. Rising high in his saddle, he made a gesture of contemptuous defiance; then spurring his steed, galloped down the road, followed by a troop of redcoats at full speed. He enjoyed the sport exceedingly, hallooing and going through the Indian warwhoop, which many of the men in that region had learned when in camp from the Catawbas. The rage of the cheated dragoons was evinced by their continually firing their pistols, without effect, however, for the fugitive took care to keep beyond their reach, turning towards his pursuers at short intervals, and making various-gestures intended to insult and irritate them. The race held on in this manner for about a mile and a half, and Esbel said it was "the prettiest race I ever had. I held in Butterfly, so as not to beat too much, you see; but just to keep about a hundred and fifty yards in advance." He was now passing the spot where the log meeting-house—burnt the summer before—had stood. The sight of the blackened space brought to his mind the last sermon he had heard preached there, and the words of the minister, "the race is not always to the swift, nor the battle to the strong," came forcibly to his recollection. Esbel had but little feeling on the subject of religion, nor had his deeds been such as he could always remember with satisfaction. Yet conscience sometimes made its low voice heard, and at this moment the idea that after all, he might be given up to final perdition, that his time might be even then at hand—that by some mischance his horse might stumble and throw him—was far from agreeable. He knew well, from the example of Capt. Land and young Will Stroud, what mercy he might expect, if captured. Possessed by a sudden fear, he turned and took to the woods, resolved to throw Rocky Creek between him and his pursuers.

Mrs. Anderson heard the tramp of his horse as he came down the hill towards her house, for some time before he appeared. When he rode into her yard, he called out—addressing her by name—" I have chased fifty red coats; no, I am not right there; I have led them a chase like a pack of fools! So here's the old canteen; will you taste a little whiskey? Now, isn't it good? 'tis of Butterfly's winning. He has carried me bravely in this race, and I would have had these fellows all day at my heels to keep them out of worse business, but as I passed the burnt meeting-house it made me a little sorry, and then I thought about the minister's last sermon, and so I thought I would just leave them." By this time the distant sound of horses' feet gave notice that the dragoons were coming. Esbel bade a hasty adieu to his neighbor, took to the ford, and having crossed, went a little way up the creek, to the top of the hill. There he blew a loud and long note on his horn. The redcoats came down to the creek, but not finding the ford readily, rode back to Mrs. Anderson's house to enquire of her if the rebels were in any considerable force. They had been chasing, they told her, a saucy fellow who, they now began to think, had been decoying them out of the way, as they judged from his extreme impudence. He would stop, they said, in the midst of his running, and call out to them, repeating his audacious defiance every little while. What was the result—as far as the

troopers were concerned—it is not our present business
to inquire; we have to do with another individual,
whom their pursuit of Esbel brought upon the stage
of action.

On the road passed in this chase, north of Ragsdale's
house, lived a man who had come to the country in
the company of one Tom Morris. Morris had none of
the best of characters, and the stranger's intimacy
with him was not much to his credit in the neighborhood. None, however, knew anything to his disad-
vantage, unless extreme poverty might be deemed so,
and that was a complaint which the ravages of war
rendered too common to be disreputable. He was so
reduced that he owned not a hunting-shirt except one
much the worse for wear, but he was willing to work,
and readily engaged to do a certain quantity of labor
for a new one. Mrs. Ferguson told her husband if he
would give him the work, she would cut and make the
garment out of some material she had in the house.
The man accordingly undertook a stipulated quantity
of grubbing, and was upon the last forty rods, when
happening to look up, to his surprise he saw a horseman—Esbel, in fact—galloping down the road, and
shortly after, the dragoons following him at full speed
and firing their pistols. Leaving his work, he ran to
hide himself; but after a while, finding all was still,
he ventured out again and resumed his grubbing.
Hardly had he begun, however, before he again heard
the tramp of horses, and spied the redcoats coming
swiftly up the road on their return. Again he was off,

lying hid all the afternoon and part of the night—and returning, finished his work by moonlight some time before day.   The next morning, wearing the new hunting-shirt his labor had procured, he set off to fulfil a resolution he had formed after seeing the redcoats— that he would go out into the range, take the first horse he could find, and make for the army under command of General Greene, then on the march towards Camden after the battle of Guilford.   He had no doubt that he would soon find a horse, for while at work he had seen many in the range.   This day, however, luck seemed to be against him, and he walked about till near noon without seeing a horse grazing, or hearing the bell commonly worn by animals thus at liberty.   At last he heard the sound of a distant bell, and followed it up a small stream that bordered a cultivated field.   In the midst of this space he saw a log cabin, with two or three little children playing on the sunny side of the house.   Coming nearer, he perceived a very young girl letting down some bars to give entrance to a sorrel mare followed by a colt, and a woman of comely appearance, who by this time had noticed the approaching stranger, and was looking anxiously towards him, as if doubtful if he were friend or foe.   As soon as he saw her, he walked directly up, and asked if she had seen any other horse in the range besides her own.   She replied in the negative, and courteously invited the stranger to walk in.   The invitation was accepted, and in the conversation which ensued, the visitor learned that the dame was a widow,

and the mother of the children he had seen; that the
young girl was an orphan she had taken to bring up,
and that she had suffered not a little from the depre-
dators infesting the country. He told her on his part
that he had been grubbing for Mr. Ferguson, that he
had resolved to join the army, having had a great fright
on account of the redcoats, and what had been his business in the woods. " I suppose," said the dame—in
whom the reader will recognise an acquaintance—
" you are the soldier Tom Morris brought with him?"
The reply to this interrogatory introduced a prolonged
and interesting conversation, which was interrupted
by dinner. At the widow's hospitable solicitation the
stranger sat down to the meal with the family, relin-
quishing, for that day at least, his project of securing
a horse. Of course he could not think of taking the
only one belonging to a poor woman! He was glad
he had not seen the animal before, for had he taken
her, she might not have found her way home after
being turned out, or might have been seized by some
one less scrupulous. Having parted from his new
acquaintance, he took his course back to Ferguson's,
much more thoughtful than he had come. The image
of the sociable dame went with him; her fair face
and handsome features, set off by soft light hair of the
hue poets call golden, with her fine form—had made
an impression which his admiration of the courage and
resolution she had shown through so many trials,
deepened and strengthened. Her lot in life was like
his own : she lived alone, with means sadly diminished

by the troubles of war, and her little family depended
on her labor for their subsistence from day to day.
When he thought of the spirit she had shown, he remembered with some mortification how he had hid
himself from the redcoats. That night it may be supposed he slept but little, having such food for reflection.
In the morning little Lizzy came to Mr. Ferguson's to
shell a bag of corn. The stranger assisted her, and
having finished shelling the corn, took the bag and put
it on the horse, offering to carry it to mill for her if
she would tell him the road. The little damsel was
not so ready to trust a person she did not know, especially as she had noticed what he said the day before
on the subject of getting a horse, and prudently declined his offer, saying she had been bidden to go herself, and she always obeyed her aunt. Her answer
caused the man no little chagrin, for he had made the
friendly proposal only that he might have a reasonable
excuse for another visit to the cabin. His conclusion
now was to go at all hazards, trusting for his welcome
to fortune and the dame's kindly nature.

It was not long before he was again at the fair
widow's house, and to all appearance on a very comfortable footing. His history was already pretty well
known to Mrs. Anderson, for she had heard the details
from Tom Morris himself. When at length he ventured the question, "I suppose, Madam, you think
well of the fellows Tom has told you of?" the frank
answer was: "I do; my ain dear Willie died the
death of a soldier."

"Then you would marry a soldier?"

"I have not thought about that; but if I ever should marry—if I think as I do now—none but a soldier would I have."

What turn the discourse took after this avowal tradition does not exactly inform us; nor how the "round unvarnished tale" which the soldier had to tell concerning himself, was received by his gentle auditor. But it is certain that, some three or four days after this conversation, the associate of Tom Morris went to Ferguson's to borrow a horse, and that he, accompanied by Nancy Anderson mounted on the sorrel mare, was riding along the road on the way to the house of the old Justice, John Gaston. After a short ceremony the Justice pronounced them man and wife, and received the fee of one dollar, all the money which the newly made husband possessed in the world.

The sudden conversion of Mrs. Anderson into Mrs. Green, gave no small offence to many of her friends, who fancied they had an undoubted right to control her in a step involving her future prospects. Not a single person of her acquaintance thought she had made a good or suitable match. They were especially scandalized that she had thought proper to dispense with formalities prescribed by the church and the cus-tom of their fathers, which required an intended marriage to be published by the minister on three successive Sabbaths. It was impossible for her to comply with this requisition, there being no meeting for public religious service in those days of desolation, but the over-strict deemed this no sufficient excuse. Nancy, however, did not suffer herself to be rendered uncomfortable by their disapprobation of her choice, or their censure of her hasty nuptials. She considered herself the most competent judge in the matter, and had decided that circumstances may modify cases to such an extent as to render proper a course which at a different time might have been ill-advised and unbecoming. She thought also that Daniel Green and herself had probably become better acquainted with each other's disposition and character in the five days preceding their marriage than many whose course of love is protracted for years; and knowing what it was to be alone and destitute, it was something to find one who could take care of her little property, aid in the maintenance of her family, and defend her in case of need. Both she and her soldier had been tried in the crucible of the Revolution, and both came forth like gold refined. They were well suited, in all respects essential to the comfort of married life, and matched in personal appearance. Nancy had no inconsiderable share of beauty of that striking order which suited her rather tall and robust figure, and though mild and amiable, possessed great energy and firmness. Daniel Green might have been called one of nature's noblemen. His appearance was commanding, his powerful frame denoting great strength, and his open and honest countenance expressed the benevolence of his heart. Frank and honorable in all his dealings, he was disposed to trust, but sagacious in discerning character,

his intellect being naturally keen and strong, and experience, without book learning, having given him
deep insight into men. It will not be inappropriate
here, to give a brief sketch of his career, especially as
part of it illustrates the benevolence of other women
who lived in those days. He was born in New Jersey,
about 1752. His parents were poor, and unable to
send him to school, but a quick perception and reten-
tive memory enabled him to gain knowledge; when
six years old, by hearing the sayings of Poor Richard
read from the almanac, he soon got them by heart,
and by close application learned to read, afterwards
teaching himself to write. These maxims strongly
impressed him; throughout his long life he was in
the habit of repeating them on all occasions, and
might have been called a second edition of the philoso-
pher who wrote them, so similar was the character of
his mind. As soon as he was old enough to contribute to the support of the family, he hired himself out
to service. In the beginning of the war he was
drafted to go to Canada. He then went to Philadelphia, about thirty miles from his home, and enlisted as
a marine with Capt. Biddle. When entering the service, he informed Biddle that he had left his business
at home in an unsettled state, and was promised a
furlough before long, when he could have an opportunity of attending to it. Notwithstanding this promise
leave of absence was refused on the ground that it had
been granted to several married men, who should have
the preference, and after applying four times in vain

for permission to go home, the Andrea Doria getting ready to sail, Daniel, with one of his fellow marines, took his departure without leave, went back to New Jersey, settled his business, and returned to Philadelphia. As he and his companion entered the city they met an acquaintance, who informed them they were advertised as deserters, and that it was in his power, had he not scorned such bad faith, to make ten pounds by arresting them. The handbills posted at the corners, offering a reward for their apprehension, confirmed this information. Green used afterwards to say, had the man attempted to secure them, he would have been killed, for both were resolved to perish on the spot rather than submit to be arraigned as deserters. Their resolution was soon taken, and going directly to the barracks—where their guns had been left—they despatched a message to Capt. Biddle, announcing their return, and requesting him to come on shore. The next morning a sergeant and guard were seen marching towards the barracks. The two delinquents stood ready, musket in hand, and when the guard came within a short distance, Green called to them to halt, accompanying his order with a look of desperate determination that could not be mistaken. The sergeant informed them the captain had sent for them; the answer was, that they had sent for the captain and did not mean to leave the barracks with any but himself. At the sergeant's order to seize the prisoners, their muskets were presented, and the clicking of the cocks was the signal for the prompt order " right about face," which the guard instantly obeyed, being out of sight at the first corner. A few hours after, they saw Biddle approaching, and wheeling out of the room into the street as he came up, at the proper distance they presented arms. The captain returned their salutation, and asked Green why he had thus treated the guard. The young man replied by reminding him of his promise of leave of absence, which was afterwards refused when solicited. His affairs required his attention; he had gone home to settle them, had returned of his own accord, and was now ready to serve his country. "You shall have justice, my brave fellow," said the captain; then taking each marine by the hand, the three marched through the streets to the wharf, and were soon on shipboard. Every eye was upon them, the sergeant having given an account of his reception, and several were heard to say they would be put to death for desertion and resistance to the guard, or at least whipped severely for an example. When the marines mustered they fell into ranks, and answered to the calling of the roll. The captain then came forward and explained the whole matter, concluding by saying, "These men are not deserters; I was to blame. I am satisfied with them, and," turning to the sergeant, "you, sir, and the guard must overlook what they did. Desperate men will do desperate acts, and you in their situation might have done the same. Let it pass, therefore, and see that every one hereafter does his duty." Thus did his humanity and candor prevent injustice and secure the confidence of his men.

Green was afterwards transferred to the Randolph, which, after encountering a heavy gale at sea, put into the harbor of Charleston, to have a new mast made. This mast in a few days chanced to be struck by lightning and destroyed, and the accident, which he regarded as ominous, so disturbed the sailor's mind that he went ashore, and finding a soldier willing to exchange places with him, enrolled himself in a regiment of continental regulars. Whenever the vessel came into port on returning from her voyages, Green always visited his old companions, being very kindly treated by the commodore, but always looked upon his exchange as providential—the poor fellow who took his place never having returned. He served in the army, was taken prisoner May 12th, 1780, and employed on board the prison ship as a boat hand to fetch water and provisions from land. In March, the following year, the boat was sent some distance up Cooper River for fresh water, two British soldiers acting as a guard. The prisoners—seven in number—suffered not the opportunity to pass; they rose on the guard by a concerted movement, disarmed them, and effected their escape. After encountering many difficulties, they reached a plantation belonging to Col. Pinckney, and were received with the most cordial hospitality by Mrs. Pinckney, who, though alone—her husband not daring to venture home, and plundered of everything by the royalists, so that she depended on her negroes for daily supplies—was ready to share what she had with them. From this place the fugitives made their way to " Buckhead," called Fort Motte, on the Congaree River, the residence of Mrs. Motte. This lady, whose patriotism was soon to be so signally displayed in the destruction, by her own consent, of her beautiful mansion, welcomed them kindly, and gave them lodging in an outhouse, where they were hid during the day, for it was thought unsafe to let the blacks on the premises know of their presence. Provisions were sent to them every day by Mrs. Motte, and she often paid them visits, accompanied by a young lady whose residence was on the north side of the river, and who was on a visit to her house. Her name, it is to be regretted, cannot be ascertained. Green, in relating the adventure, said, " These ladies were elegant and polished in their manners ; we were ragged, dirty, rough-looking fellows; yet notwithstanding our forlorn condition, they treated us as equals, spoke to us kindly, and made us feel that we had not served our country in vain. They made many inquiries about the situation of the prisoners, and informed us that all was not lost, as the British would fain have made us believe when trying to seduce us from our duty. ' Yes,' said this lovely young lady, ' the Scotch-Irish of Chester, Lancaster and York refused British protection and defended themselves ; they have fought many battles since you were immured in the prison ship, and though sometimes driven back, have rallied again. A few days ago, Sumter and his men swam the river

in this very neighborhood. These are your countrymen.' My comrades smiled, especially Tom Morris,
whom the speaker addressed, for they were men of
Chester and Lancaster. Then, with one of the
sweetest looks I ever met, she said to me, 'Green, you
keep good company,' and informed me that Gen.
Greene had lately fought the enemy at Guilford."

This young lady at length proposed to assist the
men in getting across the river. She told them she
and Mrs. Motte had decided that she was to go home
the next day, and make arrangements to send some of
her negroes to the riverside on the following night with
canoes to convey them across. Accordingly on the
appointed night, Mrs. Motte's trusty house servant
came and conducted them to the landing. Several
blacks were there with canoes; they were taken over
the river, and led up to the overseer's house, where a
table was set out, covered with abundance of provisions.
Bedclothing was also furnished, so clean and fresh,
that the hardy travellers would not soil the snow white
sheets and quilts by sleeping in them, but stretched
themselves before the fire. In the morning before they
had all risen, breakfast was on the table, and they
were invited to take for their journey as much as they
could conveniently carry. " To think,"—said Green
—" of one so accomplished showing so much kindness
and attention to us, of late so unused to humane
treatment!" In taking leave of the overseer, he
offered him the only dollar he had remaining of the
money with which they had left the banks of Cooper

River. The overseer shook his head, saying he would not take it for the world : Miss —— would never forgive him. " Why, all day yesterday," he said, " after she came home, she was riding back and forward from the great house to the quarter, ordering the killing of a hog or a sheep, and late in the evening was here with several negroes, who brought baskets full of large loaves of bread and cake, with bedclothing ; and again, she herself set out the table, putting on the provisions, and all the time keeping me in the dark. At last she said—I shall never forget her look—' I suppose you would like to know what all this is for ! I intend to send you seven men a little after dark, and you must do your best to make them comfortable. You see I have provisions pretty plenty. Mrs. Motte told me the giant Tom Morris was a great eater ; let them have plenty, and take with them in the morning. They have seen rough times; they are very dirty; but they are the finest looking men I have seen in a long time, and you know they are on our side.' No—no —sir—I can't take your money !" Green contented himself with sending by the overseer a message of heartfelt thanks to his mistress, and a wish that when she married, her husband might be as good a man as she was a woman. Two days afterwards he and Morris were safely sheltered in the house of Isabella Ferguson.

Mr. and Mrs. Green found their troubles ended with the war. Prosperity attended them : they grew wealthy, but had no children to bear the name. The children of Anderson were treated by Green as his own.

With the wealth his industry acquired he did much
good during his whole life.   He repaired the church
at Beckhamville, and built a wall around the burial-
ground of cut granite well laid in lime, which is still
entire, and to all appearance will last for generations.
For many years the church he rebuilt was used by the
Presbyterians, though it has now passed into the hands
of the Methodists, and is their place of worship.   Green
himself never belonged to any particular denomination,
but was esteemed by the members of all the different
religious societies as an excellent man and a sincere
Christian.

One who knew Nancy Green observed that if a
woman ever lived who came up to Solomon's description of the virtuous woman in Proverbs it was she.
As her life was spent in quiet usefulness, so her end
was peace, and her last moments were sustained by
the hope which gives to a Christian the victory over
death.   Her earthly course was finished in June, 1827.
The afternoon of the day of her burial, Green remarked
to one of his friends that he and his late wife had
lived together near fifty years—and had tasted far
more of real happiness than falls to the lot of most
mortals.   "We have been blessed," he said, "in our
basket and our store, flourishing like a green bay tree
beside the waters ; but this is not our abiding place
I have laid her at the head of her little granddaughter,
Nancy Anderson.   How soon I too may go the way of
all living, I know not ; but when that time comes, lay
my bones by her side, at the head of the grave of my

granddaughter, Polly Anderson." He survived Mrs. Green but a few weeks. The fatigue of nursing and watching during her protracted illness, was in all probability the exciting cause of a severe attack of fever, which shortly terminated his life. For many hours before the final yielding of the powers of nature, he was delirious, and the ruling passion of the soldier was strong in the mind's wandering; all day he was mounting guard, and fighting over again the battles of the Revolution. The last words he uttered were an order to charge and break the ranks, and even when no longer able to speak, he would make the motion of thrusting with his hand, as if charging with the bayonet.

A singular circumstance occurred not many days before the death of Mrs. Green. While she lay in so precarious a state, that every day was expected to be her last, the country was visited by one of the heavy rains common to a southern climate. The water, falling almost in torrents, swept deep hollows even in nearly level ground; the earth was washed away from the spot at Neely's bars, where, as already mentioned, William Anderson and James Barber were interred, and the bones, after the repose of almost half a century, were brought to the surface. Col. Anderson, the son, went up to Neely's place, collected the bones, and carried them to the burial-ground enclosed by Daniel Green, depositing them there beside the place where he expected soon to open a grave for his mother. It was thought that in her feeble state she could not bear

7*

to be informed of the occurrence, and her family refrained from allusion to it in her hearing; but the black nurse, having less prudence, told her what had happened. Mrs. Green expressed much regret that the bones had not been brought to her, anxiously desiring to see even one of the finger joints of the husband of her youth. Her last resting place is now a spot of remarkable interest. On either side repose the remains of her two warrior husbands: at her feet her son, Col. William Anderson—her grandchildren and great grandchildren enlarging the circle of kindred dead,—and around them is the granite wall which is a monument of the public spirit of her last chosen companion. To this solemn scene is not wanting a dirge of nature's own music; the ceaseless roar of the great Falls of the Catawba. Here lofty mountains confine the river in a narrow channel, pent as it comes nearer within walls of rock, piled on either side. Rushing over large masses of rock, it precipitates itself down the falls, the troubled waters dashing from one descent to another—a sheet of foam from shore to shore—descending in the succession of falls about one hundred and fifty feet, and abating not their impetuosity till they have passed Rocky Mount. The wildness of the steep and rugged cliffs, the grandeur of the Falls, and the picturesque scenery around—combine to render the spot an object of curiosity to travellers. It is an appropriate place for the rest of those whose spirits were tried amid the fierce conflict of political opinions and human passions—wilder than the strife of the boiling waters.

VIII.

ESTHER WALKER.

THE readers of American history must honor the memory of the noble patriot and martyr to liberty—Dr. Alexander Gaston, the father of the late Judge Gaston, of North Carolina. Others of that family were conspicuous in Revolutionary times. One of the brothers of Alexander, the Rev. Hugh Gaston, was a Presbyterian clergyman of eminent piety and learning, and well known as the author of " Gaston's Concordance," a standard theological work. Another, John, had his share in the labors and dangers of the patriots in the heroic age of our country. He was born in Ireland, but his ancestors were French, and are noticed in history as distinguished and zealous adherents of the Huguenot cause in the early part of the seventeenth century. They sought refuge in Ireland, after the revocation of the edict of Nantes.

John Gaston, the father of the subject of this memoir, emigrated to the United States about the year 1730, and some time afterwards, married Miss Esther Waugh. At this time his residence was in Pennsylvania. How long he continued there is not definitely

known ; but it is believed that he left that colony
about 1750 with some families of the Scotch-Irish,
who came to South Carolina and settled upon the Catawba River.   They gave to these new settlements
the names of Chester and Lancaster, corresponding
with those of the counties they had left.

The homestead where Mr. and Mrs. Gaston resided,
was on the south side of Fishing Creek, six miles from
its junction with the Catawba—now known, as it was
then, by the name of Cedar Shoals.   At this place
Esther was born, 1761.   She was the eleventh of a
family consisting of nine sons and three daughters.
Her parents, who were strict members of the Presbyterian church, took pains to instil into the minds of
their children those principles of piety which exercised
an influence over her life.   The father of this family
was himself a devoted Christian, as the whole course
of his life testified.   The following singular clause in
his last will and testament, written with his own hand,
is characteristic: "I leave my soul to Almighty
God, my Creator ; to Jesus Christ, my Redeemer,
and to the Holy Ghost, my Sanctifier. I leave my
body to be buried in a decent, Christian manner."

John Gaston was familiarly called Justice Gaston,
having been a justice of the peace under the British
rule.   He was also one of His Majesty's surveyors,
and celebrated for the accuracy of his plats.   When
the separation took place between the Colonies and the
Imperial Government, followed by the struggle for
freedom, although advanced in years, he took an ac-

tive part in favor of the Americans. He was in the habit of sending one of his sons weekly to Camden, a distance of nearly fifty miles, for the only newspaper published in the State—"The South Carolina and American General Gazette." A copy of this journal is in the possession of the widow of his youngest son, Joseph, and bears date February 23d, 1776. From this the old man learned from time to time the progress of British encroachments, while he nourished that spirit of resistance to tyranny, which prompted him, when the oppressors of his country endeavored to enforce submission, to meet the crisis with firmness, to maintain his own independence, and to urge his patriotic band of sons to a vigorous defence of their rights.

The darkest period of the war for the South, when South Carolina was claimed by the Briton as a conquered province, when the hopes of the people were prostrated, and they were compelled, almost every where, to accept protection by professing allegiance to the crown, did not extinguish the zeal of the patriots. The sons of John Gaston, and his nephews, McClure, Strong, and Knox, often met to speak together of the aspect of affairs and consult as to what steps were to be taken. While they were talking of the disaster at Monk's Corner,* a messenger brought intelligence that

---

* John McClure, ' a young veteran of twenty-two,' was with the company of mounted militia at Monk's Corner. They escaped with the loss of their horses, and had just reached home. He was at Justice Gaston's when the news came of Buford's defeat.

Tarleton with his cavalry had pursued and overtaken
Col. Buford near the Waxhaws, and refusing quarter,
had slaughtered his men without mercy. The wounded
had been carried to Waxhaw Church as a hospital,
while the tories had shown themselves active on either
side the Catawba below Waxhaw and Fishing Creek
settlements. At this news, the young men rose with
one accord, and undaunted by reverse, grasped each
other by the hand, and voluntarily pledged themselves
to suffer death rather than submit to the invader.
This spontaneous vow was confirmed by a solemn
oath, and thence forward they continued in arms, Dr.
James Knox being the surgeon of their company.

Such were the spirits by whom Esther Gaston was
surrounded. She was at this time about eighteen,
tall and well developed in person, and possessed of
great mental as well as physical energy. Determined
to bear her part in the work that was to be done, she
lost no time in repairing to Waxhaw church, accompanied by her married sister Martha, and Martha's son
John, a boy eight years of age. The temporary hospital presented a scene of misery. The floor was
strewed with the wounded and dying American soldiers, suffering for want of aid; for men dared not
come to minister to their wants. It was the part of
woman, like the angel of mercy, to bring relief to the
helpless and perishing. Day and night they were
busied in aiding the surgeon to dress their wounds,
and in preparing food for those who needed it; nor did
they regard fatigue or exposure, going from place to

place about the neighborhood to procure such articles as were desirable to alleviate the pain, or add to the comfort, of those to whom they ministered.

Meanwhile, the British were taking measures to secure their conquest by establishing military posts throughout the State. Rocky Mount was selected as a stronghold, and a body of the royal force was there stationed. Handbills were then circulated, notifying the inhabitants of the country that they were required to assemble at an old field, where Beckhamville now stands, to give in their names as loyal subjects of King George, and receive British protection. After this proclamation was issued, Col. Houseman, the commander of the post at Rocky Mount, was seen with an escort wending his way to the residence of old Justice Gaston. He was met on the road by the old man, who civilly invited him into the house. The subject of his errand was presently introduced, and the Justice took the opportunity to animadvert, with all the warmth of his feelings, upon the recent horrible butchery of Buford's men, and the course pursued by the British government towards the American Colonies, which had at length driven them into the assertion of their independence. In despair of bringing to submission so strenuous an advocate of freedom, Col. Houseman at last left the house; but presently returning, he again urged the matter. He had learned, he said, from some of His Majesty's faithful subjects about Rocky Mount, that Gaston's influence would control the whole country; he observed that resistance was useless, as the province lay at the mercy of the conqueror, and that true patriotism should induce the Justice to reconsider his determination, and by his example persuade his sons and numerous connections to submit to lawful authority, and join the assembly on the morrow at the old field. To these persuasions the old man gave only the stern reply—"Never!"

No sooner had Houseman departed, than the aged patriot took steps to do more than oppose his passive refusal to his propositions. He immediately despatched runners to various places in the neighborhood, requiring the people to meet that night at his residence. The summons was obeyed. Before midnight, thirty-three men, of no ordinary mould, strong in spirit and of active and powerful frames—men trained and used to the chase—were assembled. They had been collected by John McClure, and were under his command. Armed with the deadly rifle, clad in their hunting-shirts and moccasins, with their wool hats and deer-skin caps, the otter-skin shot-bag and the butcher's knife by their sides, they were ready for any enterprise in the cause of liberty. At reveillé in the morning, they paraded before the door of Justice Gaston. He came forth, and in compliance with the custom of that day, brought with him a large case bottle. Commencing with the officers, John and Hugh McClure, he gave each a hearty shake of the hand, and then presented the bottle. In that grasp it might well seem that a portion of his own courageous spirit was communicated, strengthening those true hearted men for the approaching struggle. They took their course noiselessly along the old Indian trail down Fishing Creek, to the old field where many of the people were already gathered. Their sudden onset took by surprise the promiscuous assemblage, about two hundred in number ; the enemy was defeated, and their well directed fire, says one who speaks from personal knowledge, "saved a few cowards from becoming tories, and taught Houseman that the strong log houses of Rocky Mount were by far the safest for his myrmidons."

This encounter was the first effort to breast the storm after the suspension of military opposition ; "the opening wedge," in the words of an eye witness,* "to the recovery of South Carolina." Before the evening of that day, Justice Gaston was informed of the success of the enterprise, and judging wisely that his own safety depended on his immediate departure, his horse was presently at the door, with holster and pistols at the pommel of the saddle. The shot-bag at the old man's side was well supplied with ammunition, and his rifle, doubly charged, lay across the horse before him. Bidding adieu to his wife and grandchildren, and bestowing on them his parting blessing, he left home with his young son, Joseph, who was armed and mounted on another horse. On his way, he made a visit to Waxhaw church, where his daughters Esther and Martha were still occupied with their labor of

* Joseph Gaston. His account of the events of this period was written in 1836, and printed in a country newspaper of that time.

kindness, to carry the news that "the boys," as he called them, had done something towards avenging the injuries of the poor men who were dependent on their care. A shout of exultation from the women welcomed the intelligence, and many a wounded soldier felt his sufferings mitigated by the tidings. The Justice pursued his way till he could consider himself beyond the danger of pursuit. His son Joseph returned, and marching with a detachment of men from Mecklenburg, North Carolina, in a few days joined his brothers in arms under the gallant John McClure.

Loud and long were the curses of Houseman levelled against old John Gaston. The arch rebel, he declared, must be taken, dead or alive, and the king's loyal subjects were called upon to volunteer in the exploit of capturing and bringing to Rocky Mount a hoary headed man, eighty years of age, for the crime of being the friend of his country and bringing nine sons into the field. Before the sun rose, about twenty redcoats were fording Rocky Creek, and wending their way along the Indian trail leading to Gaston's house. The thirst for revenge rankled in their hearts, and destruction and murder were in their purpose; but the God who protects those who place reliance on Him in all trial and danger, had opened a way of escape for the patriot's family. His wife and little Jenny, the daughter of his son William Gaston, providentially advised of the enemy's approach, had quitted the house. Their place of concealment was so near, that they could distinctly hear the frightful oaths of the disappointed

British soldiers, and could see the redcoats passing to and fro through the yard. Mrs. Gaston, clasping her grandchild's little hands between her own, knelt upon the ground, and in that glen, sheltered by bushes, poured out her petition to the God of the widow and the fatherless. The prayer of this aged matron, the mother of a brave race of men and women, was not only for her husband and children, but for the liberty of her country and its deliverance from evil and bloodthirsty men, who had not the fear of their Creator before their eyes. In the fervor of her supplication she prayed aloud. Her granddaughter, in describing the scene thirty years ago, said she might have been heard as far as the house, and it was fortunate that the soldiers did not discover her.

Samuel McCreary, the grandson of Mrs. Gaston, who was employed at work not far from the spot, heard the noise of the soldiers, and ascended a steep bluff within a short distance of the house, where he was concealed from view by the thick foliage, while yet he could observe every movement. He heard the heavy strokes of their broadswords on the chair usually occupied by the Justice, with the diabolical wishes that he were in it to receive the cleaving blows. The house was plundered of everything, and the stock carried off. The only article saved was the Family Bible, which Mrs. Gaston had taken with her in her flight. It is still kept in the family. She and her grandchildren spent the night at the house of Thomas Walker, the father of Alexander Walker, who was at that time the lover, and afterwards became the husband of Esther Gaston.

On the next Sabbath the Rev. William Martin preached the discourse already mentioned at the log meeting-house. As steel sharpeneth steel, so did this minister, by his stirring words, rouse the spirit of his hearers, and prepare them to meet the coming storm by taking up arms. The effect of his eloquence was soon apparent. At an early hour on Monday morning, many of the conscientious Covenanters were seen drilling on the muster-ground seven miles from Rocky Mount, under the brave Capt. Ben Land, while two miles above this, at the shop of a negro blacksmith, some half a dozen more were getting their horses shod. Those at the muster-ground were charged upon by a party of British dragoons, having no previous notice of their approach, and dispersed.* Their captain being overtaken and surrounded by the dragoons, who attacked him with their broadswords, defended himself with his sword to the last, and wounded several of his enemies severely before he fell. The news of his death was carried to his wife, who shortly after gave birth to a son. It may be mentioned, as an instance of female patriotism illustrative of the general feeling, that in the anguish of her recent bereavement, while it seemed that the prospect was utterly dark, and the hope of national freedom crushed for ever, Mrs. Land called

---

* The man who carried to the enemy the tidings of Martin's sermon, and the mustering of the Covenanters, "did not die in his bed."

her child Thomas Sumter, in honor of the American general.

The party at the blacksmith's shop was also surprised, and one man killed in the shop. The dragoons then crossed Rocky Creek, and soon found their way to the rude stone hut which was the preacher's dwelling. They found the old divine in his study, preparing a sermon which was to be a second blast, made him their prisoner, and carried him like a felon to Rocky Mount. Thomas Walker had already been arrested, and was also confined there. The country was daily scoured for the purpose of discovering and destroying the whigs, and the unoffending inhabitants were plundered. Meanwhile, the loyalists were collecting and strengthening the royal post.

The victory at the Old Field was followed by a battle at Mobley's Meeting-House, and one at Williamson's—now Brattonsville—July 12th, in which Huck* was defeated and slain. The attention of General Sumter, who was encamped near Nation Ford on the Catawba, was then directed to Rocky Mount. On the night of July 30th, the American soldiers marched near the residence of Esther Gaston. She was informed, perhaps by one of her brothers, or her lover, Alexander Walker, who found time to call, that they

---

* The name is thus printed in most historical books, although at the time spelt Huyck. It is commonly pronounced Hook through that region of country, and sometimes written Hoik. His first name was Christian. There seems to have been a Lieut. John Huyck in the army. See Hist. Suffolk Co., p. 99.

were advancing against the enemy's position. By the
morning she was in readiness to follow, and riding
about two miles to the house of her brother, John Gaston, she urged her sister-in-law to go with her to the
scene of action. The two were soon mounted, and
making their way at a quick gallop down the Rocky
Mount road. The firing could be distinctly heard. While
these brave women were approaching the spot, they
were met by two or three men, hastening *from* the
ground, with faces paler than became heroes. Esther
stopped the fugitives, upbraided them with their cow-
ardice, and entreated them to return to their duty.
While they wavered, she advanced, and seizing one of
their guns, cried " Give *us* your guns, then, and we
will stand in your places !" The most cowardly of
men must have been moved at such a taunt; the run-
away soldiers were covered with confusion, and for
very shame dared not refuse to go back. Wheeling
about, they returned to the fight in company with the
two heroines. During the action Esther and Jane
Gaston were not merely idle spectators, but busied
themselves diligently in rendering whatever services
were required, assisting in dressing the wounds of the
soldiers, and in carrying water to allay their burning thirst. A Catawba Indian, severely wounded,
was succored by them, and his last looks were turned
in gratitude on those who had soothed his pain and
supplied his wants. In these services, the training
Esther had received at Waxhaw enabled her to do her
part skilfully, and while she gave comfort to the dy-

ing, her animating words encouraged the living to
persevere. The gallant Col. Neil was here slain. The
prisoners William Martin and Thomas Walker, were
bound to the floor in one of the log huts. The enemy
knew well what reason they had to dread the effect of
Martin's stormy eloquence. He afterwards regained
his liberty, and lived to about the age of ninety, dying
in 1806. The gentleman who communicated this account, remembers to have heard him preach, and was
struck with his remarkable personal appearance. Numerous anecdotes are related of him. It was usually
his practice, when reproving, to name the person who
was the object of his displeasure. When the news
came to him that the British had evacuated Charleston, he rode about the country to carry the intelligence
to the neighbors, adding the comment, " The British
have taken shipping, and may the d——l go with
them !"

The action continued for a great part of the day.
The sharp-shooters among the whigs concealed themselves in the woods and behind rocks, and fired at
every crevice of the log houses occupied by the enemy's garrison. The British marksmen who went up
to the loft to return the fire, were brought down every
few minutes wounded or dead. The defence was
made good from the buildings surrounded by an abatis,
although the General offered a reward of four thousand dollars to any one who would fire them.* This

* So says a MS. narrative by Rev. Samuel McCreary. It appears to have been written in 1822.

was attempted by throwing faggots from rocks to the
nearest houses, but without effect. A more effectual
measure was then adopted—building brushheaps from
the rocks to the houses, but this was frustrated by the
rain which began to fall. An anecdote is told of one
of Sumter's partisans, "hopping John Miller" (so
called from being lame of a leg.) He took care to
load his piece behind a rock, but would come out
openly when about to shoot, always after deliberately
taking aim, uttering the brief ejaculation, as he pulled the trigger, "May the Lord direct the bullet!"
The same confidence in Providence and the justice
of his cause, impelled him to a desperate attempt
to dislodge the enemy. Assisted by a few others of
his own stamp, he made a brush-pile by throwing
brush over a rock that stood against the rear of the
house. Having piled it so as to reach the house,
Hopping Miller fired the heap, with a good prospect of
burning out the garrison. This time, however, fortune was in their favor; for a heavy rain put out the
fire, and late in the evening, Sumter drew off his
men. With the retreat, Esther and her sister-in-law
returned to their homes, through a heavy shower of
rain, and a night so dark that it was impossible to dis-
tinguish any one.

In the following week, the Battle of Hanging Rock
took place. Again the heroic maiden repaired to
Waxhaw Church, where the wounded claimed the care
of generous woman. Among the sufferers lay her
youngest brother Joseph, a lad of sixteen, severely

wounded in the face, pale as death, and exhausted from loss of blood. Heavy cause for mourning, indeed, had the Gaston family after that fatal encounter, no less than three of Esther's brothers, Robert, Ebenezer, and David, being numbered with the dead. Her cousin John McClure, too, was desperately wounded, and died not long afterwards. Another brother, Alexander Gaston, who was a lieutenant in the regular army, fell a victim to the small-pox in Sumter's retreat from Wright's Bluff. When news of the death of her sons was brought to Mrs. Gaston, it is said her words were—" I grieve for their loss, but they could not have died in a better cause." Nor did grief for these bereavements prevent Esther from performing her melancholy duty. Her heart was wrung by the suffering she witnessed, in many, too, whom she well knew as neighbors. Attentive only to the claims of the distressed, and wasting no time in the indulgence of her own sorrow, she spared herself no exertion nor fatigue in helping her cousin, Dr. James Knox, who performed the duty of surgeon to the wounded soldiers. She remained for a considerable time in this hospital, and afterwards went with the wounded to Charlotte, where she continued her care of her brother, and other sufferers.

When Justice Gaston quitted his home, his intention was to go to his brother Alexander at Newbern, N. C., but finding his way blocked up by the loyalists on Cross Creek, he turned back, and remained a few weeks in Iredell and Mecklenburg Counties. After the

battle of Hanging Rock, he returned home, for he observed it was at best but a few days of life that could
be murdered by his foes.   It is said he always went
armed with a brace of horseman's pistols and his trusty
rifle, all well loaded and ready for use, being resolved,
in case of attack, to defend to the death his house and
his aged partner.   The victories of his countrymen,
however, acted as a check on those who might be disposed to molest him, and the only hostile demonstra-
tion was the cutting out of his initials from a white oak
that stood where the road to his house left that to
Rocky Mount.   His useful life was closed in 1782,
(his pistols, it is said, being still under his pillow, and
the rifle beside him,) leaving the memory of his heroic
acts as a proud inheritance to his children.   Mrs. Gaston survived him seven years, surrounded by her
children and grandchildren, by whom the memory of
her excellence and piety is affectionately cherished.*

* Samuel and John McCreary, grandsons of Justice Gaston, lost
their mother in childhood, and having a stepmother of a loyalist
family, left their home and came to his house.   Samuel, a lad of
fifteen or sixteen, went out to battle with his uncles, and fought
bravely.   After the war he and his brother were taught to read by
their grandmother, having few other advantages in the way of instruction.   Samuel became an able minister of the Baptist denomination.   He had a wonderful memory, could recall any event, and
seemed to have the whole Bible by heart, besides being deeply
read in many learned works.   His constant remark was, "I owe
everything to my grandmother."   John was sheriff at an early period and for a great part of his life a member in the House of Representatives and Senate of his State, and a member of Congress

Alexander Walker was in service during the whole war. In 1775, when there was a call for men to go out against the Cherokees, in the Snow Campaign, Thomas Walker, his father, was drafted for the expedition, and Alexander, then only about fourteen, but tall and athletic beyond his years, went out in his place, serving through the campaign under the command of Capt. Steel. He was also engaged with Steel at the siege of Savannah. Among the anecdotes he was accustomed to relate was one of Ben Rowan, of the infantry, being out on a foraging party and meeting at the dead of night a number of men, with whom they exchanged a fire before discovering that they were whigs. No harm was done ; but late on the following morning, as they came towards the camp, they were attacked by a body of British. Alexander was with the dragoons under the command of Count Pulaski who were ordered to charge for the protection of the infantry. The gallant Count might be seen riding up and down the lines on his black charger, chapeau in hand, exclaiming every now and then in his imperfect English, "I am sorry for your country! I am sorry for your country!" "He was the noblest horseman," Walker used to say, "I ever beheld, except Col. Davie, who was a splendid looking officer, unrivalled in eloquence, and with a voice that could be heard at a great distance. On one occasion when we were about to make a charge at night, after everything

from the district of Pinckney. These two Revolutionary boys belonged to the debating society established by John Brown.

was ready, Davie in a penetrating voice gave the command, to ' be silent *as thought itself.*' For weeks this caution rang in my ears."

At the battle of Hanging Rock, Walker was in the division of Col. McClure, which made a furious onset on the tory camp. The account of this action, one of the most spirited and best fought during the Revolution, belongs to another memoir. Whenever the army was in the vicinity of Justice Gaston's, Alexander obtained leave of absence and visited Esther. They were married at the close of the war, and having both done and suffered so much for their country, now enjoyed the blessings of peace they had contributed to purchase. Their house was on the north side of Fishing Creek, nearly opposite the old homestead where Esther's father had lived. Her only child, a son, was named after this revered parent, John Gaston.

Mrs. Walker never lost her desire of being useful to those around her, nor refused to exercise, for the benefit of her neighbors, the medical knowledge her practice during the war had given her. She was regarded as a skilful doctoress, and was consulted in most cases of disease occurring in her neighborhood. Women in delicate health were occasionally brought to her, sometimes on litters when not able to travel, and left under her care. In cases of wounds she was frequently called upon, and generally succeeded in giving relief to the sufferer. Although this success was doubtless in great part owing to the experience she had in administering to the soldiers, she was not destitute of scientific knowledge in medicine. Shortly after her marriage, she had an opportunity of studying those branches of the subject to which she wished to devote herself. An educated physician, Dr. McCrea, boarded in her house, and under his instruction, she acquired the medical knowledge which she so often made useful in after life.

In other excellent qualities, more strictly pertaining to the female character, Mrs. Walker was eminent. She was remarkable not only for energy, but for ingenuity and industry. Like other Revolutionary matrons, she was skilful in the use of her needle, and many of the coats worn in the neighborhood bore testimony to her dexterity. She also did a great deal of cutting out for the country people. Having no daughters, she frequently took orphan girls to bring up, exercising over them the kind care of a parent, and teaching them to do the work she gave them. After educating them to industry and usefulness, she gave them in marriage to worthy young men. Thus she became the mother of the motherless, and there is no doubt that her instruction and example both in matters pertaining to usefulness in this life, and to religious preparation for another, had much to do in forming that character for industry and piety, for which the females of that vicinity were so much respected. She was not only useful in her own day and generation, but the impress of her character may be observed even now, forty years after her death, upon the neighbor-

hood in which she lived.   Truly, the price of a virtuous woman is far above rubies !

In person, Mrs. Walker was tall, stout, and erect.
The expression of her countenance was that of firmness mingled with kindness.   In advanced life she became very large ; yet she could mount her horse with
the agility of youth, and ride either by day or night
to meet the calls made upon her by those who needed
her aid.

She died in 1809, her death being attributed by her
physicians to an affection of the heart.   Her memory
has not perished with her, but is still cherished by a
large circle of relatives and friends, who admire her
talents and love her virtues.

IX.

MARY McCLURE.

MARY McCLURE was the mother of Capt. John McClure, a man recognised throughout the whole South as one of the master spirits of the Revolution. His achievements during his brief and brilliant career were important enough to render him the theme of high praise among his compatriots, to make his loss deeply felt as a public calamity, and to cover his memory with honor. Revolutionary men spoke of him as " one who disdained to shun his foe." Gen. Davie said regarding him, " of the many brave men with whom it was my fortune to become acquainted in the army, he was one of the bravest, and when he fell, we looked upon his loss as incalculable." It is not too much to say that he was indebted for his eminent qualities to maternal training.

Mrs. McClure was the sister of John Gaston. She came to South Carolina probably about the same time, and settled upon the rich table lands lying on the south fork of Fishing Creek, eight miles north of Chester Court House, where two of her grandsons, James and Hugh McClure, now reside. She was one of the earli-

est residents of that region of country, and had much
to encounter from the hostile incursions of the Cherokee Indians.   It was probably in allusion to this
experience that she was commonly called " The
Cherokee heroine."   Many nights and days did she
spend in the forts, whither the women and children
were accustomed to resort when the men were out.
At the period of the Revolution she was considerably
advanced in years, the mother of seven children of
mature age—four sons and three daughters—and had
been a widow some fifteen or twenty years.   She took
a warm interest in public affairs, and was active in
personal exertions to serve the cause of freedom.   Two
witnesses yet living—John Bishop and Mrs. Mary
Johnston, testify to her zeal, " that she did all she
could ; she urged every one to take up arms, sent forth
all her sons and her sons-in-law, and her neighbors
too."   So strenuous and successful were her efforts,
that she had not a doubtful neighbor whom she did not
bring over to the whig side.   It was, indeed, owing in
great part to the women of that vicinity, that the men
were so united and so resolute ; that they went forth,
to a man, to fight the battles of the Revolution, while
the women attended to the farms, performing the labors both of the household and the field.   Mrs. McClure
seconded the enterprise set on foot by her brother—the
surprise of the British at the Old Field.   In that encounter her son Hugh was so severely wounded that
he was left a cripple for life.   John, the leader of the
enterprise, manifested great coolness and energy in

directing and carrying it out, and was rewarded by the achievement of a brilliant victory. This bold stroke, the first symptom of reaction after an apparently hopeless prostration—had a marvellous effect, several who had previously suffered their names to be enrolled among the loyalists changing sides on that day. These were of course regarded as traitors, and some were afterwards taken prisoners and hung by the order of Lord Cornwallis. The arrival in the neighborhood of Col. Winn, of Fairfield, who came to propose a similar attack on a large body of the enemy at Mobley's Meeting-house in Fairfield District, was warmly welcomed. The same number of men, among whom were John Bratton and John Mills—went down with him, and as before, were victorious, surprising and defeating more than two hundred. They also recovered several horses which the loyalists had taken for the King's service from the whigs of Chester. Three or four of these belonging to Mrs. McClure, were brought back and delivered to her.

The success of these attempts inspiring the patriots with new hope, McClure spread his men in small parties over the country, inducing others to join them. Their numbers received daily additions in York District. They made a stand at the Iron Works of Col. Hill, exchanging a few fires, but being outnumbered, they continued the retreat—while the enemy destroyed the works—and crossing the Catawba, withdrew as far as Lincoln County in North Carolina. There they selected their position, and made preparations to receive the

British, who, however, did not advance upon them, but
facing about, retreated, making no halt till they were
within the stronghold of Rocky Mount.   The whigs,
watchful for an opportunity favorable to their return,
at length passed down the north side of the Catawba,
and formed their camp near a stream called Clem's
Branch, on the edge of Lancaster District.   This
district and that of Chester lay in front, between them
and the British posts at Rocky Mount and Camden.
On one hand were the whigs of York, on the other,
those of Mecklenburg County, which lay on the east,
the Catawba forming a defence on the west.   No position could have been more judiciously selected than
this in the heart of a whig population, and in time
came encouraging reinforcements.   It was here that
Gen. Sumter found the men who had been driven to
North Carolina, resting upon the soil of South Carolina ; the line of division probably passing through the
camp.   During the weeks they occupied this encampment, the patriots were not idle.   Sergeant Ben.
Rowan, with a few men, went back into North Carolina nearly two hundred miles, for the purpose of procuring lead, and drove pack-horses before them laden
each with about two hundred and fifty pounds weight.
Others were sent out after powder.   The smiths were
busy in every direction, manufacturing swords, and
making and repairing those twisted rifles which did
such destructive execution in the battles of the south.
The active and enterprising John McClure, with his
company of mounted riflemen, was constantly in the

field, and others were out in different directions through the country, encouraging the desponding partisans, collecting recruits, and putting down the loyalists wherever they could. These movements annoyed and alarmed the British, who regarding the province as subdued, were not disposed to brook disrespect from a few stragglers. Col. Floyd, a loyalist of York District, made grievous complaint at Rocky Mount, in consequence of which Col. Turnbull, then commander of the post, sent out Capt. Huck with his force of four hundred men. With his band of redcoats and tories he wasted the country; everywhere, it is said, cursing Presbyterians, and burning those Bibles which contained the old version of the psalms. In his second progress he visited the house of Mary McClure. Her son James and her son-in-law Ned Martin, had just returned from Sumter's camp. When the British drew near, both were busily employed in running bullets, having melted up for this purpose their mother's pewter dishes—in those days the pride of a housekeeper. So occupied were they, that the enemy had entered the lane before they were aware of their presence. James McClure, it was commonly said, had but one idea at a time, and at this particular moment, perhaps from the nature of his occupation, that of fighting was uppermost. His first impulse was to salute the intruders with a volley; but Ned objected that they were too many for them. James replied—" we can kill a good many before they get to the house, and then we can go up the stairs and kill a good many more before they can get up." "But,"—remonstrated Ned—"they will burn the house and defeat us at last." The idea of fighting, therefore, was reluctantly given up. To escape was out of the question, but James climbed the wall of the new house, and perched himself upon some plank lying on the windbeams. Here he was soon discovered and brought down, and with his brother-in-law, taken out into the yard and searched. Their pockets were full of pewter bullets, furnishing proof of their murderous designs against the king's men. While they were secured with ropes, James told them boldly that if Ned had agreed to do as he wished, both would have been saved from their present disgrace ; for, said he—" to surrender without firing a gun is too disgraceful !" His daring only made his situation more desperate, and the sentence was pronounced, that at sunrise on the morning of the 12th July, Ned Martin, James McClure and Col. Moffat, were to be hanged by the neck for the crime of having their pockets full of pewter bullets !

Mrs. McClure saw the young men bound by the redcoats, whose tender mercies she well knew. But remonstrance or entreaty would be vain, and it is not recorded that she ventured on either, though the keenest anguish must have filled her heart when she thought of their too probable fate. When they were secured, Huck stepped up to her and said, rudely, " You see now, Madam, what it is to oppose the King! Where are your other sons—John and Hugh? I should like to have them in company with this Jemmy

of yours, who impudently says if it had not been for
Ned Martin, he would never have been bound as he
now is. We'll hang your son, Madam; that is his
doom! Where are John and Hugh? Come, out with
it! Search, men; they are hid some where—grand
cowards!"

"That is a lie!" exclaimed the indignant mother,
casting upon the brutal captain a look of intense
scorn. "You, sir, know better! You have never yet
stood to meet them; and if John were here now, you
would be afraid to face him!"

"D—n him!" cried Huck, "tell me where I may
meet him."

"Go to Gen. Sumter's camp," was the reply; "there
you may possibly meet with him."

In scrutinizing the different objects around the room,
Huck laid his hands upon two books on the table
Taking them up, he asked, "What book is this?"

"That, sir, is the 'Afflicted Man's Companion.'"

"A good title—one which the d—d rebels will soon
have need of."

"It is a good book, sir," replied Mrs. McClure.

"And what book is this?"

"It is the Family Bible."

"Do you read them?"

"Yes, sir."

"It is these books," said Huck, furiously, "that
make you such d—d rebels!" and he threw them both
into the fire. The matron sprang forward to recover
them, and though he would have prevented her, suc-

ceeded in dragging them from the flames. One corner of the Bible was badly burned. It was long kept
in the family as a relic.

Enraged at her saving the books, Huck struck Mrs.
McClure with the flat of his sword. She said to him,
nothing daunted by his brutality, " Sir, that will be a
dear blow to you !"

The soldiers set fire to the new house, but Mrs.
McClure succeeded in extinguishing the flames. It
was but little, however, that her unassisted strength
could avail, and they soon entered and began pulling
down the plank partition. It happened that she had
wrapped a few gold guineas in a cloth, and hid them
in a crevice. Knowing where they were concealed,
she rushed in through the soldiery amidst the falling
plank, and when the cloth fell, placed her foot upon it,
stooped down as if hurt, and saved the money. The
others, meanwhile, were busily engaged in destroying
her property, carrying off whatever articles it suited
their inclination to take. A quantity of nails had
been purchased for the new building; these they took
and scattered them broadcast over the field as they departed from the premises, driving James and Ned before them.

No sooner were the intruders gone, than Mrs.
McClure despatched her daughter Mary in all haste
to Sumter's camp, to carry the news of the outrage
she had suffered and the captivity of the young men.
The young woman made her way to the camp, arriving late in the evening. The Americans had heard

from different persons for several days past, of the
march of Huck's party through the country, their progress being marked by cruelty and spoliation, and
some from the vicinity of Mrs. McClure's had fled to
the camp for safety. The news of the capture hastened their preparations for the expedition against
him, and just after sunset the companies of John
McClure and John Bratton—the York and Chester men
—headed by their captains and under the command of
Col. Neil, left Sumter's camp. The distance to be
marched was thirty miles, and from the intelligence
they had received, it was supposed that the enemy
would be found at White's (now Crawford's) Mills,
engaged in grinding the wheat and grain they had
been for several days gathering throughout the country. The little band of patriots, only seventy-five in
number, but resolved to peril their lives in avenging
their own and their neighbors' injuries, made directly
for the mill. Shortly after midnight they arranged
the disposition of attack. McClure took twenty
mounted men, and went up the pond, intending to go
round its head about half a mile ; but found a ford
where they could pass through the pond. McClure, putting himself at the head of his men, gave command to
swim their horses, and having reached the other side,
issued his orders in a loud voice, and the party, spurring their horses, dashed up the hill. The tramp of
their feet on the rocky ground, broke the dead silence
of night. No British were found on the hill, and so
rapid had been their advance, that the body below with

Neil and Bratton, not expecting them so soon, at first
took them for the enemy. The march was resumed,
and a little before day they passed the house of old
Mr. Adair. Observing the door ajar and light shining
from the fire place, Bratton went up gently to the
door and tapped. The old man was sitting up at the
fire, two British officers having taken his bed. From
him they learned the disposition of the enemy at Williamson's. The plan of attack was then arranged, and
McClure, taking one division, went off to enter the
lane at the further end, where the attack was to be
commenced, Neil and Bratton entering at the near
end, to take the enemy in rear. McClure, as usual
with him, took a nigh cut, and came on the side of the
lane, where he threw down the fence as he leaped over.
It was now so light that his brother James, who was
confined with other prisoners in a corncrib, recognized
him ;* but when the guard placed over them called
out " Who is there ?" James, with admirable presence
of mind, replied indifferently, " Oh, it is some of your
tory friends." The drums and fifes of the enemy now
began to play for morning parade. In an instant the
sharp crack of McClure's rifle announced that his part
of the game had commenced. The particulars of this
action have been elsewhere noticed. The guard stationed at the crib ran behind it to hide themselves from
the shots ; James McClure, though tied down so that
he was unable to move, shouted an order for them to

* One account makes the action commence rather earlier in the
morning. See Vol. i. p. 243.

leave the crib, that the prisoners might not be exposed
to the danger of being killed by their own friends.
After the fall of Huck and Ferguson, and the scatter-
ing of their forces, the tory, Col. Floyd, made his
escape on horseback. Dropping his valise, he ordered
his boy, Sam, to stop and get it. Both Sam and the
valise were captured, and the negro was sold as a part
of the booty. He was purchased by John Nixon, and
is still living with his daughter. Although very old,
he occasionally goes up to the great house, to carry
his " young mistresses" through the war. That battle
field of July 12th, 1780, made Sam decidedly a whig,
and he gives it as his opinion that " the whigs can
whip the whole world chock full of redcoats and tories
too." One other article of booty, obtained that day
and afterwards sold, was Huck's razor. It was bought
by Capt. John Steel, and is now in the possession of
one of the Gastons, having already done a good deal
of shaving, and likely, if properly taken care of, to last
for several generations to come.

McClure, mounted at the head of his men, pursued
the flying enemy for nearly thirty miles. The bushes
were the only places of safety between Williamson's
and Rocky Mount, and many prisoners were taken in
the pursuit. The effect of this victory was of lasting
advantage. Some who were loyalists that day, never
afterwards entered a British camp, although lurking
about unwilling to come out on the other side. From
all the surrounding country men flocked to Sumter's
camp   It was about this time that " the Bloody

Scout" under Cunningham, was committing unprecedented cruelties on the inhabitants of Union and Spartanburg Districts.   James Knox, who had removed thither but the year before from Mrs. McClure's neighborhood, was inhumanly butchered in his own yard, where he was occupied in shelling corn.   His family fled back to Chester, while the Thomases, McJunkins, and others of that region, repairing to Sumter's camp with a supply of powder, brought intelligence of " Bloody Bill's" whereabouts.   Another of John McClure's services was the driving of this notorious murderer from the vicinity.   He was sent out by Sumter in pursuit of him, and having understood that he had crossed Broad River to the western side of York District, he soon struck his trail and chased him across the district of Union.   Cunningham fled some thirty miles towards Ninety-Six, and barely escaped, while four of his men were captured by McClure.

The night he brought in his prisoners, Sumter broke up his camp at Clem's Branch, and marched down to Davie's camp in the Waxhaws.   The next day, while Davie with his cavalry took the road leading down the east-side of the Catawba, to place himself between the British posts at Hanging Rock and Rocky Mount, Gen. Sumter took that to Landsford, crossed the river at sunset, and marching all night, at sunrise on the 31st of July, invested Rocky Mount.   McClure's riflemen were engaged through the day.   At night Sumter drew off his men, and encamped on the ground where he was surprised eighteen days afterwards.

He then removed his camp to Landsford, where he was joined by Davie, and while there the Chester men held an election; McClure, who was constantly out with strong mounted parties, being elected Colonel, and John Nixon Lieutenant Colonel.

About sunset on the following Sunday, Sumter crossed the river, marched all night, and commenced the battle of Hanging Rock a little after daylight, August 7th. Hanging Rock is in Lancaster District, and remarkable not only for its association with that celebrated battle, but as a natural curiosity. On the east side of the creek many rocks are piled in an irregular group along the declivity of a steep hill. That called Hanging Rock is a single mass twenty feet in diameter, which on the side nearest the stream to which it gives its name, is scooped into a regular arch, under which several persons might be sheltered. Its edges are tinged with smoke, it is supposed from fires kindled there by hunters. Another boulder is poised on the edge of a larger rock, resembling a ship resting on the summit of a cliff, and looking as if a slight force would hurl it into the waters below. The battle ground is near this spot. Sumter's force in three divisions, advanced on the camp of the tories under the command of Col. Morgan Bryan.* His lines were posted on the brow of a steep hill beyond the creek, while the British camp lay nearly half

* The accounts written by McCreary and Gaston are followed. Mr. Stinson obtained that of Walker from himself, and the particulars concerning Mrs. McClure from her grandson and Hon. Judge Peter Wylie.

a mile distant.   Sumter's centre line, opposed to **Bryan's** centre, and led by the intrepid Capt. McClure, came first within the enemy's view.   The old song says:

> " Said Sumter—' Good men must be lost
>   At yonder point, I see.'
> McClure replied—' That is the post
>   For Rocky Creek and me.' "

His command received the first fire, but as the men ascended the hill the shot passed over, reaching only the tallest ; while on the right the fire did terrible execution.   The contest then raged fearfully ; bullets poured like hail ; McClure was wounded in the thigh, but plugging the wound with wadding, dashed on in front of his men, his voice, urging them forward, heard above the din of battle and the shrieks of the wounded. The direction :

> " No prisoners 'mong the tories make,
>   The British suppliant save."

showed their hate of the loyalists.   After firing, they clubbed their guns, rushing into the camp and grappling with the foe.   Where dead and wounded lay in heaps, McClure fell, pierced with several wounds, while at the same time his cousins, the four Gastons, lay bleeding around him.   Some near him ran to his relief ; but he ordered them back to the fight, and as he lay weltering in blood, his voice was still heard urging them on.   As the tories fled towards the British camp many of the whigs rushed pell-mell with them ; Alexander Walker, hurrying along in their midst, was about to fire on those before him, when one close to him caught his arm, crying, "Those are on our side !" and then, as if struck with a sudden suspicion, asked, "What is that green leaf in your hat for ?" The whigs had taken the precaution to put each a leaf in their hats that morning before going into battle. Walker pulled out the token, but the discovery was already made ; one of the tories seized his gun, the other ran a bayonet through his shirt. Letting the weapon go, he turned and fled back. "It appeared to me," he said, "that they fired fifty guns after me ; every leap I gave, I heard something fall on the leaves which I took for blood, and thought I must be badly wounded, and would soon fall exhausted. I thought of the intolerable thirst I had witnessed in those bleeding to death, and my mouth began to feel parched. I had now reached the branch, and stooped to drink." Major Nixon, who, going up the hill when the tories fired on McClure's line, had tripped on the scabbard of his sword, fallen, and thus probably escaped the bullets whistling over his head, had rushed on in the confusion, and seeing Walker turn, had also turned back. As his comrade stooped to the water he leaped over him.

"On examination," continued Walker, "I found I was not hurt, but my powder horn was severely wounded, being pierced through with a rifle ball, and having lost the greater part of its contents."

Nixon took command of McClure's division, and the

right and left lines succeeded in flanking the enemy, who gave way in every direction, while the victors with shouts of triumph took the ground. But they soon saw from the British lines on their right, towards Coles' old field, a part of the Prince of Wales' regiment marching in platoons upon them. The platoon firing and charge of bayonet were a new mode of warfare to the undisciplined American troops ; yet they boldly met the reinforcement. Again to use Walker's words —" In the distance we heard the enemy's drums and fifes as they marched towards us. We stood still to receive them. As the Prince of Wales' regiment approached, Sumter gave the order to keep cool and wait for the word to fire. They had come near when the order was given, and our fire was a fire that did credit to the Revolution ! Only one of their officers—and he an inferior one—was left standing on his feet, and one half their men were slain or wounded.* The soldiers stood petrified ; and then Col. Davie of the dragoons, being on the right flank of our line, in a voice like thunder called out—'Britons, ground your arms ! you have but one officer left ; to the ground, if your lives are worth preserving !' It was done ; the men of this regiment were our prisoners ; we took their muskets, armed our men with them, and pre-

* Joseph Gaston, who after being wounded was carried to a small stream in the rear, faint from loss of blood, says he heard the firing of the platoon on the hill at the encounter with this regiment, and anxiously enquiring of some one who came down, of the success, was answered—" we are killing them like wild turkeys." The Regiment was destroyed.

pared to meet the enemy. We met and fought them manfully in the open field, but an accident frustrated our hopes. Col. Davie, coming round on the right flank to make a charge where we had broken the ranks—was mistaken by our men for the enemy, and giving way, they retreated to the tory camp."*

McClure's command sustained the largest share of the whole loss. He himself, thus stricken down in the bloom of life, was borne on a bier from the field to Waxhaw church, where the next day his mother

* McCreary's MS. proceeds: " Sumter's men, flushed with victory, seized the arms of their vanquished enemy, with their unexpended round of cartridges, and advanced across a ravine to the British main encampment on Cole's old field. A tremendous fire ensued from.the enemy's cannon, which opened with platoons from the field. The enemy was surrounded on three squares of the field, and every thing seemed to promise complete victory, when the alarm of a reinforcement occasioned a retreat on the opposite side of the field from that of Bryan's ground ; nor could all the skill of generalship displayed by their commander on the occasion rally, until they had reached Bryan's ground, where they made a final stand. The British sounded a retreat, and sent in a flag with overtures for a truce, in which they offered to show the same care and attention to the American dead and wounded as their own. Bryan's ground was retained until biers were made for the wounded, and the retreat covered in safety to the Waxhaw by night. The engagement lasted three hours and forty-six minutes by the watch." * * " This was thought to be one of the most spirited and best fought actions by raw militia—all volunteers— against British regulars during the Revolutionary war. And although American historians have not paid it due attention, it being a mere militia affair, yet a British writer has not forgotten to do the subject justice."

came to nurse her gallant son. In a day or two the
wounded were carried to Charlotte, Mrs. McClure going
with them, and devoting to John the most unwearied
attention. On the 16th August occurred the defeat
of Gen. Gates near Camden, and during the two following days, men flying from that disastrous field
were continually coming and passing on. It is thought
that McClure's death was hastened, if not caused, by
his excitement, and anxiety to take the field again.
On the 18th, contrary to the directions of the surgeon,
he rose and walked across the room, but was suddenly
taken worse, his deep-seated wound broke inwardly and
he bled to death in a few hours. At the time there
was a report that the British were coming, and every
body was leaving Charlotte. It was proposed to bury
the corpse without a coffin, but his mother insisted on
having him decently interred, saying that the enemy,
"the servants of Satan, were bound like their master,
and could go only the length of their chain." A few
brave men remained with her, and rendered the last
offices to the dead. At the very hour, probably, that
McClure drew his last breath, his compatriots in arms
under Sumter, fifty miles below, on Fishing Creek,
were routed, slain, and flying; Sumter himself on the
road, bareheaded, making his way with all speed to
Charlotte, as did Gen. Gates two days before! The
hope of liberty was crushed to the earth, while the
gallant officer who had seemed all eye, who had never
suffered surprise, but often surprised the enemy, closed
his mortal career. In Liberty Hall, the room in which

the Mecklenburg Declaration was penned by the son
of the widow Brevard, died the son of the widow
McClure

Mrs. McClure returned to her home, bearing a heavy
load of grief for the loss of him who was the prop of
her declining years. Her kindred had fought the
battles of liberty on every field, and four out of her
brother's family had fallen. One of her nephews,
Hugh Knox, had been wounded at Rocky Mount;
another, William Strong, slain in the presence of his
mother. Her son Hugh had nearly recovered from his
wound, and James had been rescued by his brother's
prompt movement. These, with her neighbors driven
back at this time, were afterwards engaged in the
battle of King's Mountain. The matron herself did
not give way to sorrow, for she was still called to an
active part. Her eldest son, William, who had been
educated by her brother, Dr. Alexander Gaston of
Newbern, had entered the army as surgeon, and at
the surrender of Charleston was taken prisoner. He
endeared himself to the citizens by his professional
services to the sick, and his name is still remembered
with gratitude. He afterwards married and resided at
Newbern, at his death leaving a daughter, Hannah,
who was educated by Mrs. Margaret Gaston, and
became the wife of her son, the late Judge Gaston.

Mrs. McClure set out for Charleston—two hundred
miles distant, on horseback and alone—to see this son.
After crossing, on her way, the line of Chester District, she was in the midst of loyalists. Entering

Charleston, she may be said to have bearded the lion
in his den, where unrecorded cruelties were exercised,
not only on the imprisoned soldiers, but the unoffending inhabitants—women and children.   She found Dr.
McClure confined to the city limits, and spent some
time with him.   She informed him of the condition of
affairs in the upper districts, and he introduced her to
some of the whig leaders.   Yet, even while the prospect was thus gloomy, she still looked on the triumphant Briton as a *chained enemy*—and predicted that his
time was short.   She knew the spirit of the Scotch-
Irish Presbyterians of the Catawba; she knew that it
was a war of principle—the principle of Bible truth—
the right of self-government in church as well as State,
and that in centuries resistance would not be vanquished.   Such were the sentiments of one who would
dare martyrdom before she would stand by and see the
word of God consumed.

Returning home early in October, she was greeted
by the joyful news of the battle of King's Mountain, of
the promotion of some of her Chester neighbors to the
rank of officers, and in a few days of the retreat of
Lord Cornwallis to Winnsboro'.   In this retreat the
British army passed within two miles of her house.
The militia of the country *took toll* as it passed, at
every suitable thicket ; a single whig sometimes riding
up, picking off his object, and making good his escape.
This turn of the scale afforded great matter of rejoicing
to Mrs. McClure, who held forth the consolation to her
neighbors, never doubting for a moment, although the

issues of battle might be various, that the cause of right would ultimately triumph.

Col. Tarleton for a short time halted his legion at White's Mills on Fishing Creek, midway between Charlotte and Winnsboro', on a look out for the dreaded mountain torrent. It did not descend, but several of the King's Mountain men on their return took toll, and many a dragoon who left camp in fancied security, never returned. The redoubtable Colonel himself came near ending his days by the hand of a young woman, Jane Morrow. He went into a house where she was alone, and offering some insult, took hold of her; she struggled with him, and succeeded in causing him a rather severe fall on the floor. One John Owens, hearing the noise, ran in, and found the invincible Colonel lying flat on his back, Jane's knee upon his breast, and her hands grasping his throat with such force that he was black in the face ! Owens interposed and saved him; but the Morrows always blamed him for not letting Jane have her own way, and as long as he lived " he had to sneak out of any company where they were."

From the commencement of 1781, the widow's heart was gladdened by news of victories, or favorable results when the tide of battle turned against her friends. None felt more grateful than she did for the aid rendered by other states. On one occasion, when the whigs had obtained a quantity of salt by taking a fort, it was sent up by wagons to Col. Watson's in York District to be distributed by pecks among the

widows of those who had fallen in battle. Mrs.
McClure and Mary Johnston set out on horseback for
their peck. As they passed the battle ground at
Williamson's, Mrs. McClure said, " There, Mary, is
the grave of Hook, who struck me a grievous blow !
Old as I am, I could find it in my heart to get down
and dance over it ; but that would be wrong ; I should
not rejoice over a fallen enemy. God is just, and will
avenge his own cause ; let us ever trust in Him !"
At this period, though at least seventy-five, Mrs.
McClure scarcely appeared to have numbered forty-five
years. With a constitution that seemed almost to
defy the ravages of time, she was one of the finest
looking women of her day ; having a smooth, clear
and fair complexion, cheeks blooming as the rose, and
a form faultless in its proportions. Her countenance
indicated the fearless spirit she possessed. Her relations with her neighbors and acquaintance were always
friendly. The men of the Revolution, after the war,
took much pleasure in visiting " the mother of the
brave captain" as they called her. She was a Cal-
vinist in faith and always prompt to maintain the
right, in religion as in politics, regardless of consequences. She lived till about the year 1800, in the
midst of her family settled on lands she had appor-
tioned to them. Her remains were deposited in the
graveyard of Old Richardson Church, by the side of
her brothers, John and Rev. Hugh Gaston. No monument points out the spot, yet do their labors follow

them, and their country yet reaps the fruit of their services and privations.

The descendants of Mrs. McClure have exhibited a constant devotion to their native land. James, the son of James, served in Canada through the war of 1812, and James, the son of Hugh, led one of the companies of Chester volunteers to Charleston, and was for some time stationed at Bull's Island. In the late war with Mexico three of her great grandsons were in service, one in Alabama, and two in the Palmetto regiment. It is to the descendants of the patriots of '76 that our country will look in the hour of her peril. May their friendly clasp bind the Union with the grasp of the giant!

X.

ISABELLA FERGUSON.

SOME months before the destruction of the log meeting—house mentioned in a preceding memoir, Samuel Ferguson, a 'country-born,' attending service there, had looked upon the face of Isabella Barber, and had seen that she was fair. The wooing and marriage followed in due time, the last event taking place a little before the fall of Charleston. The young couple were then living in the house of Isabella's father— Samuel Barber,—the brothers, Joseph and James, having taken to themselves wives, and fixed their homes on the opposite hill. They were in the field with Sumter while Samuel was enjoying a protracted honeymoon. His brothers were rampant loyalists, and were with the royal force at Rocky Mount, James Ferguson having a colonel's commission. Samuel was a lover of hunting, and it was shrewdly suspected that in some of his forest excursions he went as far as that post ; though if he ever did so, the occurrence was not mentioned to his young wife. They had more than once talked over the subject of the war, and the differ- ence of opinion between her brothers and his own.

Samuel was never strong in argument, not being highly gifted in mental endowments, whereas Isabella had sat under the preaching of a learned minister, had been regularly catechised, and indoctrinated in the Scriptures and the political creed of her people. Her husband was thus constrained to acknowledge that to her "beautiful countenance" she added Abigail's other accomplishment—"a good understanding"—and it usually happened that she had the best in every discussion.

Col. Ferguson, having raised a hundred and fifty or more loyalists, was not a little proud of his new command, and his fine British uniform. He was a man of commanding appearance, and the honors heaped on him were very gratifying to his brothers, who like him, anticipated nothing but honor and riches in their military career. But what was to be done with Samuel and his Irish wife, whose counsels had so far prevailed with him against all their solicitations to join the King's party? At this time Col. Ferguson was preparing to accompany Capt. Huck on his expedition. With his command he left Rocky Mount one morning, dressed in full uniform and mounted on a noble charger—the music of drum and fife sounding, and the colors of Old England flying. He could not help thinking that if his young sister-in-law could see him thus in the pomp of war, she would no longer detain her husband from a chance of the like promotion. It was not much out of his way to take the road by the house,—and then his martial appearance

might have a proper effect upon that nest of Covenanters ! He pleased himself with imagining the surprise
of Isabella when she should see how much better he
looked in a splendid uniform than in tow trowsers
and hunting-shirt. In the afternoon of the first day's
march, the cavalcade of New York regulars and South
Carolina loyalists approached the house of old Barber.
A messenger was despatched to say that Col. Ferguson
of His Majesty's army wished to speak with Samuel.
Samuel presently made his appearance, looking rather
awkward, and his brother, in a formal address, invited
him to join him, saying he had come for that special
purpose. "It may be,"—he urged, "that I shall be
made a lord ; how then should I feel in hearing it said
my brother was a rebel ?"

Isabella was within hearing while the Colonel was
endeavoring to persuade her husband, and came forward at the last word. "I am a rebel !" she said
proudly—as glorying in the name :—"my brothers
are rebels, and the dog Trip is a rebel too! Now,
James, I would rather see you with a sheep on your
back, than tricked out in all those fine clothes ! Above
all, I am told you have our minister chained by the
foot like a felon ! Rebel and be free ! that is my
creed !" Then turning to her husband, "we have
often talked it over, Samuel," she said, "and you
could never justify their unhallowed practices—coming
here to make slaves of us who would die first, and
plundering, stealing cows, and the like. Now, in the
presence of the British army I tell you, if you go with

them you may stay with them—for I am no longer
your wife! You know well if Joe or Jemmy should
happen to see you in such company, they would pick
you out as a mark not to be missed."

Samuel was unable to withstand this determination of his bonny Isabel, whom he loved the better for her spirit. He requested his brother to excuse
his going at this time; he might report him a
true subject of the King, but his wife being rather
on the wrong side, he would content himself with doing what he could at home to serve His Majesty and
bring back the rebels. Could Isabel but be convinced,
he might be able to turn the whole clan of Covenanters; " for she is never afraid to speak her mind." Thus
he spoke while in his heart he felt sure that his wife
would stand firm, and doubted if after all she were
not in the right. His brothers shook hands with him,
and the Colonel bade him be faithful and have courage, and he would no doubt obtain a commission for
him.

The party scoured the country round about, punish-
ing rebel men and women, sending prisoners to Rocky
Mount, enlisting loyalists, and thrashing out wheat at
different farms, to be sent to White's Mills for grinding.
After Huck was slain in the action at Williamson's,
another of the officers, mounted his horse, which
became restive, the new rider's legs being much longer
than the Dutch Captain's, and threw him against a
stump. He died afterwards of the injuries received
in the fall. Col. Ferguson was to be seen every where

endeavoring to rally the scattered force.   A fatal shot brought him from his horse—his head striking the ground, and one of his brothers had his hand torn to pieces.   The brothers scattered with the rest of the men and were hid for weeks in the woods—their wives bringing them food in the dead hours of night.   It was particularly observed that the brothers Barber and William Anderson, who were excellent shots, fought that morning more like wild beasts than conscientious Covenanters.   Henry, a red-headed Irishman of Huck's party, had insulted Mrs. Bratton with opprobrious epithets, striking her with his sword, and driving her before him into the house.   He was wounded when taken prisoner by the whigs, and fortunately not recognised by Col. Bratton, who would have killed him for his outrage to his wife.   Her generosity saved him, while her husband was searching every where for the offender.   Adamson, who had treated her and her children with respect and kindness, driving the rude soldiers from her room, and seeing that nothing was taken from her, was nursed by her with the tenderness of a sister, and her cheeks were bathed in tears when she saw his sufferings.

This victory proved of advantage to the wives and widows of the patriots of Rocky Creek.   Samuel Ferguson, on his part, when he heard of the result of the expedition, the Colonel's death and the miserable situation of his remaining brothers, never looked on the bonny face of Isabella without a feeling of thankfulness that he had escaped a similar fate.   Her words

that day, respecting Joe's and Jemmy's shooting, he
had thought sounded like a prediction. When the
prospect seemed darkest, other movements were working out for the widows and orphans made by this un-
natural strife, a deliverance from starvation. Isabella was earnest in schemes for the alleviation of the
misery around them, while her husband, whose confidence in her judgment and good sense was stronger
than ever, listened to her plans with approval, and
sought her counsel as to the manner of assisting his
unfortunate brothers. She exhorted him to gain the
confidence of their neighbors by deeds of kindness to
the defenceless and destitute, and thus deserve their
good offices in turn. "Your brothers," she would say,
"went to their undoing, leaving their own people to
join themselves to the alien; but if they repent, there
is forgiveness for the greatest transgressor. You and
they too might have work to do in helping those who
have lost all by the war, and then the whigs would
call you friends."

About three quarters of a mile north of Rossville, at
the bend of Rocky Creek, is a deep ravine, the sides
of which are precipitous, but may be descended by
grasping the bushes along the path. In the depths of
this ravine was a cave, excavated by human labor,
about ten feet deep and as many in width. This place
at the present day is a marvel to the country people,
who are unable to conjecture at what period, or for
what purpose, the cave was originally constructed. It
was here that Samuel Ferguson deposited the articles

entrusted to his care by the benevolent Isabella, she receiving the goods from the women, for fear of involving her husband, should the royalists discover that whig property had been secreted. The corn brought to him for safe keeping Ferguson put into his own crib, and assisted the poor women by milking for them, and by various needful services. It was understood, for prudence' sake, that he leaned to the loyalist side of the controversy, while his wife was a firm whig; though in reality he had been won over, in heart, to her opinions. By their joint exertions the distresses of the neighborhood were much relieved, and his brothers found advantage in adopting the same course, deserving the good offices of the women by the kindly assistance thus rendered them. All this was brought about by the efforts of a woman, who well merited to be called, as she was by all who knew her, " the good Isabella Ferguson." Her prudence so restored good feeling between the people and the Ferguson family, that they came to be regarded rather as benefactors than enemies, and at the close of the war were almost the only loyalists permitted to remain in that part of the country. Their descendants are among the most worthy citizens of Chester District.

Isabella had her full share of trial and suffering. Her father's grey hairs were brought to the grave by the untimely death of her brothers, and the horrors enacted around them from time to time, with the blame thrown upon her husband's family, often wrung her kind heart. She was a blessing to her family and her neighbors, both in adverse and prosperous circumstances; but few knew the energy of character concealed under her quiet and unassuming manner. Samuel was for many years a ruling elder in the Presbyterian Church to which he belonged, under the pastoral care of the Rev. Robert M'Culloth, the last classical teacher of Gen. Andrew Jackson.

Mrs. Ferguson ended her days in 1820, upon the plantation on which her father settled when he first came to the country in 1773. The graves of her household are in Catholic burial ground.

XI.

MARY JOHNSTON.

THE District of Chester, so prominent in the Revolutionary picture for its brave men—a Lacy, a Davie, a Nixon, a Gaston, or a Brown, furnished patriotic women enough—were no other instances on record, to exhibit the power of female influence in the country's heroic age. Their unobstrusive example—their spirit, constancy and self-sacrifice—wrought so much good, that their memory may well be cherished with pride, not only on the ground rendered classic by its stirring associations, but by the whole nation.

The name of Johnston is conspicuous on the list of those justly entitled to the meed of praise. David Johnston, the grandfather of the subject of this sketch, born in 1688, married Mary Boyd. His son Matthew, the sixth of seven children, was born in 1734, and married Jane Gaston, the daughter of John Gaston, a cousin of the Justice. These parents of Mary emigrated from the neighborhood of Ballymoney in the county of Antrim, Ireland, in the year 1769, the daughter at that time being eight years of age. They landed at Charleston, and removing to Chester Dis-

trict, settled near the residence of Mrs. McClure.
Some time afterwards, yet before the commencement
of the war, their nephew James Johnston, the uncle
of the present Chancellor Johnston—came from Ireland, and made his home in their house. This James
went out with Matthew Johnston against the Cherokee
Indians in 1776, and both were at Fort Moultrie when
it was attacked. James was at the siege of Savannah, and in nearly all the campaigns of the war. The
affection between the cousins in time grew into love,
and in 1780, just after the British had taken possession of Charleston, James and Mary were united in
marriage. They had but little time for the enjoyment
of each other's society, the state of the country calling
to action all who counted not their lives dear for the
achievement of independence. The Johnstons were
among the foremost ; they were with McClure in the
action at Mobley's, and also at Williamson's, Rocky
Mount, Hanging Rock, and the taking of Carey's
Fort. They were with Sumter's army at the surprise
on Fishing Creek, and made their escape with others,
picking up their guns as they fled. After they had
passed up the road some distance, they were charged
upon by a troop of dragoons, and Matthew Johnston
was shot down. James turned, and taking deliberate
aim at one of the troop, fired, and saw him fall from
his horse. At the same instant a ball reaching him,
struck against a pocket book in his vest, which turned
its course under his ribs, inflicting a severe wound.
The dragoons, seeing one of their number fall, wheeled

about; the freed horse ran towards the spot where James lay unable to move, and his friend Samuel Morrow, a man of great strength, caught the animal, flung Johnston upon him, and mounting himself behind, bore him safely to Charlotte. This Morrow is living at the present date.

It was a dark and disastrous period. The defeat of Gates, followed by the surprise of Sumter and the butchery of so many men in his camp, completely prostrated the country's rising hopes. Those who had saved their lives by flight, were hurrying from the neighborhood or returning to their homes. The news of Matthew Johnston's death, with that of Capt. Pagan and others, was carried to their friends; there were no men to render the last offices, and it devolved upon women to go down to the battle ground and see that the dead received sepulture. Mary Johnston, accompanied by Miss Mary McClure, went the same night to Justice Gaston's, and found at home only the Justice, Mrs. Gaston and their granddaughter, Margaret McCreary. The house had been plundered of everything, and that night the aged couple slept upon *cowhides*, the two young women and Margaret occupying other cowhides stretched on the floor. The next morning they prevailed on Margaret to accompany them to the field of the dead. They passed near the house of widow Steel, but did not stop. As they drew near the spot of the disaster, with a natural reluctance to go alone where they must encounter so appalling a spectacle, they called at the house of one

Rives, and asked him to go with them. He was a loyalist, and somewhat afraid of the consequences of being seen with rebel women ; but finally yielding to their persuasions, he consented to accompany them. It happened that he and some negroes had buried Matthew Johnston and the slain dragoon. He was under the impression that the corpse was that of old William Stroud ; but when the grave was opened, probably at Mary's request, she recognized the body as her father's by a cut on one of the shoes. No pen can portray the feelings of the bereaved daughter when the truth thus broke upon her. She cut off a piece of the dress to take to her mother, and the corpse was recommitted to the earth. Unwilling to view the battle ground, they did not go further. but on their way home they met two of their neighbors, Mary Gill and Isabella Kelso, going down to look after the body of Capt. Pagan.

Mary's husband recovered of the wound he had received, and was afterwards generally known as " Adjutant Jemmy Johnston" under Colonel Lacy. He was promoted, and served as captain in the State troops ; was at the battle at King's Mountain, and with Gen. Sumter till the close of the war. As Secretary Peters, in the halls of Congress, was said to be engaged in building up the republic with wit and pleasantry, so was it with Johnston in the army ; for he kept the company in camp in a roar of boisterous laughter, while he was fighting the republic into existence With a fine person he had excellent conversational powers, and a large fund of humor and ready wit.   During his absence it was Mary's part to attend to the home business for her mother, as well as to perform most of the labor on the farm.   It has been mentioned that she went with Mrs. McClure on horseback for the peck of salt distributed at Watson's.   Not only did the labors of the field devolve on the women during this period, but they frequently had to devise means of assisting or sheltering the hunted whigs.   Their friends could not venture on a visit home without watching their opportunity.   North of this settlement lay the blackjack region, now thickly covered with blackjack, but at that time an open prairie, on which persons could be seen at a great distance.   The patriots coming to visit their families, always endeavored to pass over this plain by night, though to do so, they were often under the necessity of lying by all day.   As they approached their homes, they usually discovered some signal hung out by the women, by which they understood whether or not they could enter their houses with safety.   Mary McClure gave the cue to all the operations of the women of her vicinity, and notwithstanding the popular notion that a female can never be trusted with a secret, it is certain that the women of Fishing Creek neighborhood kept their countersigns as inviolate as ever Washington and his Generals preserved the secrets of their councils in the American army.   They had the knowledge, as far as their observation extended, that the church-going people—the Scotch-Irish Presbyterians—with few exceptions espoused the cause of the country; while in the ranks of the loyalists were generally found the outlaws —horse thieves, Sabbath breakers and the like. The respective parties being generally of this description, Mrs. Johnston says it formed a reason, to her mind, why a mere handful of whigs could scatter a body of three or four hundred tories. On the one hand, the men fighting for their inalienable rights, their homes and families, had confidence in the justice of their cause; on the other, plunder was the only object; there were neither fixed principles nor settled aims to direct men's efforts, and having no high impulse or worthy purpose to overcome the fear of death, on the least reverse they would take to flight, and lurk about like thieves even when threatened with no immediate danger. They exercised power, when it was in their hands, with cruelty, often with wanton barbarity, and the consciousness of deserving no mercy tended to increase their apprehensions. The whigs, on their part, while they frequently showed unexpected clemency, seldom evinced a want of courage or address. This was proved in numerous exploits, among which might be mentioned the feat of Mills and Johnston in capturing and carrying off two British officers in view of the army of Cornwallis. Gen. Sumter was aptly denominated "the Game Cock;" and the captains by whom he was supported, Nixon, Steel, McClure, Johnston, Mills, and others on the Catawba, proved themselves possessed of the qualities which contributed to his success.

Some years after the Revolution, James and Mary Johnston removed from Chester to Fairfield District, and settled on Wateree Creek. The inhabitants of this district, with the exception of a brave band— the Wynns, the Durhams, Buchanan, Strother, Milling, and others, had generally submitted, and joined the British when they overran the country. In this locality James and Mary performed, in the peaceful walks of private life, a nobler work than at the stormy period of the war. They agreed between themselves that they would never introduce the subject in the presence of their new neighbors. It might be a sore one to them, and they reasoned—"it would be cruel to wound their feelings; they have been on the wrong side, and are now convinced of it; it was their misfortune if they lacked knowledge, or wanted courage to pursue the right; they have good hearts, and it is in our power to make them friends, and while treating them as friends, now in time of peace, we may mould them into good citizens, doing ourselves and the country a service. Why should we act the cowardly part of trampling upon a humbled foe? let us rather take them by the hand and raise them up." Thus it was— while Starke and Durham, who had suffered by the loyalists, refused to countenance any, that the jovial Johnston would be surrounded by crowds of them, causing them nearly to split their sides with laughter. They would say to one another—"We used to fear him as the devil, but he knows how to treat us! Who would not stand up for Johnston, equally brave in war and peace?"

When we consider the state of feeling in the country, it will appear that there was no little heroism in this course. The same generosity was shown by many of the patriots, who, heartily forgiving their " erring brethren," refrained from wounding their feelings, and evinced their confidence by elevating them, in some cases, to official positions of power and influence. This magnanimous conduct might rebuke the political demagogues of the present day, reminding them that the proscriptive spirit of party was not that of the patriots of Seventy-six. In Chester, many sons of the tories were not surpassed by any in devotion to the republican party, and in the war of 1812, they rallied to the country's standard, as well as those of Fairfield District, now esteemed one of the most patriotic in the State. It may not be amiss to mention, as illustrative of the good feeling that prevailed in the Johnston family towards their late opponents—that Ellen, a sister of Mary, was married to John Ferguson, a son of the tory Colonel who fell in the action at Williamson's.

James Johnston died in 1795, leaving seven children. His widow experienced to the full the trials peculiar to her bereaved state, and well performed the duties that devolved upon her. Her sons went out in the war of 1812, under their uncle, William Johnston, who headed a company of volunteers from that neighborhood.

In narrating incidents of the Revolution, Mrs. Johnston shows exact knowledge of the details learned from the information of others, as well as those which passed under her own observation. Yet she says: "Had I continued to live among my good old neighbors of Fishing Creek, I should have remembered more; but in Fairfield we agreed not to talk of it." From her infancy she was nurtured in Presbyterian doctrines, and was a constant attendant at Fishing Creek church—then under the pastoral charge of Rev. John Simpson—till some years after her marriage. When they removed to Wateree, she joined Mount Olivet church, and ten or twelve years since, removing with her son John to Chester, and settling within the bounds of Catholic—she regarded it as her peculiar good fortune, that in each of these churches she enjoyed the singing of the Psalms according to Rouse's version. Till lately she has been able—though in her eighty-ninth year—to ride on horseback five miles to church; but happening to get a fall while walking, she was so injured as to be obliged to use crutches. She is fond of conversation, and occasionally enters into it with so much spirit, that a listener might imagine her to be still in her youth. She is tall in person, her eyes are full of intelligence, and her face is strongly expressive of the energy of her nature. Her life has been one of industry, and even now she is continually engaged in some useful occupation. When asked why she so constantly applied herself to labor, she answered—"It gives me pleasant sleep. Others may work to make a living; I work to keep myself alive, for this body requires exercise. It is true, I have no clog to bind me to earth; for long since I gave all my worldly estate to my children, and I am left alone by those whose existence commenced with mine. I know not how soon it may be the will of my Master to remove me; yet life is a desirable thing, and it is my duty to take care of this mortal body, that it may last with comfort to myself, as long as it may please God to suffer me here to remain." In conversing with such an one, the past and the present are both before us; she carries the mind back to scenes in our country's history now only remembered in tradition, while she is not regardless of more recent occurrences. Her long and eventful life has been spent usefully to the communities in which she has lived, and in the service of her Creator. Having been sole head of her family for more than half a century, she has seen the children she trained become respectable and useful members of society. She has thus finished the work assigned her, and with the meek patience of a Christian awaits her appointed time.

XII.

~~~~~~~~~~~~

JANE BOYD.

It will be remembered that one of the chief sufferers
from British vengeance in Fishing Creek neighborhood,
was the Rev. John Simpson. He was distinguished
throughout the country for the zeal with which, at the
earliest period of the struggle, he espoused the cause of
liberty. He came from Delaware, where he had married a Miss Remer, and took up his residence in Chester District, being the first regular pastor of Fishing
Creek church. He had been preceded in the work of
planting the Gospel in this thinly settled and destitute
portion of country, by the Rev. William Richardson,
who, coming as a missionary and settling in the Waxhaws, preached daily in the different settlements, often
extending his visits to the distance of sixty and seventy miles from his home, and being occasionally absent
on his tours for months at a time. Mr. Simpson followed in his footsteps, preaching with a like zeal, and
laboring as earnestly in the work of spreading the
blessings of true religion. He collected and organized
many of the now flourishing congregations of Chester,
York, and adjacent districts. In those days the in-

habitants thought it no hardship to ride fifteen or twenty miles to hear preaching, and that, too, on week days, and in all kinds of weather. Nor had they the comfortable houses in which their descendants now worship; but often in the grove, with logs for their seats, and a rude structure of boards for the pulpit, they offered up their meed of devotion to the God of their fathers.

The Rev. John Simpson was regarded as the head and counsellor of the band of heroes who had so signally defeated the enemy at the Old Field and Mobley's —and it was determined that his punishment should be speedy. In pursuance of this resolution, a party took their way to the church, where they expected to find the pastor with his assembled congregation, intending, as was believed at the time, to burn both church and people, by way of warning to other " disturbers of the King's peace." This was on Sabbath morning, June 11th, 1780. Mrs. Simpson, who was sitting at the breakfast-table with her children, heard the report of a gun, which caused her much alarm, for such a sound was unusual in that vicinity. She afterwards heard that it was at the house of William Strong, and that he had been killed by the enemy on their way to the church. Their design of murdering more victims was frustrated. On the Friday previous, Mr. Simpson had shouldered his rifle and marched to the field, under the command of Capt. McClure, who had been reared from infancy under his ministry. There the pastor, taking his place in the ranks with the brave men of York and Chester, encouraged and stimulated them by his counsel no less than his services, performing the duties of a private soldier, and submitting to the rigorous discipline of the camp.

While the destroyers were at the church, some of the negroes overhearing them declare their intention to go to Mr. Simpson's house and "burn the rascal out," hastened to carry information to his wife, urging her to save herself and family by immediate flight. Mrs. Simpson looked out, and saw a body of men coming down the lane. Stopping only to gather up a set of silver tea-spoons, most valued by her as a gift from her mother, she took her four children and went out at the back door, concealing herself in the orchard in the rear. Here she was enabled to watch the movements of her enemies, without being herself discovered.

They rifled the house of everything valuable, took out four feather beds, and ripped them open in the yard; collected all the clothing, from which they selected such articles as they fancied for their own keeping, and having exhausted their invention in devising mischief, finally set fire to the house, which was soon burned to the ground. Just as they were going away, they noticed an outhouse, which contained a valuable library, and was usually occupied by Mr. Simpson as a study. This was soon also in flames. The men now left the premises, and as soon as they were out of sight, Mrs. Simpson hastened back to the house, rushed into the study and carried out two aprons' full of books. She could save no more, and in doing this, was much burn-

ed and had nearly lost her life. The feathers in the
yard had taken fire, but she succeeded in saving
enough for one bed. She then went to the house of
one of her neighbors, where she remained till after her
confinement, which took place in four weeks. As soon
as she recovered, she returned to her own place, and
took up her residence in a small outhouse which had
escaped the enemy's vengeance. Here she contrived
to live with her five children and a young Miss Neely,
receiving continual assistance from the people of her
husband's charge, but not yet free from depredation
and danger. At one time, when she had procured
some cloth, out of which to make clothing for her children—the spoilers having left them nothing—she
had cut out and was making up the garments, when a
company of tories came along and plundered her also
of these. She complained to the leader of the party,
and he ordered his men to give them back. Some of
this gang were dressed in Mr. Simpson's clothes, and
strutting before her, tauntingly asked if they were not
better looking men than her husband; telling her at
the same time, that they would one day make her a
present of his scalp! This marauding party took off
her stock of cattle. Mrs. Simpson begged them to leave
her one milch cow for her little children, but her
request was refused. The property was restored, however, in an unexpected manner; after going two miles
further on their way, the robbers put the cattle in a
pen till morning; two large steers broke out during

the night, opening a way for the rest, and the whole flock returned home.

During the time that Tarleton was encamped at White's Mills, three of his dragoons, all intoxicated, came to Mrs. Simpson's. One of them falling asleep in a chair, the others went away without him. Miss Neely suggested the propriety of killing their unconscious foe, saying, " These fellows have killed our friends, and if our men were here, would they not despatch him ? What they would do, ought we not to do to assist them ?" To this Mrs. Simpson replied that it would be extremely wrong ; " Our friends would only take him prisoner, and exchange him for some one of our men who are prisoners at Camden." They then consulted upon the expediency of binding him fast, and carrying him as a prisoner to Charlotte ; but on the reflection that they could not conveniently go with him, this project also was abandoned.

Jane, the subject of this notice, was the eldest of Mr. Simpson's children, and at that time about ten years of age. She remembers seeing the redcoats and tories, and has a distinct recollection of the scenes of trial and distress through which her mother passed. The facts above stated were related by her, having passed, for the most part, under her own observation. Her father remained with the army till the tories were quieted, and the country delivered from the power of the aggressor, and she thinks he was engaged in most of the battles fought. After the war he continued in charge of Fishing Creek and Bethesda Churches, occasionally supplying Catholic and other small congregations. He could never feel confidence in those among his hearers who had sided with the oppressor in the country's extremity, though no remains of enmity were in his heart. They appeared to perceive this, and withdrew from his charge when churches of other denominations sprang up around them. Between 1790 and 1800, Mr. Simpson removed to the district of Pendleton, where his days were ended. To brilliant talents he united eminent piety and excellence of character, with a superior education, which, in lieu of worldly estate, he bestowed on his sons and daughters. Some of these sons became ornaments to the learned professions. One married a daughter of Gen. Pickens ; another a daughter of Col. Moffat ; another —Dr. James Simpson—a daughter of Col. John Bratton, and two others into the family of the Sadlers. Jane was married first to James Neely, of Fishing Creek, and after an absence of one or two years, returned to the place of her nativity. She had one son —named after her father—and two daughters by her second marriage with John Boyd. She has been a widow more than twenty-five years, and her son died about ten years ago. One of her daughters is the wife of James Drennan, the other of Mr. Reid. Mrs. Boyd resides with them, having her grand children around her. Her countenance is expressive of the energy of her character, and her sprightliness of disposition renders her conversation delightful. She has a heart full of the kindliest feelings towards her fellow-creatures, and is always ready to do a good act, and give assistance to her neighbors in sickness. Faithful to the lessons of her early life, when she was taught not to absent herself from the sanctuary unless engaged in ministering to the sick, she may be found in her seat on every Sabbath. How solemn must be her reflections, as on each returning day of rest, she takes her place in the house of prayer! It was here she first heard the truths of the Bible expounded by the lips of her venerated father. But she meets no more those friends and neighbors who began with her the journey of life, and whose voices mingled with her's in hymns of praise; although their descendants of the third and fourth generation, bearing the same names, recal by their features the memory of those who are gone. As she walks through the large churchyard, the tombstones with their brief inscriptions call back the past more vividly; here rests an aged matron whom in youth she loved and venerated; there an old man, whose words of counsel aided in moulding her youthful character, or some friend of her brightest days, whose joyous youth promised a length of years equal to her own, or some brave man to whose protection she looked in the hour of danger. Their dust has returned to kindred dust, and she, "beneath the burden of fourscore," waits her appointed time, trusting her all, both here and hereafter, to Him who has promised to pass with her "through the valley of the shadow of death."

Mr. Stinson, who communicated the above details,

had requested a friend to procure from Mrs. Boyd the incidents of her life. She told him she would write out the sketch, and shortly after sent it in her own handwriting. The diction and neat penmanship would have done credit to any young lady in a modern school, and this is the more remarkable, as for many years she has had but little occasion for the exercise of the pen. The education she received from her father was a substantial one, contrasting with the superficial kind fashionable at the present day, and has contributed to her usefulness and happiness even to the latest period of life. Instructed in the principles of true religion, trained to correct habits of thought, unwavering in her Christian faith, industrious in doing offices of kindness to those around her, respected by every one and regarded by all as a friend—her character presents a suitable example for the imitation of her sex in the present day.

XIII.

JANE GASTON.

"THE old homestead," the residence of Justice John Gaston—a place memorable for the resolution to which the members of his family so solemnly pledged themselves, to die rather than submit to the invaders —is now the home of his daughter-in-law. It seems fitting that the soil thus consecrated to the memory of brave men who were active in the national struggle for freedom, should be still in the possession of a representative of those times—a living witness of the horrors of civil strife. Jane Gaston is the widow of Joseph Gaston, whose blood mingled with that of his three brothers—David, Ebenezer, and Robert—on the battle-field of Hanging Rock. August 7th, 1780. It was her lot to pass her early years in the midst of distress and suffering, but her life has been prolonged beyond the term of fourscore years, enabling her to see her country rise from its calamities into a prosperity far beyond what the most ardent patriot could have anticipated. Since the period of her trials she has been crowned with blessings through her lengthened life, and happy in the respect and affection of a nu-

merous circle of friends, many of whom have listened
with interest to her oft-repeated account of the events
her childhood witnessed.

Jane Brown was born April 10th, 1768, in the
county of Mecklenburg, North Carolina, where her
parents, Walter and Margaret Brown, had first settled
after their emigration from the county of Antrim, in
Ireland. When Jane was about a year old, they
removed to Chester District, South Carolina, and fixed
their home upon Fishing Creek, about two miles south
of the mill-seat now owned by Major N. R. Eaves.

In the early part of June, 1780, John Brown, the
brother of Jane, then about seventeen years old, joined
the company under John McClure. His father was
then not more than fifty-five, but in very feeble health.
It will be remembered that after the first attack on·
the British at Beckhamville, and at Mobley's Meeting-
house, a strong party was sent under the command of
Huck, in pursuit of McClure and those who had joined
him, and that the whigs, retreating through York
District, were driven as far back as Lincolnton, N. C.
About this time Col. Locke defeated a large party of
loyalists under Col. Moore, at Ramsour's Mill. The
whigs, gaining strength every day, now turned upon
Capt. Huck, who in his turn retreated, making not
much delay till he and his men were again safe at
Rocky Mount. On this first incursion of the royal
troops into the remote parts of the State, many outrages were committed upon the helpless families where
they passed. On Sunday morning, June 11th, the

10*

troops under Huck arrived at the house of Mr. Strong, near Fishing Creek Church. They immediately entered and plundered the house of everything, carrying away also the corn and wheat. Some of the grain being accidentally scattered in the yard, a tame pigeon flew down and picked it up. The brutal captain struck the bird, cutting off its head at a blow with his sword ; then turning to Mrs. Strong, he said : "Madam, I have cut off the head of the Holy Ghost." She replied, with indignation : "You will never die in your bed, nor will your death be that of the righteous." The prediction thus uttered was in a month signally fulfilled. Mrs. Strong was a sister of old Justice Gaston.

After this insult and blasphemy, some of Huck's men went to the barn, where her son, William Strong, had gone shortly before their arrival. He had taken his Bible with him, and was engaged in reading the sacred volume. They shot him dead upon the spot, and dragged him out of the barn. The officers then began to cut and hack the dead body with their broadswords, when Mrs. Strong rushed from the house, pleading with all a mother's anguish, to the officers, that they would spare the corpse of her son. They heeded not her agonized entreaties, till she threw herself upon the bleeding and mangled body, resolving to perish as he had done by the cruel hands of her enemies, rather than see her child cut to pieces before her eyes. Such outrages were of common occurrence, and the example set by officers of the royal army, in the

slaughter of boys of too tender an age to become soldiers, and in the plundering of houses defended only
by women or aged men, gave encouragement to the
loyalists, who followed their banner to practise similar
cruelties. Robbery, spoliation and murder were everywhere the order of the day.

The brother of Jane being one of McClure's band,
the house of Mr. Brown was occasionally visited by
gangs of robbers, sometimes in the dead hours of night,
and his life often threatened. One day a large party
came to the house, plundered it, tore up the floor, and
carried away several large bolts of homespun cotton,
taking the cords of the beds to tie up their plunder.
The same party of marauders went to the house of
Daniel Elliot, in the neighborhood, and robbed it of
everything they could find. Mr. Elliot offered neither
resistance nor remonstrance, till they proceeded to
bridle one of his best horses; he then interfered, laying
his hand upon the rein. He was instantly shot dead.
His son Ebenezer, terrified, fled from the murderers;
but Margaret, his daughter, walked boldly up, jerked
the bridle rein from the tory's hand, and pulled it off
the horse. The man threatened to kill her; she defied
him. The murderers, however, did not venture to stay
long, probably fearing they might be surprised by some
of the neighbors. When they departed, Margaret,
missing her brother, went over to Mr. Brown's to ask
if they had seen anything of him. The family had
heard the report of the gun, and feared some mischief
was going on at Elliot's house. Margaret learned that

they had seen nothing of her brother, and then burst
into a flood of tears, exclaiming : " Oh, they have
killed my father !" " Oh, my father !" she would
repeat, again and again, in agony : " They have
wickedly killed him without cause !"

Mr. Brown and his family, already stripped of everything they possessed, gave all requisite attention to the
burial of their neighbor.   It was then necessary to seek
a place of greater safety for themselves, and with their
children, Jane, Walter, Robert, and an infant that died
young, they set out in June, on foot, upon their
journey.   Well said the old song—

> " Carolina, south and north,
>   Was filled with pain and wo ;
>   The tories took their neighbors' worth,
>   And away a whig must go."

The fugitives travelled about thirty miles, and
sought shelter at the house of David Haynes, whose
wife, Molly Caruth, was one of their relations.   While
they remained there, the whigs who had been driven
back by the British, returned and formed their camp
not far below, on Clem's Branch.   At this time, a son
of old Mr. Haynes was about starting to join the
fighting men in this camp.   When his mother bade
him adieu, she gave her parting counsel in the words :
" Now, Alick, fight like a man.   Don't be a coward !"
After two weeks had elapsed, Alexander was brought
home from the battle of Rocky Mount badly wounded
in the face.   Mrs. Haynes received him without testi-

fying any weakness or undue alarm, and seemed proud that he had fought bravely, and that his wound was in front. He was taken thence to Charlotte. The hospital being not far from the house of Mr. Haynes, Jane Brown went frequently with others to see the wounded soldiers. Many of the wounded of Buford's command were there, and disabled men from the battles of Rocky Mount and Hanging Rock were lying in rude log-houses, upon boards covered with straw, laid across the sleepers for their resting-place. Some had but one arm, some had lost a leg, and some were deprived of both arms, or both legs. Jane heard them laughing and joking with one another, and her attention was particularly attracted to one who had lost both arms, and was threatening to knock down a fellow-sufferer. It was common thus to see cheerfulness manifested in the midst of misfortune, by these martyrs to liberty. Mrs. Gaston also remembers having seen there her neighbors Henry Bishop and the noble John McClure, both mortally wounded.

On the approach of Cornwallis to Charlotte, Mr. Brown took his family and went further north, to the house of James Haynes, a brother of David, who lived upon the road leading north of Cowan's Ford on the Catawba River. Here Mr. Brown procured an outhouse on the plantation for the accommodation of his family. While they remained here, Morgan passed with his prisoners—in January, 1781—and was soon followed by the British in pursuit. These last stopped at the house of James Haynes, plundered it, and made the owner a prisoner. There happening to be eight or ten bushels of meal in the house, they took the bed-ticks, emptied them, and carried off the meal in them. Mrs. Haynes, thus forced to part with her husband, sent for Mrs. Brown to come and stay with her, and she came with her children. The afflicted matron herself conducted family worship that night. She prayed fervently for peace ; but she prayed especially for the deliverance and freedom of her country, invoking the interposition of a protecting Providence for the rescue of her captive husband. " God prosper the right !" was frequently repeated by her in the prayer. It seemed that her earnest petition was providentially answered; late on the following evening Mr. Haynes arrived at his home, nearly exhausted with fatigue.

The next morning, as nothing in the way of provisions remained on the premises, Mrs. Brown went into the meal-room and swept up the meal scattered on the floor, from which she prepared a little hasty-pudding for the children. These and similar scenes are indelibly impressed upon the memory of one who bore such a part in the hardships encountered by her kindred. The scene of violence was for the present changed—the British forces being occupied in the pursuit of Greene. The following verse of a popular Revolutionary song was appropriate :

> " General Greene, Rhode Island's son,
>   Commissioned from on high,
> In that distresséd hour did come,
>   And away our fears did fly."

Mr. Brown now resolved on returning home, knowing that his countrymen had bravely and successfully maintained their cause against fearful odds, and that order would soon take the place of the desolation spread by unbridled rapine throughout the country. The family went back, and were informed of many strange things that had happened since their flight. John, coming home from camp, had gone over on Rocky Creek to the house of his uncle, David McQueston, the only relative he had in the country. The loyalists dogged and followed him, and soon after, arriving at the house, called at the door. McQueston pushed the young man into a back room, and then opened the door. The tories entered, went into the back room and searched it ; but missing the corner in which he was concealed, went back to the fire inquiring for him. John heard their questions, and fearing they might bring a light and discover him, slipped out at the back door. As he sprang over the fence, they caught a glimpse of, and shot at him. He made his escape, however, unhurt. Other incidents of the kind were detailed in the hearing of the returned family. During their absence many of their acquaintances had fallen in battle ; many had been killed in their own houses ; some had perished in Camden jail, and some had been taken to Charleston and put on board the prison ship. During the period of tory ascendency, the friends of American liberty were hunted like deer, and chased from one place of shelter to another. High-handed robbery and murder were committed.

daily by a set of outlaws who styled themselves British subjects, and took advantage of the general state
of confusion to gratify their love of plunder and
bloodshed. One incident may serve to illustrate the
state of the times. Among the most noted of these
desperadoes were two, Wood and Warren, who having
been the terror of the country for the outrages they
perpetrated, pursued their vocation rather longer than
it was safe to do so. It had not apparently occurred
to them that after the royal troops had taken their departure, some of the whigs might venture back to the
homes from which they had been driven, and that
they might chance to be surprised in their accustomed
avocation of rapine. While they were intent on this,
it happened that Hugh Knox and William (commonly
called Governor) Knox, reaching home, heard that
these fellows were in the neighborhood carrying on
their old business. Following their trail, they came
to the house of Ann McKeown, and questioned her as
to the direction in which the marauders had gone.
She expressed apprehension for the safety of " the
Knox boys," for she knew Wood and Warren to be
desperate characters, well armed with gun and sword,
always ready, and appearing to fear nothing. " They
have done a heap of killing," she observed ; " and
what, my boys, can you do with such men ?"

" We will put a stop to them, if we get up with
them," replied William Knox.

Ann then informed them that the men had gone in
the direction of Alexander Rosborough's house. " And

it is likely," added she, " that they will kill him as they have done others."

' Governor Knox' answered, " Upon my modesty" —a favorite phrase of his—" we must be going !"

" Well, my lads," said the woman, " here is a cup of old rye whiskey. It will keep your blood warm while you are engaged in a good deed." As they went off, she shouted at the top of her voice, " Success ! success to you, my brave boys !"

It was growing late ; the sun was sinking in the west, and the shadows stretched far along the ground. Wood and Warren were busy in their work at Rosborough's, having tied him hand and foot, while they went through the house collecting plunder, and bidding him pray, as his time was short—his life depending on the quantity of goods he might possess. As the desperadoes were ascending the stairs, the shadows of the Knox boys fell upon the logs of the building. The fumes of the whiskey making them less cautious, they had come up on the wrong side of the house. The robbers thus got the start. Wood, having his fusil swung on his shoulder, put it through a crevice, and aimed at one of the Knox boys. His gun flashing, he missed fire, and both then started to run. Hugh Knox fired after Warren and slightly wounded him ; the two then closed in a fierce struggle, on which their lives depended. The conflict was long and hard ; in the meanwhile, Wood ran through the fields, and William Knox close after him.

" Upon my modesty," said the Governor, in relating

the occurrence, " I did not like to shoot the poor devil running. I just wanted to take him prisoner, and let Capt. Steel try him by King's Mountain law ; but as he jumped the fence, I struck at him to stop him, and it proved an unlucky blow ; I happened to strike a little too hard, and killed him ! When I returned, Hugh had mastered his man, and was washing himself, being as bloody as a butcher. Going into the house, I unbound Rosborough, without thinking that he would be in a passion. He took one of the guns and struck Warren, and was as unlucky as myself, for he broke his skull. I felt bad, for I disliked the killing of prisoners."

William never told this without shedding tears, and always concluded his narration with, " Upon my modesty, I never could kill a prisoner!" So it turned out, however ; and they had both the robbers to bury. When they had dug the grave, Hugh Knox would have his own way, and placed both the bodies with the face downwards, saying, " Let them go down to h—, whither their doings will carry them!"

It was not long before the patriots had driven off the most notorious of the marauders, and those whose crimes were pardonable having been suffered to remain on the promise of reformation, the disorder and confusion everywhere prevalent, were exchanged for a better state of things. The militia was regulated, and every man required to do his duty by serving his country when called upon. When Mr. Brown returned to his home, in the winter of 1781, he had to begin the world afresh. John came back after the battle of Eutaw, having been in most of the battles of that season. When the war was over, he assisted his father in his business; but as he intended to pursue a course of study, he enlarged his means by teaching school, and was one of a number of young men who organized a debating society. They made a collection of all the books they could procure, and established a circulating library. While John thus availed himself of every opportunity of improvement, aided by his father with every means in his power, his mother and Jane were active and unwearied in their efforts to assist him, and provide in every way, by their industry and care, for his comfort.*

* The career of Rev. John Brown, D.D., was a remarkable one. He taught school to defray the expenses of his education in the classics, and having graduated, studied divinity with the Rev. Archibald and Rev. James Hall. For more than half a century he was engaged in the ministry, and was one of the most eloquent preachers of his day, yet the greater part of his time was spent in teaching. He had charge of the High School at Wadesboro', N. C., for several years, and a flourishing academy at Salisbury. Thence he removed to Columbia, S. C., where he held a chair in the college. He then took the Presidency of Franklin College at Athens, Georgia, and was afterwards at the head of an academy at Monticello, ending his days at Gainsville. Whereever he taught, he preached, and when travelling, collected the people every night to expound the Scriptures. When more than eighty years of age, he was still active in his Master's service, preaching with all the zeal of his early labors. H s influence was great on the destiny of the church in the States of North and South Carolina and Georgia.

Although young at the time of the war, it will be
seen that this daughter of a patriotic family not only
bore her part in privation and suffering, but contributed her aid in doing good to the defenders of her country's rights.   On the 20th April, 1790, Jane Brown
was married to Joseph Gaston, the youngest son of
Justice John Gaston.   The homestead was the inheritance of Joseph, both his father and mother being
dead at the time of his marriage.   This union was in
every respect a suitable one ; both had endured severe
trials throughout the Revolutionary contest, and had
been stripped of their worldly possessions ; yet both
were favored with a vigorous constitution and unimpaired energy of mind, with active and industrious
habits—an excellent foundation with which to commence the world anew.   Both had been reared in the
instruction of the Presbyterian Church, and had im-
bibed the principles of the Roundhead faith ; the conduct of both through life was guided by principle—
that principle being drawn from the precepts of the
Bible.   Joseph Gaston was a ruling elder in his
church from youth, and was also placed in the magis-
terial office when very young, continuing to exercise
its duties till his death.   He spent a long life on the
plantation where he was born, uniformly respected
by all who knew him, and died October 10th, 1836.
His family consisted of two sons and four daughters,
all of whom were married before his death, except his
youngest son, Capt. J. A. H. Gaston, who still lives
with his mother at the old place.

Mrs. Gaston is truly, to use her own words, "blessed in her children." Of those who began life at the same period with herself, and have passed through as many changes, how few can say that within fifteen miles of the parental residence, live all their children, grand-children, and great-grandchildren! Mrs. Gaston has lost but one daughter, who left ten children. And while most other families are divided and dispersed, their members emigrating to the far West, or scattered over different parts of the world, her children seem to have been bound by some powerful attraction to the spot of their nativity, a spot hallowed by so many in-teresting recollections—and cling to their venerable parent with a devotion only equalled by her maternal affection for them.

If it is a commonly received truth, that the children of believing parents are the seed of the church, it is equally true that the "expectancy of the State" is of those descended from the patriots whose lives have been devoted to the service of their country. Walter Brown, the brother of Mrs. Gaston, though but a child in the Revolutionary struggle, served in the succeeding war, being sent from Tennessee, and died in the camp, leaving six orphan children, one of whom is Dr. Robert Brown, of Winston county, Mississippi. Isaiah Walker Lewis, the grandson of Mrs. Gaston, was one of the Chester volunteers in the Palmetto Regiment of South Carolina, that served in the war with Mexico. He was the first victim in the regiment of the fatal disease which left but a remnant to return to their homes.

In person, Mrs. Gaston is of the medium size, inclining to stout, with a noble countenance, and combining great dignity with ease of manner; bearing, it is said, a striking resemblance to her brother, the Rev Dr. Brown. She retains, in remarkable vigor, the faculties of her mind, and has an unusual flow of spirits for one so advanced in years. It is a pleasing sight to see this venerable matron surrounded by her numerous throng of children's children, all happy in their relations one with another, and enjoying the rational and pleasant discourse of her who is so highly respected and so tenderly beloved among them. Even now, in the eighty-second year of her age, when she speaks of the trials and perils encountered by her own family and her acquaintances during the Revolution, her interest in the theme brings new fire to her eye, and gives a deeper energy to her language; she describes those days with graphic vividness, and often, with earnest thankfulness, pauses to congratulate those around her upon their freedom from political and religious oppression, and to exhort them to a suitable improvement of the great privileges of their day and generation. Being thus able to look back on a long life spent in the promotion of good to others, she enjoys rest in the remnant of her days, grounded in the humble faith of a Christian, expecting ere long to be called hence by the Master she has served, to reap her reward in the future of never-ending happiness to which she looks as her portion through the merits of a Redeemer.

XIV.

SARAH McCALLA.[*]

FEW of the women whose lot was cast amid the scenes of our Revolutionary contest, had more to do personally with what was passing around them, than the subject of this sketch. The account of her experience, therefore, is a portion of the history of the country. She had a hereditary right to be a patriot ; her mother was Hannah Wayne, a first cousin of Gen. Anthony Wayne. She was born in Chester County, Pennsylvania, in Piqua township, within forty-five miles of Philadelphia. In 1775 she was married to Thomas McCalla. In the following year, when the British were in New York, the young husband was called out to serve in the militia, and was stationed for some time at Powles' Hook, being there the day on which the battle was fought upon Long Island. He could hear the firing all day, and from Bergen Heights, where he lay. that night, saw plainly the blaze of artillery. When he had served out the time for which

[*] The materials of this memoir were obtained by Mr. Stinson from Mrs. McKown, the daughter of Mrs. Nixon, and from Samuel McCalla, who resides at Bloomington, Indiana.

the militia had been called, he received a dismissal and returned home.   Soon, however, the scene of action was brought near them.   When the British marched from the head of Elk to Philadelphia, McCalla was again in the field, and at the time of the battle of Brandywine his wife, but three miles distant, could hear the firing of every platoon.   In this scene of trial and peril she did not abandon herself to the paralyzing effects of terror, nor shrink from performing services which humanity taught her were a duty.   Many a wounded soldier had cause to bless her heroism and benevolence while she dressed his injuries with her own hands, rendered all necessary offices of kindness, or offered the consolation and encouragement which bear so soothing an influence from the sympathizing heart of woman.   It was a part of her daily business to aid the cause of her suffering countrymen by every means and exertion in her power.   She was in full hearing of the cannonade at Mud Island, and the explosion of the British ship Augusta.   In all the conflicts of that eventful period her husband bore an active part, nor would she be idle while he was exposed to danger.   She continued indefatigable in her labors, succoring the distressed as far as her ability extended, tending the sick and wounded, consoling those who suffered, and encouraging the wavering and irresolute to brave all in the righteous cause, entrusting themselves to the protection of a Providence that is not blind chance.   The good wrought by such women, full of zeal for their country and anxious desire to alleviate the miseries they witnessed, is incalculable. It could be appreciated only by those who received the benefit of their humane efforts, and therefore it had no reward, save "the blessing of those who were ready to perish."

In the latter part of the year 1778, Thomas and Sarah McCalla removed from Pennsylvania to Chester District in South Carolina. David McCalla, a brother of Thomas, had previously gone to this State, and was then residing with Capt. John Nixon. The first place at which the emigrants stopped, after their arrival, was Nixon's; but they afterwards fixed their home on a plantation upon the roadside, now belonging to William Caldwell. It was at this place, marked by " the mulberry tree," that the volunteer company of the 27th regiment used to muster. These dwellers in an almost wild region had but a humble home; they lived in a log cabin, cultivating the ground for daily bread, and trusting in Divine protection from the evils surrounding them incident to a primitive state of society, and from the more appalling dangers rapidly approaching with the desolating footsteps of civil strife. They were here when the war entered Carolina to penetrate her recesses, and during the severe campaign of 1780, when the struggle between the whigs and the British aided by gangs of tory outlaws, was carried on amid scenes of bloody contest and deeds of unprecedented cruelty. It was no time for a patriot to remain a mere spectator of what was going on, although to join the whig cause was apparently to rush on certain destruction. McCalla did not hesitate to cast his lot with the few brave spirits who scorned security purchased by submission. Repairing to Clem's Branch, he joined himself to the " fighting men," and was in every engagement from the beginning of Sumter's operations against the royal forces, till the evening of August 17th, when he obtained leave of absence to visit his family. Thus he was not with the partisans at the disastrous surprise on Fishing Creek. Intending to join the whig force at Landsford, he made his way thither soon after ; but was there informed that Capt. John Steel had passed down to the battle ground, and was rallying and sending on the men towards Charlotte. The following morning McCalla succeeded in joining Capt. Steel at Neely's, but it was for him a most unfortunate movement. An hour afterwards they were surprised ; Steel and some others made their escape, but McCalla was taken prisoner and carried to Camden. There he was thrown into jail, and threatened every day with hanging ; a threat the British did not often hesitate to fulfil in the case of those who fell into their hands, having been found in arms against the royal government after what they chose to consider the submission of the State.

While this brave man was languishing in prison, expecting death from day to day, his wife remained in the most unhappy state of suspense. For about a month she was unable to obtain any tidings of him. The rumor of Sumter's surprise, and that of Steel, came to her ears ; she visited the places where those

disasters had occurred, and sought for some trace of
him, but without success. She inquired, in an agony
of anxiety, of the women who had been to Charlotte
for the purpose of carrying clothes or provisions to
their husbands, brothers, or fathers, not knowing but
that he had gone thither with the soldiers ; but none
could give her the least information. Imagination
may depict the harrowing scenes that must have
passed, when females returning to their homes and
children after carrying aid to the soldiers, were met by
such inquiries from those who were uncertain as to
the fate of their kindred. To these hapless sufferers
no consolation availed, and too often was their suspense terminated by more afflicting certainty.

In the midst of Mrs. McCalla's distress, and before
she had gained any information, she was called to
another claim on her anxiety ; her children took the
small-pox. John was very ill for nine days with the
disease, and his mother thought every day would be
his last. During this terrible season of alarm, while
her mind was distracted by cares, she had to depend
altogether upon herself, for she saw but one among her
neighbors. All the families in the vicinity were visited
with the disease, and to many it proved fatal. As
soon as her child was so far recovered as to be considered out of danger, Mrs. McCalla made preparations
to go to Camden. She felt convinced that it was her
duty to do so, for she clung to the hope that she might
there learn something of her husband, or even find
him among the prisoners.

With her to resolve was to act, and having set her house in order, she was in the saddle long before day, taking the old Charleston road leading down on the west side of the Catawba River. The mountain gap on Wateree creek was passed ere the sun rose, and by two o'clock she had crossed the river, passing the guard there stationed, and entered Camden. Pressing on with fearless determination, she passed the guard, and desiring to be conducted to the presence of Lord Rawdon, was escorted by Major Doyle to the head-quarters of that commander. His lordship then occupied a large, ancient looking house on the east side of the main street. The old site of the town is now in part deserted, and that building left standing alone some four hundred yards from any other, as if the memories associated with it had rendered the neighborhood undesirable. It was here that haughty and luxurious nobleman fixed his temporary residence, "sitting as a monarch," while so many true-hearted unfortunates whose fate hung on his will, were languishing out their lives in prison, or atoning for their patriotism on the scaffold.

Into the presence of this august personage Mrs. McCalla was conducted by the British Major. Her impression at first sight was favorable; he was a fine looking young man, with a countenance not unprepossessing, which we may suppose was eagerly searched for the traces of human sympathy by one who felt that all her hopes depended on him. His aspect gave her some encouragement, and being desired to explain the

object of her visit, she pleaded her cause with the eloquence of nature and feeling; making known the distressed situation of her family at home, the fearful
anxiety of mind she had suffered on account of the
prolonged absence of her husband and her ignorance
of his fate, and her children's urgent need of his care
and protection. From Major Doyle she had at length
learned that he was held a prisoner by his lordship's
orders. She had come, therefore, to entreat mercy for
him; to pray that he might be released and permitted
to go home with her. This appeal to compassion she
made with all the address in her power, nor was the
untaught language of distress wanting in power to
excite pity in any feeling heart.

Lord Rawdon heard her to the end. His reply was
characteristic. "I would rather hang such d——d
rebels than eat my breakfast." This insulting speech
was addressed to his suppliant while her eyes were
fixed on him in the agony of her entreaty, and the
tears were streaming down her cheeks. His words
dried up the fountain at once, and the spirit of an
American matron was roused. "Would you?" was
her answer, while she turned on him a look of the
deepest scorn. A moment after, with a struggle to
control her feelings, for she well knew how much depended on that—she said, "I crave of your lordship
permission to see my husband."

The haughty chief felt the look of scorn his cruel
language had called up in her face, for his own conscience bore testimony against him, but pride forbade

his yielding to the dictates of better feeling. "You should consider, madam," he answered, "in whose presence you now stand. Your husband is a d——d rebel——"

Mrs. McCalla was about to reply—but her companion, the Major, gave her a look warning her to be silent, and in truth the words that sprang to her lips would have ill pleased the Briton. Doyle now interposed, and requested his lordship to step aside with him for a moment. They left the apartment, and shortly afterwards returned. Rawdon then said to his visitor, with a stately coldness that precluded all hope of softening his determination: "Major Doyle, madam, has my permission to let you go into the prison. You may continue in the prison *ten minutes only*. Major, you have my orders." So saying, he bowed politely both to her and the officer, as intimating that the business was ended, and they were dismissed. They accordingly quitted the room.

Thus ended the interview from which she had hoped so much. What had been granted seemed a mockery rather than an alleviation of her sorrow. Ten minutes with the husband from whom she had been parted so many weeks, and that, too, in the presence of the royal officer ! A brief time to tell how much she had suffered—to relieve his anxiety concerning the dear ones at home, inquire into his wants, and learn what she must do for him ! But even this indulgence, the Major informed her, had been reluctantly granted at his earnest intercession; and he took occasion to blame her own exhibition of spirit. The whig women, he observed, who had come down to see their friends, had shown a more submissive disposition; none had dared reply to his lordship angrily, or give him scornful looks, and he was therefore not prepared to expect such an expression of indignation as that which had escaped her. " It was with great difficulty," he said, " that I got permission for you for ten minutes. His lordship said : ' D——n her, she can cry, and I believe she can fight, too ! did you see what a look she gave me ? Upon my soul, Major, such a woman might do much harm to the King's service ; she must not be permitted to pass and repass, unless some one of the officers are with her. She must stay only ten minutes, and it must be in your presence.' "

A Spanish general, it is said, once excused himself for ordering to execution a prisoner whose little boy had just suffered him to cut off both his ears, on the promise that his father's life should be spared—by saying: " The father of such a child is dangerous to Spain ; he must pay the forfeit of his life." Lord Rawdon seems to have reasoned much in the same manner ; the husband of such a woman must be strictly watched, as a dangerous enemy to the royal cause.

The sight of the prison-pen almost overcame the fortitude of the resolute wife. An enclosure like that constructed for animals, guarded by soldiers, was the habitation of the unfortunate prisoners, who sate within on the bare earth, many of them suffering with the prevalent distemper, and stretched helpless on the ground, with no shelter from the burning sun of September. "Is it possible," cried the matron, turning to Doyle, "that you shut up men in this manner, as you would a parcel of hogs!" She was then admitted into the jail, and welcome indeed was the sight of her familiar face to McCalla. The time allotted for the interview was too short to be wasted in condolement or complaint; she told him she must depart in a few minutes, informed him of the state of his family— inquired carefully what were his wants, and promised speedy relief. When the ten minutes had expired, she again shook hands with him, assuring him she would shortly return with clothes for his use, and what provisions she could bring, then turning, walked away with a firm step, stopping to shake hands with young John Adair and the other captives with whom she was acquainted. The word of encouragement was not wanting, and as she bade the prisoners adieu, she said : "Have no fear; the women are doing their part of the service." "I admire your spirit, madam," Doyle observed to her, "but must request you to be a little more cautious."

Mrs. McCalla was furnished by the Major with a pass, which she showed to the officer on duty as she passed the guard on her return, and to the officer at the ferry. She rode with all speed, and was at home before midnight; having had less than twenty-four hours for the accomplishment of her whole enterprise; in that time riding one hundred miles, crossing the

river twice, and passing the guard four times—visiting
her husband, and having the interview with Lord
Rawdon, in which probably for the first time in his
life he felt uneasiness from a woman's rebuke. It
convinced him that even in the breast˜of woman a
spirit of independence might dwell, which no oppression could subdue, and before which brute force must
quail, as something of superior nature. How must
the unexpected outbreaking of this spirit, from time
to time, have dismayed those who imagined it was
crushed forever throughout the conquered province!

It is proper to say that Mrs. McCalla met with kinder
treatment from the other British officers to whom she
had occasion to apply at this time, for they were favorably impressed by the courage and strength of affection evinced by her. Even the soldiers, as she passed
them, paid her marks òf respect. The tories alone
showed no sympathy nor pity for her trials; it being
constantly observed that there was deeper hostility towards the whigs on the part of their countrymen of
different politics, than those of English birth.

Mrs. McCalla began her work immediately after her
arrival at home; making new clothes, altering and
mending others, and preparing the provisions. Her
preparations being completed, she again set out for
Camden. This time she had the company of one of
her neighbors, Mrs. Mary Nixon, whose brother, John
Adair, has been mentioned as among the prisoners.
Each of the women drove before her a pack-horse,
laden with the articles provided for the use of their

11*

suffering friends. They were again admitted to the presence of Lord Rawdon to petition for leave to visit the prisoners, but nothing particular occurred at the interview. His lordship treated the matron who had offended him with much haughtiness, and she on her part felt for him a contempt not the less strong that it was not openly expressed. From this time she made her journeys about once a month to Camden, carrying clean clothes and provisions ; being often accompanied by other women bound on similar errands, and conveying articles of food and clothing to their captive fathers, husbands, or brothers. They rode without escort, fearless of peril by the way, and regardless of fatigue, though the journey was usually performed in haste, and under the pressure of anxiety for those at home as well as those to whose relief they were going. On one occasion, when Mrs. McCalla was just about setting off alone upon her journey, news of a glorious event was brought to her; the news of the battle of King's Mountain, which took place on the 7th of October. She did not stop to rejoice in the victory of her countrymen, but went on with a lightened heart, longing, no doubt, to share the joy with him who might hope, from the changed aspect of affairs, some mitigation of his imprisonment. When she reached Camden, an unexpected obstacle presented itself; she was refused permission to pass the guard. It was not difficult to see whence this order had proceeded ; but submission was the only resource. She took off the bags from the horse that had carried

the load, and seated herself at the root of a tree, holding in her hand the bridle-reins of both horses. No
friend or acquaintance was near to offer aid, and
she made up her mind to spend the night in that
place, not knowing whither to go. She was not,
however, reduced to this; for before long one of the
inhabitants of the village came to her assistance, took
her horses and tied them in the back yard of his
house, and helped her to carry in the packs. This
piece of kindness called forth her feelings of gratitude,
and was often mentioned by her in after life as an
unexpected and gratifying instance of good will.

The next day she had another interview with Lord
Rawdon, which was abruptly terminated by one of
her impulsive answers. To his rude remark, that he
ought to have hung her rebel husband at the first, and
thus avoided the trouble he had been put to with her
—she promptly replied: "That's a game, sir, that
two can play at!" and was peremptorily ordered out
of his lordship's presence. Her friend Major Doyle,
however, benevolently interfered to plead for her,
representing her distress, and at length obtained permission for her to go to the prison with the food and
clothing she had brought. She said to this officer:
"Your hanging of the whigs has been repaid by the
hanging of the tories." In reply, Doyle assured her
he had never approved of such a course, and that the
responsibility must rest solely upon his lordship. The
consciousness of guilt in the exercise of these cruelties doubtless often harassed his mind, and it was not

surprising he should testify uneasiness or anger when allusion was made, as in her retort, to the subject. Mrs. McCalla then informed the Major of the news of the action at King's Mountain. It was the first intelligence, he said, that had reached him of the battle, though he had no doubt Rawdon was already in possession of the news, he having within a short time shown so much sternness and ill-humor that scarce any one dared speak to him. Though ill tidings spread quickly, it does not seem wonderful that the knowledge of an action so disastrous to the British arms should be concealed as long as possible from the soldiers and prisoners, and thus that the earliest information should be brought by an American woman, living among those who would be first to hear of it.

About the first of December, Mrs. McCalla went again to Camden. On the preceding trip she had met with Lord Cornwallis, by whom she was treated with kindness. Whatever hopes she had grounded on this, however, were doomed to disappointment; he was this time reserved and silent. She was afterwards informed by the Major that a considerable reverse had befallen His Majesty's troops at Clermont, and the annoyance felt on this account—Doyle said—was the cause of his not showing as much courtesy as he usually did to ladies. "You must excuse him," observed the good-natured officer, who seems to have always acted the part of a peace-maker on these occasions; and he added that Cornwallis had never approved of the cruelties heretofore practised.

Towards the last of December the indefatigable wife again performed the weary journey to Camden. McCalla's health had been impaired for some months, and was now declining; it was therefore necessary to make a strenuous effort to move the compassion of his enemies, and procure his release. Rawdon was in command, and she once more applied to him to obtain permission for her husband to go home with her. As might have been anticipated, her petition was refused : his lordship informed her that he could do nothing in the premises; but that if she would go to Winnsboro' and present her request to Lord Cornwallis, he might possibly be induced to give her an order for the liberation of the prisoner.

To Winnsboro', accordingly, she made her way, determined to lose no time in presenting her application. It was on New Year's morning that she entered the village. The troops were under parade, and his lordship was engaged in reviewing them ; there could be no admission, therefore, to his presence for some time, and she had nothing to do but remain a silent spectator of the imposing scene. A woman less energetic, and less desirous of improving every opportunity for the good of others, might have sought rest after the fatigues of her journey, during the hours her business had to wait ; Sarah McCalla was one of heroic stamp, whose private troubles never caused her to forget what she might do for her country. She passed the time in noticing particularly every thing she saw, not knowing but that her report might do service. After the lapse of several hours, the interview she craved with Cornwallis was granted. He received her with courtesy and kindness, listened attentively to all she had to say, and appeared to feel pity for her distresses. But his polished expression of sympathy, to which her hopes clung with desperation, was accompanied with regret that he could not, consistently with the duties of His Majesty's service, comply unconditionally with her request. He expressed, nevertheless, entire willingness to enter into an exchange with Gen. Sumter, releasing McCalla for any prisoner he had in his possession. Or he would accept the pledge of Gen. Sumter that McCalla should not again serve until exchanged, and would liberate him on that security. "But, madam," he added, " it is Sumter himself who must stand pledged for the keeping of the parole. We have been too lenient heretofore, and have let men go who immediately made use of their liberty to take up arms against us."

With this the long tried wife was forced to be content, and she now saw the way clear to the accomplishment of her enterprise. She lost no time in returning home, and immediately set out for Charlotte to seek aid from the American general. She found Sumter at this place, nearly recovered of the wounds he had received in the action at Blackstock's, in November. Her appeal to him was at once favorably received. He gave her a few lines, stating that he would stand pledged for McCalla's continuance at home peaceably until he should be regularly exchanged.

This paper was more precious than gold to the matron whose perseverance had obtained it; but it was destined to do her little good. She now made the best of her way homeward. After crossing the Catawba, she encountered the army of Gen. Morgan, was stopped, being suspected to be a tory, and taken into his presence for examination. The idea that she could be thus suspected afforded her no little amusement, and she permitted the mistake to continue for some time, before she produced the paper in Sumter's handwriting, which she well knew would remove every difficulty. She then informed the general of her visit to Winnsboro' on the first of January, and her sight of the review of the troops. Morgan thanked her for the information and dismissed her, and without further adventure she arrived at her own house.

A few days after her return, the British army, being on its march from Winnsboro', encamped on the plantation of John Service, in Chester District, and afterwards at Turkey creek. Mrs. McCalla went to one of those camps in the hope of seeing Lord Cornwallis. She succeeded in obtaining this privilege; his lordship recognised her as soon as she entered the camp, and greeted her courteously, questioning her as to her movements, and making many inquiries about Sumter and Morgan. On this last point she was on her guard, communicating no more information than she felt certain could give the enemy no manner of advantage, nor subject her friends to inconvenience. At length she presented to the noble Briton the paper which she

imagined would secure her husband's freedom.   What
was her disappointment when he referred her to Lord
Rawdon, as the proper person to take cognizance of
the affair !   The very name was a death-blow to her
hopes, for she well knew she could expect nothing from
his clemency.   Remonstrance and entreaty were alike
in vain ; Cornwallis was a courteous man, but he
knew how, with a bland smile and well-turned phrase
of compliment, to refuse compliance even with a request that appealed so strongly to every feeling of
humanity, as that of an anxious wife pleading for the
suffering and imprisoned father of her children.   She
must submit, however, to the will of those in power ;
there was no resource but another journey to Camden,
in worse than doubt of the success she had fancied
just within her reach.

It was a day or two after the battle of the Cowpens
that she crossed the ferry on her way to Camden.
She had not yet heard of that bloody action, but observing that the guard was doubled at the ferry, concluded that something unusual had occurred.   As she
entered the village, she met her old friend Major Doyle,
who stopped to speak to her.   His first inquiry was if
she had heard the news ; and when she answered in
the negative, he told her of the " melancholy affair"
that had occurred at the Cowpens.   The time, he observed, was most inauspicious for the business on
which he knew she had come.   " I fear, madam," he
said, " that his lordship will not treat you well."

" I have no hope," was her answer, " that he will

let Thomas go home ; but, sir, it is my duty to make efforts to save my husband. I will thank you to go with me to Lord Rawdon's quarters."

Her reception was such as she had expected. As soon as Rawdon saw her, he cried angrily, " You here again, madam ! Well—you want your husband—I dare say ! Do you not know what the d——d rebels have been doing ?"*

" I do not, sir," replied the dejected matron, for she saw that his mood was one of fury.

" If we had hung them," he continued, "we should have been saved this. Madam ! I order you most positively never to come into my presence again !"

It was useless, Mrs. McCalla knew, to attempt to stem the tide ; she did not therefore produce, nor even mention the paper given her by Sumter, nor apologise for her intrusion by saying that Lord Cornwallis had directed her to apply to him ; but merely answered in a subdued and respectful tone by asking what she had done.

" Enough !" exclaimed the irritated noble. " You go from one army to another, and Heaven only knows what mischief you do ! Begone !"

* Judge Wylie, the son of one of the prisoners, says that in attempting their escape, they loosened some bars about the door, but daylight surprising them, they replaced every thing but the spring bar, which they could not get back. When the keeper opened the door, he received a blow from the bar that nearly killed him. It was probably this attempt to escape that so enraged Lord Rawdon. Another account states that the prisoners actually got out of the jail, and were retaken before they had left Camden.

She waited for no second dismissal, but could not refrain from saying, as she went out, in an audible voice, " My countrymen must right me." Lord Rawdon called her back and demanded what she was saying. She had learned by this time some lessons in policy, and answered with a smile, " We are but simple country folk." His lordship probably saw through the deceit, for turning to his officer, he said, "Upon my life, Doyle, she is a wretch of a woman !" And thus she left him.

That great event—the battle of the Cowpens— revived the spirits of the patriots throughout the country. Everywhere, as the news spread, men who had before been discouraged flew to arms. The action took place on the 17th of January, 1781 ; on the 22d of the same month, six wagons were loaded with corn at Wade's Island, sixty miles down the Catawba, for the use of Gen. Davison's division. The whole whig country of Chester, York and Lancaster may be said to have risen in mass, and was rallying to arms. Mecklenburg, North Carolina, was again the scene of warlike preparation ; for the whigs hoped to give the enemy another defeat at Cowans or Batisford on the Catawba. On the 24th of January Gen. Sumter crossed this river at Landsford, and received a supply of corn from Wade's Island. His object was to cross the districts to the west, in the rear of the advancing British army, to arouse the country and gather forces as he went, threaten the English posts at Ninety-Six and Granby, and go on to recover the State. While

Cornwallis marched from his encampment on Service's plantation, the whigs of Chester, under the gallant Captains John Mills and James Johnston, were hovering near, watching the movements of the hostile army as keenly as the eagle watches his intended prey. Choosing a fit opportunity as they followed in the rear, they pounced upon a couple of British officers, one of whom was Major McCarter, at a moment when they had not the least suspicion of danger, took them prisoners in sight of the enemy, and made good their retreat. By means of this bold exploit the liberation of McCalla was brought about, at a time when his wife was wholly disheartened by her repeated and grievous disappointments. When Gen. Sumter passed through the country, a cartel of exchange was effected, giving the two British officers in exchange for the prisoners of Chester District in Camden and Charleston.

The person sent with the flag to accomplish this exchange in Camden was Samuel Neely of Fishing Creek. As he passed through the town to the quarters of Lord Rawdon, he was seen and recognized by the prisoners, and it may be supposed their hearts beat with joy at the prospect of speedy release. But in consequence of some mismanagement of the business, the unfortunate men were detained in jail several weeks longer. Neely was in haste to proceed to Charleston, being anxious, in the accomplishment of his mission in that city, to get his son Thomas out of the prison-ship, and in his hurry probably neglected some necessary formalities. His countrymen in Cam-

den were kept in confinement after his return from
Charleston with his son.   Capt. Mills was informed of
this, and indignant at the supposed disrespect shown
by Lord Rawdon to the cartel of Gen. Sumter, wrote
a letter of remonstrance to Rawdon, which he entrusted
to Mrs. McCalla to be conveyed to him.

Our heroine was accompanied on this journey by
Mrs. Mary Nixon, for she judged it impolitic that the
letter should be delivered by one so obnoxious to his
lordship as herself.   Still she deemed it her duty to be
on the spot to welcome her liberated husband, supply
all his wants, and conduct him home.   The distance
was traversed this time with lighter heart than before,
for now she had no reason to fear disappointment.
When they arrived at Camden, they went to the jail.
John Adair was standing at a window ; they saw and
greeted each other, the women standing in the yard
below.   Perhaps in consequence of his advice, or pru-
dential considerations on their part, they determined
not to avail themselves of the good offices of Major
Doyle on this occasion.   Adair directed them to send
the jailor up to him, and wrote a note introducing his
sister to the acquaintance of Lord Rawdon.   The two
women then proceeded to the quarters of that nobleman.   When they arrived at the gate, Mrs. McCalla
stopped, saying she would wait there, and her companion proceeded by herself.   She was admitted into
the presence of Lord Rawdon, who read the note of
introduction she handed to him, and observed, referring
to the writer—that the small-pox had almost finished

him ; still, he had come very near escaping from the
jail; that he was "a grand 'scape-gallows." On reading the letter of Capt. Mills his color changed, and
when he had finished it, turning to Mrs. Nixon, he
said in an altered tone : "I am sorry these men have
not been dismissed, as of right they ought." He
immediately wrote a discharge for eleven of the prisoners, and put it into her hands, saying : "You can
get them out, madam. I am very sorry they have
been confined so many weeks longer than they should
have been." At the same time he gave Mrs. Nixon a
guinea. "This," he said, "will bear your expenses."

His lordship accompanied her on her way out, and
as she passed through the gate his eye fell on Mrs.
McCalla, whom he instantly recognized. Walking to
the spot where she stood near the gate, he said, fiercely :
"Did I not order you, madam, to keep out of my presence?" The matron's independent spirit flashed from
her eyes, as she answered : "I had no wish, sir, to
intrude myself on your presence ; I stopped at the
gate on purpose to avoid, you." Unable to resist the
temptation of speaking her mind for once, now that
she had a last opportunity, she added : "I might turn
the tables on you, sir, and ask, why did *you* come out
to the gate to insult a woman ? I have received from
you nothing but abuse. My distresses you have made
sport of, and I ceased long since to expect anything
from you but ill-treatment. I am now not your sup-
plicant ; I come to *demand*, as a right, the release of
my husband !" So saying, she bowed to him con-

temptuously, wheeled about, and deliberately walked off, without stopping to see how her bold language was received.   Mrs. Nixon hastened after her, pale as death, and at first too much frightened to speak.   As soon as she found voice, she exclaimed : " Sally ! you have ruined us, I am afraid !   Why, he may put us both in jail !"

Mrs. McCalla laughed outright.   " It is not the first time, Mary," she replied, " that I have given him to understand I thought him a villain !"   The two made their way back to the prison, but even after they got there Mrs. Nixon had not recovered from her terror.   She was informed that it would be some time before the prisoners could be released.   The blacksmith was then sent for, and came with his tools.   The sound of the hammering in the apartments of the jail, gave the first intimation to the women who waited to greet their friends, that the helpless captives were chained to the floor.   This precaution had been adopted not long before, in consequence of some of the prisoners having attempted an escape.   They were then put in hand-cuffs or chained by the ankle.   These men left the place of their long imprisonment and suffering in company with the two women, and as they marched through the streets of Camden, passing the British guard, they sang at the top of their voices the songs of the " liberty-men."   They were eleven in all, among them Thomas McCalla, John Adair, Thomas Gill, William Wylie, Joseph Wade, and Nicholas Bishop ; the last a man eighty years of age, and per-

fectly deaf. The crime for which he had been torn
from his home and immured in jail was that of being
the father of eight or nine fighting men, enlisted under
the banner of their country. His thirteenth child, John
Bishop, was then in the camp.

After the liberated prisoners had marched a mile or
two on their way, it was concluded that those who
were able to travel should go on as rapidly as possible,
leaving McCalla and Adair, with the females, their
horses and luggage, to follow them as their strength
should permit. With this last party Joe Wade remained, being a stout able-bodied man, and willing to
render assistance to his invalid comrades. This patriotic individual—the brother of the late George Wade of
Columbia, S. C.—suffered much from British cruelty
—having been caught in arms after taking protection.
Garden states that he received a thousand lashes, and
died under the infliction. Joe, however, did not die,
but recovered of his wounds, and being unable to
overcome his propensity for fighting, he was again so
unfortunate as to be taken, was carried to Camden,
and there kept for some time in prison. He was
one of those who attempted to break jail, and
as the irons were put on the delinquents, he
said facetiously to the officials performing this duty,
that he " would prefer having a pair of stockings."
They therefore accommodated him with heavy irons on
each ankle. But this did not fetter the captive's
spirits ; he would rattle his chains merrily, telling his
fellow-prisoners they knew nothing of the pleasures of

a plurality. "Your single chain," he would say frequently, " can only go—whop !—but I can jingle
mine, and I will soon give you the tune of 'Yankee
Doodle,'" suiting the action to the word, and jingling
to the amusement of all who could hear him.   Many
a night Joe thus performed his musical airs with these
novel instruments, as a pastime to himself and those
who like him were at a loss for diversion, and to the
great annoyance of the keepers of the jail, whom he
prevented from sleeping.   He was proof, however,
against their murmurings and menaces, and continued
in spite of remonstrance, to keep his fellow-captives in
music and songs, while John Adair taught them to
play at cards, by way of getting rid of their superfluous
time.   Yet Joe had a soul that could be touched,
though his spirit was unconquerable ; his heart was in
the right place, and could feel for the misfortunes of
others, prompting to active exertions for their relief.
He saw now that his neighbor and fellow-sufferer, Adair,
who had been a prey to the small-pox in prison, had
scarcely strength to walk, and without hesitation he
took him upon his back and trudged along under the
weight.   "Never mind, my boy," he would say when
John remonstrated ; "you are not quite so heavy as a
thousand lashes !   My back is a little rough, so hold
on tight !   Why, if I had only thought of bringing the
chains along, I might have played you a tune as we
are going !   No matter ; when we stop to rest, John,
you shall out with the pack of cards, and we will have
the odd trick."

The honest patriot was bearing on his furrowed back—in that pale and emaciated stripling—a hero of after times ; one who, a third of a century from that date, led the hunters of Kentucky to the field, together with Andrew Jackson, another youth of the Catawba, on the banks of the Mississippi. Yes ! the lad whom Joe Wade then carried from the jail that had so nearly been his place of death, afterwards on the banks of the monarch of rivers, cancelled the debt of the thousand lashes, owing to his old friend ; for nearly thrice that number of Britons were numbered among the wounded and slain, two or three of them general officers in their army ! How strange that two boys of Catawba River who had been maltreated by the despotic English, should become instrumental in obtaining over the invincibles of Wellington's command—the haughty conquerors of Europe's master—the victory in one of the most splendid battles recorded in ancient or modern times ! But without looking into the future, the kind-hearted Joe had his present reward in the pleasure of doing a service to a youthful but resolute patriot, and through him, of serving the cause of his country. It could not have been difficult to discover that no common spirit animated that boy's wasted frame. He distinguished himself, indeed, in several battles, and aided to form the constitution in the conventions of the States of Tennessee and Kentucky—devoting his whole life, in short, to public service.

To return to our travellers. They stopped, the first

night, at the house of Mrs. Weatherspoon, who welcomed them with cordial kindness.   She had little to
offer in the way of refreshment, having only one cow;
but she made a potful of mush, and this with the new
milk, formed a delicious repast for supper and breakfast, seasoned as it was with the love that makes "a
dinner of herbs" more savory than the costliest dain-
ties.

When Thomas McCalla reached the home he had
so long desired to see, he found his affairs in an em-
barrassed condition, and little remained to him even
for the supply of the most ordinary comforts.   Mrs.
McCalla's frequent journeys, the necessity of providing
articles to be carried to Camden, and the impossibility
of her balancing the account meanwhile by thrifty
management, or by profitable labor, had sadly diminished their means.   Not only this, but she had been
compelled to contract debts, which her husband was
unable for years fully to repay.   Her disposition was
generous to a fault; in carrying provisions to Thomas,
she could not forget those who suffered with him, and
whose bitter wants were evident to her eyes; she bestowed liberally of what she had, and might in truth
be said to have fed and clothed the Camden prisoners.
Who could blame this liberality, when her neighbors
were willing to supply her, knowing the use that
would be made of their loans!   She and her husband
took upon themselves the responsibility of repayment,
and she spared not the labor of her hands for this purpose during many years.   Thomas, broken down in

health, was unable for some time to work, but with
returning strength applied himself faithfully to the
task, which through persevering toil was at last accomplished. He never received from the country any
remuneration for his losses, nor held any office. Yet
the unobtrusive patriots had their reward in the consciousness of having done well and nobly, and having
worthily served the good cause. If by their expendi-
tures for the relief of others, a bar was placed to their
attainment of riches, their poverty was honorable, and
they enjoyed the respect of the virtuous and good
among all their acquaintance. God gave them the
blessing of children, whom they trained up in the
right way. These became members of the same
church with their parents, and patriotism was to them
a household inheritance; the knowledge of the
duties of good citizens, as well as the principles of
piety, being instilled into them as their earliest and
most important lessons.

Lord Rawdon's aversion to Mrs. McCalla was not
without foundation; she was a very shrewd and independent person, and bore in her countenance the inef-
faceable stamp of her character. Her eye was keen
and penetrating as the glance of the eagle, and though
remarkable for self-control, she often expressed by the
rapid play of her features, the emotion called up at
the moment, which she did not deem it prudent to
utter in words. She often had secret interviews with
the leading men of the American party, to whom she
gave information, and who had entire confidence in

her representations, and high respect for her opinions
on military affairs.   She was not, however, indiscriminate in her disclosures, for she knew whom to
trust, and could keep a secret whenever it was necessary.   On her return from one of the trips she made
to Camden, she chanced to meet two of her whig acquaintances—John McWaters and Thomas Steel—
upon the Wateree.   They were seeking information
from Camden—the whigs at the time meditating a
visit to this post of the enemy.   She communicated to
them all she knew, informing them of the position of
the British in the town, and the guard stationed at
the river ;   and so satisfied were her friends of the accuracy of her account and the correctness of her judgment, that in consequence of the intelligence brought
by her, the projected enterprise was abandoned for the
time.

Regarding the enemy she always expressed herself
with candor.   The British soldiers she described as
uniformly polite and respectful to women, and frank
and manly in their deportment ; the loyalists of American birth she invariably condemned as coarse, vulgar,
rude and disgusting in their manners.   The New York
volunteers, she said, were " pilfering, thievish, con-
temptible scoundrels."   She generally spoke well of
the British officers, some of whom she thought an
honor to the service ; but in her praise always except-
ed Lord Rawdon.

In person Mrs. McCalla was of medium size.   Her
constitution was vigorous, her temperament ardent,

though her self-possession was striking, and it seemed impossible to take her by surprise. With a strong will and steadfast purpose, she had great quickness of perception and reach of apprehension, and her measures were always proportioned to the difficulties to be overcome. Though firm of resolution as a rock, her heart was full of all gentle and generous impulses; the sight of distress was sufficient to melt her at once into sympathy, and she would hesitate at no sacrifice of her own interest, nor endurance of privation—to afford relief to the sufferer. She preserved throughout life her habits as a fearless equestrian, and when she was near the age of seventy, travelled on horseback all the way alone to the State of Indiana and back to her home, to visit her daughter, then married to Thomas Archer, the grandson of Katharine Steel.

Mrs. McCalla has been dead many years, and with her husband lies buried in Catholic graveyard near the place of her residence. She had five sons and several daughters. Her son Thomas died in the last war with Great Britain, in the service of his country. Her children and descendants have now all removed to the West, except the two children of John, who are living in Abbeville District. South Carolina might regret the loss in them of some of her best and most patriotic citizens, but they still serve their country, having borne with them to the great West the lessons of earnest piety and disinterested patriotism, taught them in early life by an exemplary mother. Thus the good seed sown by her was not lost, but is springing up to bear abundant fruit in another soil, not less genial than their native one. One of the sons, Samuel McCalla, lives near Bloomington, Indiana; David, at Princeton, in the same State. They are zealously attached to their country, and aim to serve its best interests. In person they bear the impress of their brave parentage so strikingly, that were a military commander selecting among a thousand, men who would be foremost in scaling a height to dislodge the foe, or who would willingly die in the last trench of Freedom, the choice would probably fall on these two

---

MARY ADAIR, with her husband, William Adair, lived on the south fork of Fishing Creek. Their sons—James, William and John—enlisted at the commencement of the war, with an orphan whom they had adopted and brought with them when they removed to South Carolina. This was Edward Lacy, who rose to the rank of Colonel after the death of McClure, and was colonel of the Chester men at the battle of King's Mountain, and till the close of the war. After the war he became a General, and was one of the first county Judges. If the services of this distinguished man have conferred honor on his district and his State, how deep a debt does the country owe to the noble matron whose early protection and careful training formed him for usefulness, and incited him to his honorable career!

It has been mentioned that Huck's party stopped at Adair's on their way to Williamson's. After having

taken the silver buckles from Mrs. Adair's shoes, the
rings from her fingers, and the handkerchief from her
neck, they took her husband out, put a rope about his
neck and were about to hang him up because his sons
were out with the rebels, when some of the tories
pleaded in his behalf that the old man was not so much
to blame ; it was the mother who had encouraged her
sons, and urged them to their rebellious course. The
officer then drew Mrs. Adair apart, and remarking that
he had understood her sons were fine young men, and
that her influence over them was such that she could
persuade them to anything she pleased, promised, if she
would bring them over to the King's service, to obtain
for each a commission in the army. The matron
replied that her sons had a mind of their own, and
thought and acted for themselves. The call made by
the whigs before daylight the next morning—July 12th
—has been noticed. After they were gone, Mr. and
Mrs. Adair left the house quietly, leaving the two
officers who had quartered themselves upon them, in
bed, for they knew that in a short time there would
be warm work at their neighbor's. They had scarcely
reached the shelter of a thicket when they heard the
first gun, and for an hour or more while the firing
continued they remained in agitating suspense. At
length venturing within sight of the road, they saw the
redcoats and tories flying, and soon afterwards the
gallant McClure in pursuit, and then no longer in fear
they returned to the house. When they went to the
battle ground, Mrs. Adair helped to dress the wounds

of the captain who had insisted that she should send
her sons to him, and reminded him of the order.*   His
reply when she showed her sons was : " It is a little
too late."   The sons removed their aged parents, with
their moveable property, to Virginia, and then came back
to the camp.   John, who afterwards became so distinguished, was at school in Charlotte at the beginning
of the war, and left Liberty Hall to enter the army.
Although but a stripling he obtained a lieutenant's
commission, and was engaged in several battles.   He
made his escape at the time of the surprise of Sumter,
and reached Charlotte, whence he was sent out
a day or two after on some errand, and with another soldier, George Weir, was made prisoner at a
house on the road.   They might have effected their
escape the night after their capture, but John Adair had
set his heart on having two fine horses in possession of
the enemy, and the opportunity was neglected which
did not again occur.   They were then taken to Camden, and examined by Lord Rawdon, who thought he
could obtain from them some important information.
His lordship was acquainted with Weir—they having
been boys together in Ireland ; but he failed in ex-
tracting anything from either of the prisoners.   Though
both were taken out with halters around their necks—
they boldly persisted in saying " we have no disclosures to make."   Adair was kept in jail about seven
months, and suffered from hunger and want of clothing,
and from a severe attack of the small-pox.   Yet he

* See Vol I., p. 245.

did his best to keep up the spirits of his fellow-prisoners, among other devices for their amusement teaching
them to play at cards with a pack he had procured.
These unfortunate captives owed much to the kind-
hearted women of Chester and York, who shared among
them the provisions and clothing they had brought
their relatives, and encouraged them to bear their
privations with cheerfulness. Not long after Adair had
gone to the West, his parents removed from South
Carolina. Mrs. Adair lived to see him rise to distinction in the councils both of Tennessee and Kentucky,
become the chief magistrate of the latter State, and
general of the Kentucky forces in the war of 1812, and
return to his home covered with the laurels of victory,
respected and honored by all who knew his worth. As
a shock fully ripe she was gathered to the tomb in
1819.

MARY NIXON, the daughter of William and Mary
Adair, was married in 1774 to Capt. John Nixon, who
had left Ireland some years before. He was among
the foremost of the fighting men at the outbreak of the
war. When the British had possession of the country
in 1780, he raised a company, having much influence
in his neighborhood, and the unbounded confidence of
his men, and in every action acquitted himself with
distinction. From the period of Gates' defeat till the
7th November, the tories had the ascendancy through

the country, carrying off the property of the whigs, in some cases taking possession of their plantations with all that appertained—negroes, stock, etc., and parcelling out the property among themselves. A letter written by one of the patriots of that day says—" All the other parts of my estate, except my lands, have fallen into the hands of the enemy. They drove off at one time between ninety and a hundred head of cattle to Winnsboro' : they have also got all my sheep, and the greatest part of my hogs, plantation tools, household furniture, and every other article that was of any value, so that I am properly situated for a soldier, and am determined to see the event of our cause or fall in the attempt."* A party of loyalists from Newberry, assisted by some from Sandy River, had collected a great deal of plunder from the whigs of Chester. Nixon got on their trail and pursued them to the line of Newberry and Union Districts. They took refuge in a house, from which, as it was strongly fortified, they could not be dislodged. Nixon went up alone, and was in the act of firing the house, when he received the shot which terminated his career not long afterwards. His name, while he lived, had been a terror to the loyalists, and even after his fall they were bent on vengeance upon his family. Col. Winn, of Fairfield, hearing of their intentions, sent a message in haste to Mrs. Nixon, advising her to remove with her property. She left home that very night with her negroes and as many articles as could be carried in a

* MS. letter of D. Hopkins—Dec. 20th, 1780.

wagon, and made her way to the Yadkin in North Carolina. The tories arrived the next day at her house, and took what was left, destroying what they could not carry away. In the winter of 1781 she returned, and in March accompanied Mrs. McCalla to Camden for the purpose mentioned. She afterwards married David McCalla, who had been with Nixon in camp, and was engaged in the hard-fought battle of Eutaw. She was the mother of eight children. The McCallas have removed to the West, but her daughters by the first marriage, Mrs. McKown and Mrs. Mary Hemphill, still reside together in Chester District, where their high standing, and the respect and esteem of a large circle of acquaintance, testify to the general appreciation of their exemplary character. They have been widows for many years, and have reached the appointed limit of human life : yet in the influence they command, and the example presented to those around them, they continue to act a useful and important part in society. The gentleman who has collected all these Revolutionary incidents of the Catawba region, has enjoyed their acquaintance for half a century, and describes them as of striking and noble appearance, and possessing every quality—in respect both of mental endowment and moral excellence —which contributes to the perfection of female character : as fit representatives, in short, of the patriotic families to which they belong—of Nixon and Adair.

XV.

MARY MILLS.

THE rich lands within the bounds of Fishing Creek congregation were well adapted for the growth of wheat, which was extensively cultivated by the 'Pennsylvania Irish' settlers. The harvest was in June; but all the men able to bear arms, with their minister John Simpson, having taken the field, none remained to secure the crop on which the support of their families depended. It was at this crisis that the young women of the neighborhood, with spirit equal to that of their gallant brothers, in the summer of 1780 formed a company of reapers for cutting and garnering the grain. Their names were Mary, Margaret, and Ellen Gill, Isabella and Margaret Kelso, Sarah Knox, Margaret, Elizabeth and Mary Mills, Mary McClure, and Nancy Brown. These young women went day after day from one farm to another, and reaped the crop with the assistance of the matrons and a few old men. The only question they asked was—"Is the owner out with the fighting men?" and an affirmative answer was sufficient to engage them at once in the labor. It was no small undertaking, five or six weeks of unceasing toil being necessary to gather in the harvest through the country. It seemed that Providence smiled on the generous enterprise; there were no storms during that period to ravage the fields, and it was related for years afterwards as very remarkable, that some of this season's crops were secured several weeks after the grain was fully ripe. Scarcely was the work accomplished, before British and tories were plundering everywhere and laying waste the country, determined to vanquish the spirit of resistance by distressing rebel families.*

The female laborers forming this band were by no means uncouth in person or rude in manners, but might have compared with any in grace of deportment, and in qualities that constitute the excellence and beauty of female character. Mr. Stinson, who had a personal acquaintance with them, has obtained material for a brief notice of two of their number.

MARY GILL—the daughter of Robert Gill, was born in October, 1758, in the colony of Pennsylvania. Soon after her birth her father removed to South Carolina and settled on the south fork of Fishing Creek, upon the plantation known as the Lowrie place. In his removal he was accompanied by another family going to the same settlement. On the first Sabbath

* When the Connecticut and Jersey militia were at New York and on Long Island, in daily expectation of the landing of the enemy, the women and elderly men of those States got in the harvest. A Whig paper of July 25th, 1776, says: "The most respectable ladies set the example, and say they will take the farming business on themselves as long as the rights and liberties of their country require the presence of their sons, husbands and lovers in the field."

morning after the commencement of their journey, the
neighbor, while getting his team ready, inquired of
Gill if he were not going on.   Gill, who was reading
some religious book, replied that he should rest on the
Sabbath, and advised his companion also to remain.
The other answered that he could not afford to lose so
much time as every seventh day for six weeks.   They
parted, and he journeyed on, while Gill read the Bible
and catechised the children, thus occupying himself
for the six Sabbaths he was on the road.   On Friday
or Saturday he overtook his neighbor, who passed him
in his turn on the following Sunday ; but towards the
end of the journey Gill passed him earlier in the week,
and finally arrived at the place of his destination
several days before him.   He was one of the early
settlers and took an active part in establishing a church
in the wilderness.   At the period of the Revolution he
was too much advanced in years to bear arms, but
encouraged his sons—Thomas, Robert, Archy, John
and James, to do their part from the commencement
of the war.   The first two were taken prisoners and
carried to Camden, where Robert died in jail, Thomas
being released after seven months' captivity.   Archibald served to the close of the war in the State troops,
and continued to have much influence and a high
character in the community.   He owned the celebrated
fishery at the Falls of Catawba, and would never
tolerate the pursuit of the business on Sunday.   His
son Robert was a captain in the regular army in 1812,
and at the time of his death Attorney General of

Louisiana. His daughter, Mrs. Crowford, is still living near Fishing Creek.

Such training and associations early formed the daughter's mind to the heroism displayed in time of need. On the night that Col. Neil's men under Bratton and McClure were going to Williamson's after leaving White's Mills, two of them came to Gill's house. It was late, and a very dark night, and the men, anxious to get up with Neil, had lost their way. As soon as Mary was satisfied that they were libertymen, though her father tried to dissuade her, she went with them to show a path leading out to the main road. It was so dark, she was obliged to tie a white cloth upon her back, that they could see to follow her, and the distance was several miles. Some years after the war one of the men—named Hunter—travelling through the country, and stopping for the night at the old court house at Walker's, inquired for the noble girl who had done him this service.

While Tarleton's corps encamped at White's Mills, a party of troopers came to the creek where Mary and her sister Margaret were, and perceiving a flock ef geese, started in chase of them, cutting off the birds' heads with their broadswords. Mary picked up a stick and frightened the geese into deep water. When the dragoons swore at her, holding up their bloody swords, and saying they meant to cut off the rebels' heads in like manner, she answered boldly—"If these rebels were here you would run like wild turkeys." Relating such occurrences in after life, she would say

—" I seemed to fear nothing after the disastrous surprise of Sumter." She went with Isabella Kelso to
that battle-ground. They could not find the body of
Capt. Pagan, but from the description of his clothing
were convinced that he had been buried—the hogs
having rooted about the earth thrown slightly over
many of the bodies, so that parts of them were uncov-
ered. After returning home, Miss Gill and Isabella
went to Charlotte with clothes for their friends there.
Hearing not long after that her brothers were in
Camden jail, and suffering for want of provisions
and clothing, she made several trips to that place, in
company with other women, driving pack-horses laden
with various articles. On one occasion when she was
accompanied by Elizabeth McKenny, they failed to
reach Camden that night, and stopped at a small cabin
in the pine woods. Mary had her suspicions of the
place, which were confirmed when she saw a man go
out at the back door as they asked admittance; but
they were unable to go further, and concluded to avail
themselves of the shelter. She determined, however,
to keep watch, and having tied the horse to the hasp
of the door, seated herself on the step, holding the
reins in her hand. The tory within the cabin, not
long afterwards, having parched some corn on the
hearth, invited her with much importunity to come
and take some. She left the horse for a moment to do
so ; but on returning to the door found the rope cut
and the horse gone. She charged the tory with having
a hand in this piece of villany, and threatened to

punish him ; but he protested his innocence, and her companion interceded to save him from a beating. On her arrival at Camden, Miss Gill complained to a British officer, who promised to attend to the matter ; but the horse was never recovered.

The spirit of this young woman was enshrined in a frame of unusual strength : her figure was of majestic height and proportions, and there was much dignity in her bearing. It is said that at one time the British suspected her of being a spy in female apparel, and she had some trouble to convince them of their mistake. Like many other damsels of the country, she had a lover in camp, expected his visits whenever he had opportunity to come home, and looked forward to the close of the war as the period of their union. This was John Mills, a near neighbor, of whose brave exploits she continually heard. When the enemy was driven down the country, some of these soldiers seized the opportunity of a short furlough to lead their betrothed fair ones to the altar. The marriage of Mary and John took place May 21st, 1782. Mills had been among the first who took up arms, and early distinguished himself, being with Sumter from the time he formed his camp at Clem's Branch to the termination of his campaigns. He obtained the commission of captain in the State troops—and might be called with propriety ' Sumter's right arm.' Their intimate friendship commenced in camp, continuing during Mills' life. He kept a diary of the times of the Revolution, recording every event of the war. This volume was carefully preserved by Mrs. Mills, but when she died it came into the possession of her son, and after his death was probably destroyed. Had it been saved, much of the unrecorded history of Sumter's campaigns might have been given to the public. Yet, though this is lost, tradition has preserved the remembrance of some bold acts, strange as deeds of romance. On one occasion, either before the fall of Charleston or after its evacuation, Mills was sent into the city by Sumter to draw money for the troops. Observing that his steps were dogged by an individual of suspicious appearance, he turned and entered into conversation with him, finally inviting him to his room after he had made his arrangements to leave the city. A decanter of French brandy stood on the table, and Mills, having locked the door, took out a pistol, and told the man he must drink up the brandy on penalty of being shot. No alternative was left, and the fellow, perhaps thinking the matter a joke, emptied the decanter. Mills left him drunk, mounted his horse and left Charleston.

Not long after his marriage, returning home after dark, he was fired upon by one unseen. Walking coolly into the house, he took down his gun and went out in pursuit of his enemy. The country was infested for years after the war by gangs of horse-stealers, formed into regular societies, and extending from Georgia to Virginia. They had certain passwords by which to recognize each other. Mills and David Cook, in pursuit of horses taken from the neighborhood, fell in with some of these thieves, and discovering their countersigns, introduced themselves into their deposit for stolen horses, in one of the mountain passes, found the missing animals, and watching their opportunity to secure them, made good their escape. Mills afterwards became colonel of the militia regiment of the district, and till his death enjoyed great influence and popularity. He died in 1795, and was buried with military honors by his Revolutionary associates. His widow was left alone with four young children and but little property, but by industry and good management gave her children the advantages of education. Thomas Sumter Mills, her eldest son, settled on Beach Island, where his widow and children live. They have several little presents of books, etc., sent to him while a boy, by General Sumter. Mrs. Mills resided with her son Robert, whose fine talents and excellent character secured the esteem of all who knew him. Forty years ago he waged war against the vice of intemperance ; he was an influential legislator, and commissioner of the public works of his native State, and his death was deplored as a public calamity.

Towards the close of the war of 1812, when the troop was taken from the country to the defence of Charleston, a report reached the back country that good provisions were not furnished the soldiers. Mrs. Mills expressed her indignation, and hearing that Captain James McClure had sent back the bad rations to the commissary with a message that if he did not furnish better, he would march down his company and take them by force,—her countenance brightened, and

she said : " That is so like a McClure ! I am thankful
there is still left the spirit of Seventy-six !"

The chief praise of Mrs. Mills belongs to her as a
mother who made it the object of her life to instil into
her children's minds the purest and highest principles.
In them she had her reward, and by their children her
influence is still felt.   She died in 1841, in her eighty-
fourth year.   Her only child now living, is Mrs. Alexander Pagan, from whom Mr. Stinson obtained some
of the particulars mentioned.

IsABELLA WYLIE was the daughter of Samuel Kelso,
who in 1780 lived on the north side of Fishing Creek
churchyard—some vestiges of the settlement remaining at the present day.   Most of his children were
grown at the time of the war, and took part in its
scenes.   Isabella heard the gun fired at Mr. Strong's
house—a few hundred yards distant—on the 11th of
June, and going there saw the murdered youth, and
witnessed the heart-rending anguish of his mother.
Kelso's house was robbed of everything, and the
swords he had been manufacturing were carried off.
Had he been at home he would probably have been
slain ; but he and his two sons were in the American
camp.   They were engaged in most of the battles of
1780 and the following year.   At Sumter's surprise
young Samuel had his whiskers cut off by a bullet,
and George, severely wounded, was left on the ground
for dead, but crawled to a loose horse, mounted him

with difficulty, and effected his escape. While Tarleton lay at White's Mills, his mother's house was plundered, and Isabella went to make complaint; but received for the stolen property nothing but curses and blows. One tory said to her sarcastically, " So, you rebels have killed all the redcoats down at Fishing Creek !"—a taunt that made his presence intolerable to her even long after the war.

When inquiries were made of women who had been at Camden, concerning the prisoners there, it required no great penetration to discover that the fair Isabella took a special interest in one among them ; for the name of William Wylie was never uttered without a blush like the rose. This soldier, a few weeks after he obtained his liberty, was united to the beautiful maiden by the Rev. Mr. Simpson. He was the eldest son of Peter Wylie, the poet of the day, who has left a volume of unpublished verses. His home was at the Big Spring, six miles north of Chesterville. William was in military service from the commencement of hostilities ; fought under Gen. Williamson, and was with Moultrie on the retreat from Black Swamp to Charleston ; was in McClure's company under Col. Washington at the surprise at Monk's Corner, and did his part bravely in the succeeding battles. While the whigs were at Clem's Branch, he and a comrade obtained leave to visit their homes. As they lay by on their way, Wylie fast asleep on the ground while his companion was washing his shirt in the stream, he was awakened by a kick, and looking up saw a

British dragoon standing over him with his sword
drawn. The two prisoners were taken to Rocky
Mount, whence Wylie made his escape on the morning of July 12th. He met on the road the redcoats
flying from the battle at Williamson's, and shortly
after his gallant captain, McClure, scouring the country in pursuit. He joined him, and was with him on
his last field. Being on separate duty he was not at
the surprise of August 18th, but in December was
sent by Col. Lacy—who had formed a camp on Turkey Creek in York District—to Morgan's camp, then
at his father's house. He was accompanied by the
brave " Hopping John Miller," and on Sandy River
fell in with a large tory party under the command of
one Nichols. Both took to flight, but were closely
pursued, and when Wylie's horse began to fag, Miller,
seeing that the enemy gained on them, proposed to
turn and fight. Wylie, however, saw that they were
too many, and insisted on Miller's saving himself. He
then dismounted and leaped over a fence, hoping to
make his escape ; but Nichols cleared it on horseback
after him. Wylie posted himself at a tree, determined
to sell his life dearly, and was about to fire on Nichols
when he called to him that he should have quarter.
He then threw down his gun, but would have been
killed by the other tories when they came up, had not
their leader thrown himself between them. They
took his jaded horse, flung away the saddle, and
mounted him, tying his legs and arms, and went on.
The first place at which they stopped was the house

of William White—a thorough whig, whose wife Jane
had the spirit of a Revolutionary matron. In her
broad Scotch dialect, she asked—" Weel, Willie, lad,
hae ye had onything to eat the day ?" and when told
he had not, and was very hungry—" Then ye maun
tak' a bit of bread, and a wee sup o' buttermilk," she
said, " till keep up your strength ; for by the company
ye are in I trow ye hae a long ride afore ye." " No!"
exclaimed one of the loyalists ; " I'll be d——d if he
does ; we'll hang him !" On hearing this Mrs. White
turned round, and poured out such eloquent denuncia-
tions against all tories and redcoats, that the men were
glad to make haste and be out of the reach of her
tongue. At night they stopped at the dwelling of a
poor family, where little was found in the way of provision. Wylie was put into a back shed, where late
at night he was visited by Nichols, who crept in on his
hands and knees, to give his prisoner a piece of bread
and encourage him by kind words. He had not abso-
lute control over his gang, but promised better treatment when they arrived at Winnsboro'. This attention
Wylie long remembered, and on hearing afterwards
that Nichols had been taken and hung by the liberty-
men, said he would have ventured his life to save him.
Early the next morning they reached Winnsboro', and
Wylie was taken to the quarters of Lord Cornwallis,
where Tarleton was at the time. His lordship asked
him many questions about the rebel army, and ordered
some liquor to be given him. The prisoner drank
sparingly, for he suspected the motives of such an

indulgence, and was determined to give no information that could injure his friends. Cornwallis and Tarleton were walking the room, and frequently spoke together in a low tone while conducting the examination. The tory Col. Philips was standing by, and at length beckoned to Wylie, whom he well knew—having lived near his father in Ireland. When the prisoner went to him, he said in a persuasive manner—"William, gang home, bring in Frank and Jemmy, an' quit the rebels, or ye will be caught and hung, as ye ken they did McClurkie of Rocky Creek !" The advice, it need not be said, was lost upon Wylie. On the day that Tarleton marched from Winnsboro' to attack Morgan, he was sent with a guard to Camden, where he lay the greater part of the winter in jail, being liberated at the same time with McCalla.

After his marriage, Wylie enlisted in the State troops with Capt. John Mills, in the regiment under Col. Henry Hampton, where he served as sergeant to the end of the war. He was a man of great bodily strength and an invincible spirit ; withal something of a poet, and possessed of a fund of wit and humor. These qualities made him the delight of the soldiers, and his shrewd and piquant sayings were long afterwards treasured up by his acquaintances as well worth repeating. During his absence in camp, Mrs. Wylie lived with her father and father-in-law, and after his return they remained for many years at the Big Spring. In 1820 they removed to Perry County, Alabama. Most of their children went to the West, and there are remaining only Mrs. Walker and Peter Wylie of Chester District. The father died in 1830.

It was in the quiet domestic circle that Mrs. Wylie so well performed her part, exercising through her unobtrusive and unappreciated labors an influence that has not yet ceased to be felt. By the diffusion of the principles in which her youth was trained, she wrought incalculable good. When after the war was ended, some southern churches suffered the infliction of ministers destitute of vital religion, and men of the Revolution were led astray, Mrs. Wylie, with other women of the neighborhood, exhibited an unwavering spirit in rebuking infidelity, setting a bright example of firm faith and devotion to the precepts of the Bible. Her constant reading of the Scriptures, and religious conversation, were never forgotten by those who had the advantage of her training, and the good effect of such lessons has been proved by the patriotism **and** usefulness of her descendants.

XVI.

JANE WHITE.

In the centre of Chester District, two miles south of Chesterville, stands Purity Church, on the Rocky Mount Road, branching from the main Columbia road which forms, as it were, the back bone of the district, passing through its entire length, and separating the waters that flow into the Broad River from the tributaries of the Catawba. About a mile below the church, at an equal distance from either of these roads, may yet be seen the upright trunk of a weeping willow, that marks the spot where for more than half a century stood the residence of the subject of this sketch. Jane Brown was born in the county of Antrim, Ireland, in 1758. Her father died when she and her only brother were very young; her mother married again in a year or two, and in a short time the family emigrated to South Carolina. William White, who became the husband of Jane, was born in the same county in 1753, and removed about the same time. The farms on which they lived in youth were adjoining; their close neighborhood brought them much together, and being of congenial dispositions, their in-

timacy soon grew into a lasting attachment. They
were married and had one child when hostilities commenced in the South. Two of William's sisters were
married, and three others lived upon his premises.
When it became necessary to take sides in the contest,
White and his brothers-in-law had no difficulty in
making up their minds, their language being that of
the patriots of the Old Dominion: " Give me liberty
or give me death." White was not with McClure in
the surprise at Beckhamville, not having been apprised
by the runners sent out by Justice Gaston that such
an expedition was meditated, but eight of his neighbors, including Walker, his brother-in-law, were there.
A few days after this exploit, he joined McClure in the
attack on Mobley's Meeting-house. This stood on the
banks of Little River in Fairfield District. A number
of people from the vicinity had assembled in obedience
to a summons from the commander at Rocky Mount, to
take protection and enlist in the royal army, a suitable person being there from headquarters with a force
sufficient to sustain him in any necessary movement.
This functionary after a while became wearied in the
performance of his duties, and indulged himself with
a nap, on awaking from which, some one accosted him
with the question : "What if McClure should come
upon us ?" He replied; " I wish to heavens he would,
for I am full of fight." This same redoubtable champion
was found after the battle ensconced in the chimney
corner.

In making his attack on this place, McClure surrounded three sides of the house, the fourth being

guarded by a precipice down which it was supposed
no one would venture to leap, though more British and
loyalists perished in the attempt to escape this way
than by the rifles of his sharp-shooters. White was
next with Sumter at the taking of Carey's Fort, and
at the surprise on Fishing Creek. His brother-in-law,
Lieut. Kennedy, was preparing some food by the camp-
fire, while William, with no other clothing than his
hunting-shirt, sat nodding by it. When Kennedy had
finished the cooking, he bade him wake up and eat;
and White, only partially awake, in starting up
struck his foot against the vessel containing the food,
and upset it. When fully aroused he saw the wings
of Tarleton's cavalry enclosing the encampment, and
his comrades flying in every direction or cut to pieces
by the enemy. Snatching up his trusty rifle, he fled
for life. His course was directed to Charlotte, where
he arrived with many of the American soldiers. The
son of Mary Martin, one of his neighbors, was brought
thither wounded. As soon as the mother heard of it,
she set off for Charlotte with Mrs. White and Mrs.
Kennedy, who brought clothes for their husbands.
This dark hour was the harbinger of brighter prospects;
for far up among the mountains and on western waters,
were gathered bands of patriots under partisan leaders,
who descended not long afterwards from their heights
to spread confusion among the invaders. Of the nine
hundred men selected near the Cowpens from the army
of these mountaineers, William White was one.
While Ferguson hastened to secure himself an advan-

tageous position for contending with them, he left one
of his men concealed in the cellar of a house on the
road-side, whose business it was to ascertain the number and character of those who were pressing on his
rear. This spy making himself rather conspicuous,
was taken by the pursuing whigs, and forced to give
the very information they desired. The practice among
their riflemen of picking off the officers in an engagement, had produced much confusion in the British
ranks, and it being known to the leaders, they had
adopted the expedient of disguising themselves before
going into action. This prisoner, bidden to answer
truly on pain of death, was asked if Ferguson went
to battle in uniform. He answered unhesitatingly in
the affirmative. "But does he wear no disguise?" "He
has a large check shirt which he wears over his uniform;
by this you may recognize him." William White
was present at this examination; and the information
being spread among the soldiers, it is easy to
account for the fact that Col. Ferguson was shot
through the arm at the very commencement of
the battle of King's Mountain; his fine white horse
being seen not long after, dashing down the hill without a rider. White always spoke of these mountain
men in terms of high praise. Many, he said, previous
to the engagement took off their hats and tied hand-
kerchiefs about their heads, and being nimble fellows,
were so eager for the fight that they ran at full speed
up the mountain. He and Robert Miller, who afterwards married his sister, were rushing up together,

firing occasionally at the enemy, while they sheltered themselves from their fire as well as they could. Miller fell, and when White asked if he were hurt, supposing he had stumbled over the rough ground, he received no answer. He lifted him up, and perceiving he was badly wounded in the thigh, carried him to a place of security. Soon afterwards he walked over numbers of the fallen enemy to the spot where lay Ferguson's lifeless trunk, wearing the check shirt which had been described.

During all this time Mrs. White, who was occupied in attending to her house and carrying on the business of the farm with the aid of her sisters-in-law, knew not what had become of her husband. All the liberty-men in the neighborhood had fled to the mountains, and she was visited repeatedly by the tories, who took from her on each occasion the little articles she had managed to collect during the intervals between their visits. The most notorious among these marauders, one Edmund Russell, had driven off the cows belonging to her and Mrs. Kennedy. His retreat at Sandy River was known to many of the whigs who had suffered from his depredations. When, after the battle of King's Mountain, White with nineteen of his comrades ventured home to see how matters were going on, he found his wife and sisters in the field with a basket of wheat, which they were beginning to sow. He alighted from his horse to show them " the cast of the hand," as he called it, not venturing more, for he knew that his movements were watched, and was

aware of the doom pronounced against those who had
been engaged in the affair at Mobley's. Cornwallis at
the time was lying at Winnsboro', nearly thirty miles
distant; yet that night he received intelligence that
William White was at home sowing wheat, and sent a
detachment of men in the morning to capture him.
White, however, had other occupation, having started
at daylight with his nineteen associates in quest of
Russell, of whose doings his wife had informed him.
The robber, afraid to live above ground, had made
himself a den in the earth some distance from his
house, where he had provisions brought to him. This
den was in the woods, and so covered as to be undistin-
guishable from the ground about it. When the whigs
were approaching his house, they met two children
carrying a bottle of milk, but could obtain from them
no information as to the whereabouts of Russell, or the
destination of the milk. One of the party suddenly
exclaimed—" Here is smoke issuing from the ground;"
and presently Russell sprang out and ran away. Fear
lent him wings, but it was of no avail, seventeen guns
being fired at him in such rapid succession that it was
impossible to tell who had laid the victim low. The
detachment sent by Cornwallis heard this firing, but
learning that twenty whigs were together, would not
venture to attack them, though their own number was
more than quadruple, excusing themselves as well as
they could to his lordship for not bringing White to
atone for his crimes by hanging on a tree.

When Cornwallis was marching from Charlotte to

Winnsboro', he encamped for some days on the plantation of John Service, two miles east of White's residence. During his stay here, his soldiers robbed Mrs.
White of all her clothing, provisions and cattle, taking
also some lambs on which she set a high value. She
went to the encampment, and through Service presented her petition for redress to his lordship; but that
great man drove Service from his presence with angry
oaths. Mrs. White was thus compelled to submit to
the spoiling of her goods, but her tongue was a free
and fearless member, and she did not often fail to give
her spoilers some of its lessoning in the information
that a day of retribution was not far distant.

On the day of the action at Blackstock's, White
drove a wagon to bring flour, for which Col. Taylor
had been sent with a detachment of fifty men to a
mill in the vicinity. The understanding was that
Sumter would remain where he was until Taylor's return; but shortly after his departure information came
that Tarleton was advancing to the attack, and the
general in consequence moved off to secure a more
advantageous position. Taylor knew nothing of
Tarleton's approach, and when he returned with the
flour and did not find Sumter, he was not a little dis-
pleased. His men were very hungry, and he allowed
two or three hogs to be cleaned and cooked, and some
of the flour made into bread. White was engaged in
baking the bread, in the fashion of johnny cake, on a
piece of pine bark, at the moment when Sergeant Ben
Rowan and Major Hannah, who had been sent out by

Sumter to reconnoitre, dashed up in fiery haste to bring the news that Tarleton was just at hand. The hogs and the dough were thrown into the wagon uncooked, and Rowan used to say that William drove the wagon into camp at a full gallop. White said as he turned the corner of a little stable the firing commenced, and a ball passed through the sleeve of his hunting-shirt. He saw 'Irish Johnny Walker,' and asked where two individuals were, whom he called by name. He replied that he did not know, but had last seen them running over the hill. "What shall we do?" then inquired White, and Walker answered—"Stand to them: we'll beat them any how." White put three balls into his mouth to have them ready, and went into the fight. While this was going on, James Wylie partially parried a blow dealt upon a whig by one of Tarleton's dragoons. A friend near him shot the dragoon, and Wylie seized his sword, which he took home and afterwards gave to his son Peter, who wore it when a captain in command of his company, and a few years since carried it with him to Florida.

While Cornwallis was engaged in the pursuit of Greene, William White ventured home, where he continued in painful suspense, being unable to obtain any information concerning the movements of these generals. Early one morning he and Jane perceived three men approaching their house by an old road that came down the hill on the other side of a small stream. Mrs. White, suspecting treachery, begged her husband to run away, but he refused to move, and presently,

13*

seeing that the men were unarmed, took his gun—which
is now in the possession of his youngest son, as well as
the old family Bible containing ' David's Psalms in
metre'—and ordered them to halt and give an account
of themselves. He then commanded them, on pain of
being shot in case of refusal, to declare immediately
all they knew respecting Cornwallis and Greene.
They entreated him not to fire, protesting that they
had no intention of molesting him, and stated that
they were from the army of Cornwallis, that an action
had taken place between him and Greene at Guilford,
and that Cornwallis had kept the ground, though the
advantage lay on the side of Greene. These men
were Fairfield loyalists, on their way home ; they were
very hungry, having eaten nothing for three days, and
begged for some food. Mrs. White gave them the
breakfast she was preparing for her own family, and
they went on their way.

At the close of the war White returned to his home
and resumed his agricultural pursuits. It was always
his peculiar delight to describe to his youthful acquaintances the Revolutionary scenes through which
he had passed, and in such recitals, even when more
than three score and ten years had rolled over him, all
the fire of his youth seemed re-kindled in his breast
He was often urged by his friends to apply for a pen-
sion, but his invariable answer was—" my country
once needed my services ; perhaps she now needs her
revenue more than I do, and I am both able and willing to work for my living."   In extreme old age he

became convinced that it was his duty to accept what his country offered ; but he did not live to receive it. He died in 1833, in the eighty-first year of his age.

In person Mrs. White was tall and stout, yet well proportioned and active ; her manners were simple and unassuming, and she was frank and unreserved. She was a firm believer in a particular Providence adapting trials and burdens to those called to sustain them, and thus accounted for the strength given her, in the protract- ed absence of her husband, "to labor out and labor in"— and for the fact that the sower had seed and the eater bread when the fruit of her toil was often consumed by very unworthy eaters. She was merciful and kind al- most to a fault, and would leave her own business by night or day, when called upon to minister to the neces- sities of her neighbors. Though tender of the feelings of others, she never scrupled to give fearless utterance to her thoughts in the presence of friend or foe. The an- ecdote of her in the sketch of Mrs. Wylie illustrates this trait of character. Major Kennedy, who is still living, mentions another. In the war of 1812, he wished to raise recruits for his troop of horse, and knowing that Mrs. White had a fine supply of sons, he rode to her house to make known his business. All her sons were in the field at work except the youngest, whom she called, and in her broad Scotch-Irish dialect, bade him "rin awa' ta the fiel' an' tell his brithers ta cum in an' gang an' fight for their counthry, like their father afore them." She was the mother of eight sons and one daughter. Two of the sons signalized them-

selves under Jackson in his war with the Creeks;
five others were at Charleston as volunteers in 1812,
and one of her grandsons obtained much distinction in
the Black Hawk war, in which he was at length severely wounded.

Being of the strictest sect of Presbyterians, Mr. and
Mrs. White were opposed to all innovations or new-
fangled measures, and all despotism, civil or ecclesias-
tical; it was this principle that impelled them to count
no sacrifice too great in the acquisition of that liberty
which cannot be prized too highly by those who inherit its blessings. Mrs. White survived her husband
eight years, dying in 1841, in her eighty-third year.
Her remains and his rest side by side in Purity churchyard, where none but those incapable of generous emotion can read the inscription on their tomb-stones without resolving to imitate their virtues.

The friend to whom I am so much indebted mentions some incidents in the history of a single family,
which present a remarkable contrast. Before the
breaking out of the war there lived in the district of
Fairfield a man named John Philips, a man of wealth,
talents, and many personal advantages, who had
brought with him from Ireland two nephews——John
and Robert Buchanan——sixteen and eighteen years of
age. As soon as war was declared, both the young
men left their uncle and enlisted in the American army.
At the siege of Savannah one had risen to the rank

of captain, the other of lieutenant. Both were taken
prisoners, probably at the fall of Charleston, and sent
to James Island. A young widow from Fairfield—
Mrs. Milling—who happened to be in the city, interested herself in their favor, and obtained permission
for them to return on parole to Fairfield and remain
until exchanged. John availed himself of the offer,
but Robert refused to accept any favor at the hands
of a British officer, and died a prisoner. John afterwards married the generous widow, whose two daughters by her first marriage were united to Thomas and
John Means of the same district. Buchanan had no
children, but was for the greater part of his life Judge
of the court of ordinary for his district, and one of its
most exemplary and highly respected citizens, inso-
much that to be called " as excellent a man as John
Buchanan" was esteemed great praise. The influence
of his name in the community secured a kind reception
for others of his family who came to the country, and
the election of his nephew, though an alien and a
stranger, to fill his place on his decease. Far different
was the fate of Philips, who took part against the
country's liberties, and was called during the war
" Tory Col. Philips." On one occasion, when pursued
by the whigs, he threw himself on the mercy of Capt.
Milling, who told him to go to the loft and cover himself with a pile of flax, and when his enemies came
to search, put them off his track. One of the party
asked for a new gun that lay on the rack, which
Milling took down and gave him. Although Philips

thus owed his life to this man, when Lord Cornwallis took possession of Winnsboro' he endeavored to get him executed on the charge of aiding and abetting the rebels by furnishing the gun ! At another time when with his loyalists he accompanied Tarleton to Little Rocky Creek, he took a young man—McClurkin—who was ill of the small-pox, from his bed, and hung him on a tree by the roadside. This act of barbarity aroused the Irish spirit of Rocky Creek, adding the instinct of revenge to military opposition. One of the whigs, Thomas Standford, came alone in the dead of night to Tarleton's encampment on the creek, and picked off several sentinels as he passed from one point to another, being so well acquainted with the ground that he easily avoided the reconnoitering parties. Tarleton, ignorant of the enemy's force, was so much alarmed that he ordered to horse, and went off in the night. Several articles were left and dropped in the haste of departure, and some were found about the place many years afterwards. Many other acts of cold-blooded cruelty are attributed to Philips. He returned to Ireland, but even there was not safe from the vengeance he had provoked; he was shot in the street in Ballymoney by one of McClurkin's brothers, and after living in fear of the avenger of blood, pursued by the terrors of a guilty conscience, died a drunkard, in poverty and disgrace, leaving his family to destitution. Buchanan never spoke of his uncle's misdeeds without shedding tears. Their different history may show by a striking example that virtuous and vicious courses often meet their reward even in this life.

XVII.

REBECCA PICKENS.

REBECCA CALHOUN, the wife of General Andrew Pickens, was born in the year 1745. She was the daughter of Ezekiel Calhoun, who resided near "Hopewell Meeting-House," Calhoun Settlement, Abbeville District, South Carolina, and grew up under the education common at that period in a frontier settlement. Her father was an amiable and intelligent gentleman, and possessed what in those days was considered an independent estate. In 1761, the settlement made on Long Cane, Abbeville District, was nearly broken up by a massacre of the Indians, and many of the best citizens were murdered at the Long Cane bridge near Calhoun Settlement. Ezekiel Calhoun, with his young and interesting family, escaped to the Waxhaws, on Catawba River. It was there that Gen. Pickens became acquainted with Miss Calhoun. He afterwards went to Calhoun Settlement and married her, in 1763. She was considered very beautiful and attractive, and tradition says it was the 'largest

wedding' ever known in that section of country. As
was the custom in those days of simplicity and cordial
hospitality, all were invited, far and near, to join in the
festivities, which, it is said, lasted three days without
intermission. The beauty of the bride was the theme
of all tongues. She had extensive connections of the
highest respectability, and the hospitality of her parental home was proverbial. The bridegroom was in
the full flush of joyous manhood, and was not of the
kind that " said never a word," and " stood dangling his
bonnet and plume ;" but was " as faithful in love, as
dauntless in war."   On this great festive occasion all
were contented and happy ;

> " Soft eyes looked love to eyes which spake again,
> And all went merry as a marriage bell."

" *Rebecca Calhoun's wedding*" was long talked of
as a great event in the neighborhood, and old people
used it as a point of time to reckon from, while many
' lads and lasses' dated their first emotions of tenderness and love from that joyous occasion. She was
remarkable for the elasticity of her form, with delicate
and fair complexion, and a girlish playfulness that
never deserted her, even in her old age. Pure was her
heart as the dew-drop hanging from the bosom of the
mountain flower—and light was her step as the fawn
playing upon the mountain's brow. Bright rose her
morning star, and not a cloud hung around it. Ah !
how little did her young heart know of the trials and
dangers that lay before her in the future !

During the perilous scenes of the Revolution, her devotion and fidelity cheered and sustained her gallant husband amidst all their difficulties, and made his home ever bright and dear, even through the blood and carnage of those terrible days. The frontier settlements of South Carolina had not only to encounter the British in their invasions from the sea-coast, but the savages from the mountains, and the tories in the neighborhood of their homesteads. It was with them literally "war to the knife, and from the knife to the hilt." Neither night nor day were they safe. Their houses were plundered and burnt by the tories, and their children often massacred by the Indians. Mrs. Pickens was on many occasions compelled to abandon her husband's residence, near where Abbeville Court House now stands, and to secrete herself and children for days ; while at these times she and her infant family were sustained and supported by their faithful and devoted negroes.* She endured all with a fortitude that never failed. True to her country, she never forgot that she was a soldier's wife. If he

* General Pickens had a faithful African, Dick, who followed him throughout the war, and often fought by his side. This servant swam the Broad River twice, in a cold winter's night, to get to the camp of his master—mistaking the enemy's camp once. At the 'Cowpens,' a wounded British officer lying against a tree, asked Dick to bring him a little water. He brought it in his hat, and then immediately put out his knee and asked to draw his boots. The officer said—"Surely, boy, you will not take them before I die ?" Dick replied—"Him mighty fine, and massa need him mighty bad !"

met with dangers in the open field, her perils were not less in her situation, and her trials were to be borne without the stimulus of ambition, or the expectation of fame's reward.

Before the breaking out of the Revolution, Gen. Pickens had built a block-house at his residence, as a place of refuge to the settlement in case of danger from the Indians. Into this the inhabitants were often driven, and many a youthful warrior received his first training there, and caught the fire of that spirit which prepared him to be a freeman, and made him a soldier in the cause of his country. It was on these occasions that Mrs. Pickens exerted her powerful influence upon those who were forced to gather round her husband's standard. Her kindness and cheerfulness in entertaining those who were thus thrown upon her hospitality, made all feel that they were welcome, and that they were united together as brothers in a common cause. Her active spirit shed a soft light upon all their councils. These were the scenes in which she received her education. These were the courts in which she acquired her graces.

After Gen. Greene was forced to fall back from before Ninety-Six, and retreated over Saluda River on his way towards North Carolina, it was generally supposed that South Carolina would soon be conquered, as the British held Ninety-Six, Granby, Camden, and Charleston, with the intermediate country. Many whig families, fearing to remain, fled to Greene's camp, to follow and claim the protection of the retreat-

ing army. Among these was the family of Gen.
Pickens, who with his command, (although holding
his commission from South Carolina,) was then with
Greene's army. It was supposed, of course, that Gen.
Pickens would provide for their safety ; but he immediately sent them back to share the common sufferings
of the country, and thereby to show that the struggle
was not over, but that the spirit of resistance was undying. Mrs. Pickens, with Roman fortitude, and the
devotion of a true woman, met the difficulties of her
situation, and sustained herself and her children
through all reverses, amid the perilous times that fell
upon her home and her country. Her husband's
younger brother was a captain in the service, and was
killed at the " star redoubt," Ninety-Six. He was a
brave officer, devoted to her and her children, and
often rendered her great assistance when Gen. Pickens
was absent. After his death she was obliged to struggle almost alone.

With elasticity of spirits remarkable even in one of
her sex, she had the peculiar faculty of rigid government over her children, who all feared and loved her.
Her sons often spoke of it in after life. She was very
playful with children even in old age,—and

  —— " When wild war's deadly blast was blawn,
   And gentle peace returning,"

her house was the delight of young people, and her
playful spirits enlivened their evening sports. She
was kind and unostentatious, and full of charity and

meekness. She was a member of the Presbyterian
Church, and her even piety was without the slightest
tinge of bigotry, She died in 1815, and a marble slab
marks the spot by the side of her husband, where her
earthly remains repose, in the sweet and hallowed vale
that surrounds the "Old Stone Meeting-House" of
Pendleton.

She had three sons and six daughters. Her sons
graduated at Princeton and Brown University, and
two of them became members of the bar. One was
afterwards lieutenant-colonel in the tenth regiment,
U. S. Army, in Canada, during the war of 1812, and
before the termination of that war was chosen one of
the colonels in a State brigade raised in South Carolina for the war. Judge Huger was the general, and
Drayton the other colonel. This son in 1816 was
chosen governor of South Carolina, and was afterwards, in 1825, appointed by the Alabama legis-
lature the first president of their State bank. The
brother of Mrs. Pickens, Col. John E. Calhoun, was a
very eminent lawyer, and also a senator in Congress
from South Carolina. The Hon. John C. Calhoun is
her cousin.

At a Roman banquet, a dispute arose between the
distinguished revellers as to who had the best wife,
and it was agreed that it should be decided by visiting that night each one's wife, to observe her occupation. One, who afterwards exercised great influence
upon the destiny of her country, was found busily engaged with her maidens in preparing her wool for the

loom. She was immediately pronounced by all the
best wife. If judged by this Roman standard, Mrs.
Pickens would be pronounced the best of wives; for
the woof and the distaff were never neglected by her.
She did not pretend to any of those accomplishments
which modern ladies are too apt to think the only
things necessary in life. She knew nothing of the
fashionable etiquette borrowed from the upstart manners in city life, and which has too much of late
pervaded the interior of our country, corrupting that
ancient and cordial hospitality which was once the
pride and glory of South Carolina. But in all the
genuine dignity that becomes a woman, in ease and
affability of deportment, in gentleness and kindness
of disposition and manners, she had few equals;
while in all the pure and high virtues which adorn
the female character, she had no superiors.*

* This sketch is communicated by a descendant of Mrs. Pickens.
It seems appropriate to close the picture of the war in the Catawba region with a notice of the wife of so eminent an officer.

XVIII.

SARAH BUCHANAN.*

The history of the trials and sufferings of the early settlers of Tennessee, in their more than ten years of border warfare with the Delawares, Shawnees, Creeks and Cherokees, lives only in the memory of a few of their descendants. Yet in the midst of those trials and sufferings were enacted deeds of heroism and chivalry which might well challenge a comparison with those of the Pequod war and King Philip, in the early settlement of New England, or with those of a later date, in which Daniel Boone and Simon Kenton obtained their legendary fame.

About the year 1772, a few adventurous spirits in Virginia and North Carolina, allured by the tales told by hunters and trappers of beautiful valleys and meandering streams beyond the Alleghany Mountains, sought new homes in the lovely valley of the Watauga,

* I am indebted for this sketch to Milton A. Haynes, Esq., of Tennessee, who obtained the materials from Mrs. S. V. Williams, the daughter of Mrs. Buchanan, and other members of the family. Some MS. papers have been consulted for the historical facts; see also Haywood's History of Tennessee from 1770 to 1796.

now the Holston River, in the region now called East
Tennessee.   One of these hardy pioneers was the father
of Sarah Buchanan, Capt. George Ridley.   In December, 1773, in one of the rough block-houses used for
the double purpose of fort and dwelling, was born the
subject of this memoir--one of the first, if not the
first-born daughter of Tennessee.   Her earliest im-
pressions were received amid scenes of strife, in which
the inhabitants of the Watauga were continually engaged with their Cherokee neighbors.

In the year 1779, several parties made preparation
to strike out still further into the wilderness, to establish
if possible a new colony west of the Cumberland
Mountains in the valley of Cumberland River.
Gen. James Robertson, of North Carolina, in concert
with Col. Donaldson, started from Watauga about the
middle of December, the former leading a land expedition, the object of which was to cross the mountains,
proceed to a place then known as the Big Salt Lick,
now Nashville, establish a fort, build houses and open
fields; the latter conducting a flotilla of rudely constructed flat-boats, which bearing the old men, women and
children, and the baggage of the pioneers, descended
the Holston, for the purpose of following Tennessee
River to some point beyond its pass through the
mountains.   The land party was to join the flotilla
somewhere on the great bend of the Tennessee, and
conduct them to their new home in the valley of the
Cumberland.   Of this party was the father of Sarah
Buchanan with his family.   It was a dark and fear-

ful voyage, that descent of the Watauga and Tennessee, through the dark and bloody grounds of the warlike Cherokees and Creeks. To daily attacks from the Indians, who from the shores of the narrow river fired on the voyagers as they descended the rapid current in their frail open boats, now and then boldly pushing out in their canoes to assault them, were added the dangers of the rapid and meandering stream, where sunken rocks and dangerous rapids threatened to engulf the frail barks in its boiling eddies. To aggravate these horrors, when the voyagers, their numbers reduced by disease and the murderous savages, reached the head of the Muscle-Shoals, no sign could be discovered of Gen. Robertson. Col. Donaldson and his party found themselves environed by dangers which might have unnerved the stoutest heart. An unexplored wilderness on either side, seven hundred miles of up-stream navigation behind them, with thousands of armed warriors ready to fall upon them, while in advance was heard the roar of the turbid waters as they dashed amongst the projecting rocks of the Muscle-Shoals. It was a fearful alternative, but death was certain in the rear or on either flank, and after weighing well all the dangers of his situation, Col. Donaldson determined to descend the Tennessee to its mouth and attempt to reach the Big Salt Spring by the ascent of the Cumberland. Many instances of female courage are mentioned in connexion with this voyage; but their history does not properly belong to this sketch.

On the 24th of April, 1780, four months and two

days after Col. Donaldson left Watauga, those who survived of this adventurous party of pioneer voyagers reached the spot where Nashville now stands. Here they met their friends who had succeeded in reaching the same place some weeks before. Interesting indeed was the reunion, but not without its sorrows; for many a father, mother, brother, sister, looked in vain for the pride of their hearts. The painter who loves to depict upon the canvas the varied and conflicting emotions of the human heart, might find in the landing of these wayworn voyagers at the French Lick a fit subject for his pencil. The parties of Donaldson and Robertson, and two small ones conducted by Capt. Rains and Major John Buchanan, father and son, having met here, constituted the entire colony of Cumberland Valley, numbering less than five hundred souls, of whom one hundred and fifty were all that were able to bear arms. It would be an agreeable task for the historian who loves to trace a state from its foundation, to follow the rise and progress of this infant colony step by step down to the present time; but this task belongs not to the humble biographer.

From the landing of these pilgrims at Nashville, they were regarded by the various tribes of Indians around them as intruders, and a war of extermination was waged upon them by the Creeks, Cherokees, and Shawnees for fifteen years. Never was the history of any colony so marked by bloody opposition. Its settlers thus by the force of circumstances driven at once into a state of war from the moment of their settlement, every man became an armed occupant, who held his life and his fort or block-house only by the strength of his arm.

The situation of these early pioneers was most adverse to the formation of polished and elegant society. Living in forts, each containing half a dozen or more families, they were compelled to work their small fields with guns by their sides. Books, schools, churches, academies, they had none. Toil and danger were their only school-masters, and stern necessity their only pastor and lawgiver. Capt. Ridley had established a small fort near Nashville, in which military rule was necessarily preserved, while various persons, pursuing the bent of their own interest established others, in which they rallied their friends and retainers to repel the assaults of Indian marauders. In the space of thirty miles around Nashville were a dozen such forts, and in and around these were all the inhabitants of the valley. Of necessity, social intercourse was kept up by occasional visits from one to another; but the road being often rendered dangerous by Indian ambuscades, it required more than a common share of bravery for small parties, especially of females, to venture, though the distance between the forts was only two or three miles.

On one occasion Sarah and a kinswoman named Susan Everett were returning home from a visit a mile or two distant, careless of danger, or not thinking of its presence. It was late in the evening, and they were riding along a path through the open woods, Miss

Everett in advance. Suddenly she stopped her horse, exclaiming, "Look, Sally, yonder are the red skins!" Not more than a hundred yards ahead was a party of Indians armed with rifles, directly in their path. There was no time for counsel, and retreat was impossible, as the Indians might easily intercept them before they could gain a fort in the rear. To reach their own block-house, four or five hundred yards distant, was their only hope of safety. Quick as thought Sarah whispered to her companion to follow and do as she did, and then instantly assuming the position of a man on horseback, in which she was imitated by her relative, she urged her horse into a headlong gallop. Waving their bonnets in the air, and yelling like madmen, they came furiously down upon the savages, who had not seen them, crying out as they came—"clear the track, you d—d red skins!" The part was so well acted, that the Indians took them for the head of a body of troopers, who were making a deadly charge upon them, and dodging out of the path, fled for very life—and so did Sally and Susan! Before the savages had recovered from their fright, the two girls were safe within the gates of the fort, trembling like frightened fawns at the narrow escape which they had made.

It was no doubt in consequence of this and similar instances of intrepid bearing and excellent horsemanship, that Sarah won the title of "the fast rider of Mill Creek." Soon after this period she won the heart and accepted the hand of the gallant Major John

Buchanan, and was married to him at the age of eighteen. He was a widower, over thirty years of age, and on account of his intrepidity in repelling Indian aggressions, had become the terror of the savages, as well as the pride of Cumberland Valley. His family originally emigrated from Lancaster, Pennsylvania. He had come with his father in 1779 from South Carolina, where he had been a soldier under Col. Pickens. In several battles with the Indians he had been greatly distinguished for personal bravery, as well as for tact and skill as a commander. It is said he was dressed in buck-skin from head to foot, equipped with rifle and powder horn, starting out on a scouting expedition, when he came to address his future bride, and asked her to become the commander of Buchanan's Station—a fort two miles east of her father's block-house. Sarah had scarcely been transferred to her new home, before it was her lot to see her husband's father shot down at the gates by the Indians. Not long afterwards her brother-in-law, Samuel Buchanan, also an inmate of the fort, having gone a few hundred yards from the station, was surprised by a party of Indians, who cut off his retreat, so that his only means of escape was to gain a bluff twenty-five or thirty feet high on the bank of Mill Creek, and precipitate himself from its summit. This he did; but in the fall dislocating his knee, was overtaken by the Indians, who killed and scalped him within gun shot of the fort. Such scenes of blood, brought so near to her door, were calculated to unnerve the tender spirit of woman ; but Mrs. Buchanan seemed to gather new energy and power from every trial and danger by which she was surrounded.

On another occasion, when her husband and all the men of the fort were absent, two celebrated horse-thieves who had taken refuge with the Indians, came and demanded of Mrs. Buchanan two of the Major's fine horses. Knowing their lawless character, she pretended acquiescence and went with them to the stable, but on arriving at the door she suddenly drew a large hunting-knife from under her apron, and assuming an attitude of defiance, declared that if either of them dared to enter the stable, she would instantly cut him down. Struck by her intrepid bearing, they fell back, and although they tried to overcome her resolution by threats and bravado, she maintained her ground, and the marauders were compelled to retire without the horses.

In 1792, the population of East Tennessee had increased to near ten thousand, and that of the Cumberland Valley, principally around Nashville, to seven thousand. Of these about one thousand were men of arms, many of whom had for twelve years battled with the Creeks and Cherokees. General Washington as President of the United States, had sent for and received at Philadelphia a large delegation of Indian chiefs, in order if possible to establish amicable relations between the settlers of Tennessee and the red men of the forest. In pursuance of his instructions, Gov. Blount had held a peace talk about the beginning of May, 1792, in which the Cherokees and Creeks pretended to be reconciled to their white brethren. Bloody-Fellow and John Watts, two Cherokee chiefs, were so earnest in such protestations that Gov. Blount called them the champions of peace, and President Washington conferred upon the first the title of General.

The report of the pacific disposition of the Indians soon spread over the Cumberland Valley, and although some of the old men shook their heads, as if distrusting the signs, yet the effect was to cause the mounted rangers, who had been for some time kept as a guard for the frontier, to be disbanded. The people watched less carefully, and ventured out more boldly and in smaller bodies, and nearly all began to rejoice at the return of the halcyon days of peace. But there was one to whom these signs of amity between the red men and the Anglo-Saxons of Cumberland Valley were any thing but pleasing. This was the Spanish Governor of Florida, at Pensacola. Distributing presents in arms and clothing to the Creeks and lower Cherokee towns, he invited and obtained a conference with the chiefs, in which he arrayed them all except Bloody Fellow against their neighbors. In consequence of this conference, about the middle of August John Watts assembled the principal warriors at Will's Town, and having hoisted the Spanish flag, appealed to the young warriors to join his standard, and march with him to exterminate the people of the Cumberland. Bloody-Fellow alone spoke against the war, and declared that he would have no part nor lot in it. Among the hostile chiefs were the Shawnee Chief, and the son of the White Owl, who boasted that they had killed three hundred white men, and could kill as many more. During this talk, Bloody-Fellow taunted Watts for wearing a medal given to him by General Washington, while he was waging war against the whites. At this Watts tore off his medal, threw it upon the ground, and stamped upon it.

The war party prevailing, Watts was chosen as the commander of about a thousand warriors, principally Creeks and Cherokees, including about one hundred Shawnees, commanded by the Shawnee Chief. It was resolved immediately to send two refugee Frenchmen, who lived with the Indians, to the Valley. They were bearers of letters from Watts to Gen. Robertson at Nashville, professing great friendship; and were to return in ten days and report the situation of the country. Arriving at Nashville, these Frenchmen immediately informed Gen. Robertson of all that had been done at the late conferences; adding that the Indians would attack the Cumberland settlements in ten days. This report caused great alarm. Five hundred mounted men were immediately assembled at Nashville, and scouts sent out in every direction, but especially towards the Tennessee River, to discover the advancing Indians whose invasion was thus foretold; yet each returning scout reported none.

In the meantime Watts and his confederates, ignorant of the treachery of their spies, were busily pre-

paring their warriors and supplies for the invasion.
They had despatched several written messages to Gov
Blount at Knoxville, in the name of Bloody-Fellow,
professing great friendship, and artfully detailing the
efforts of Watts to get up a war-party, which was represented as a failure. Gov. Blount and Gen. Robertson were thus deceived, although both had been warned
of nearly all that had happened. The hostile Indians
were assembled on the Tennessee River, below Chatta-
nooga, having organized and equipped an army to attack and destroy the settlements in Cumberland Valley,
while one of the young chiefs, who was to join the expedition, was at Knoxville, eating at Gov. Blount's
table, and receiving presents for the chiefs, as a reward for their friendship. So skilfully had these
adroit savages blended falsehood with truth, that
Blount sent an order to Gen. Robertson, at Nashville,
by express, about the 20th September, directing him
to disband his troops, as the Indians were all peaceably disposed. On the same day the Indians, having
waited in vain two weeks for the return of their French
spies, crossed the Tennessee River. It seemed as if
the fate of Cumberland Valley was to be decided by a
mere chance. Gen. Robertson, knowing the lawless
character of the semi-barbarous Frenchmen who had
alarmed him with news of the intended invasion, and
had kept the troops two weeks beyond the longest period fixed, wholly disbelieved their tales, and looked
upon them only as rogues who sought, under the

alarm which they had created, to cover a retreat with stolen horses.

In this state of affairs, Gov. Blount's orders came; and yielding alike to his own convictions of duty and the orders of his governor, on the 28th Sept. Robertson disbanded the five hundred militia who had been assembled to repel the invasion. Every man sought his own home in one of the twenty or thirty stations scattered over Davidson and Sumner Counties; some rejoicing at the prospect of a respite from "war's rude alarums," while not a few hastened quickly to their families, feeling a presentiment that some dreadful calamity was about to descend upon the Valley. At this very time a murderous army of Indian warriors were within thirty miles of Buchanan's station, and not a company of armed men remained west of the Cumberland mountains. A few men had thought it blindness to disperse the soldiery at such a crisis, and among these was Major John Buchanan. His station was four miles east of Nashville, on the farther side of Mill Creek, being the outpost toward the Indian Nation, and necessarily exposed to the first assault. Having no power to alter the orders of Gen. Robertson or Gov. Blount, he yet felt that the very state of affairs which he deplored, imposed upon him a double responsibility. Having about a dozen men living in his station, he quietly prevailed on half a dozen young men on whose courage he could depend, to pass a few days with him. Yet, though uneasy at his exposed condition, he dared not breathe his fears; for the first

14*

sign of alarm on his part would have been a signal
for the departure of half his little garrison, consisting
of nineteen men, a few women and slaves, whose natural instinct would lead them to seek safety in some
fort less exposed, and more in the rear. He spoke of
his fears to but one—his wife; for he knew her firmness, and was not afraid to trust her discretion. Having put all the arms in order, and prepared the doors
and gates to resist the expected assault, he calmly, but
anxiously awaited the result.

On Sunday night, about the hour of midnight, while
the moon was shining brilliantly, the Indian army under Watts and the Shawnee, advancing in silence, surrounded Buchanan's station. In order to effect an
entrance into the fort by a coup de main, they sent runners to frighten and drive in the horses and cattle.
This was done, and the animals came dashing furiously towards the fort; but the garrison, wrapped in
slumber, heeded them not. The watchman, John
McCrory at this instant discovering the savages advancing within fifty yards of the gates, fired upon
them. In an instant the mingled yells of the savage
columns, the crack of their rifles, and the clatter of
their hatchets, as they attempted to cut down the gate,
told the little squad of nineteen men and seven women
that the fearful war-cloud which had been rising so
long was about to burst upon their devoted heads!

Aroused suddenly from deep slumber by the terrible
warwhoop, every man and woman felt the horror of
their situation. The first impulse with some was to

surrender, and it is related of one woman that she instantly gathered her five children and attempted to go with them to the gate to yield themselves to the Indians. Mrs. Buchanan seized her by the shoulder, and asked her where she was going.

" To surrender myself and children to the Indians—if I don't they'll kill us any how," exclaimed the terrified woman. " Come back," said Mrs. Buchanan, " and let us all fight and die together." An old man who waked up as it were in a dream, seemed paralyzed, and exclaimed in a plaintive voice—" Oh, we shall all be murdered !"

" Get up then and go to fighting !" exclaimed Mrs. Buchanan ; " I'd be ashamed to sit crouched up there when any one else is fighting. Better die nobly than live shamefully !"

In the meantime Major Buchanan had arranged his men in the block-houses so as to rake the Indians by a flank fire, and was pouring a galling fire into the head of the assaulting column. Yet nothing dismayed, the daring foe crowded against the gates, their blows falling faster and heavier, while now and then they attempted to scale the pickets. At length, unable to do this or to force open the well-barred and ponderous gate, the bold warriors advanced to the block-houses, and standing before them, pointed their guns in at the port holes ; both sides sometimes at the same instant firing through the same opening. It was the policy of Major Buchanan to impress upon them the idea that the fort contained a large garrison. To do this it was necessary for his men to fire their guns often, and occasionally in volleys. At this crisis the whisper went round—"All is lost. Our bullets are out!" But there were guardian angels whom these brave men knew not of. Scarcely had the words been spoken, when Mrs. Buchanan passed around with an apronful of bullets, which she and Nancy Mulherrin, the Major's sister, had moulded during the fight out of her plates and spoons. At the same time she gave to each of the tired soldiers some brandy which she carried in a pewter basin. During the contest they had thus moulded three hundred bullets. Not without their fun were these hardy men in this hour of peril. In order to keep up a show of good spirits, they frequently cried out to the Indians, "Shoot bullets, you squaws! Why don't you put powder in your guns?" This was understood, for Watts and many others spoke very good English, and they replied by daring them to come out and fight like men. In the midst of these banterings, Mrs. Buchanan discovered a large blunderbuss which had been standing in a corner during the fight and had not been discharged, and gave it to an Irishman named O'Connor to fire off. In telling the story afterwards the Irishman said : "An' she gave me the wide-mouthed fusee and bade me to shoot that at the blasted creeturs, and Jimmy O'Connor he took the fusee, and he pulled the trigger when the rest fired, for three or four times, and loaded her again every time, and so ye see, yer honor, when I pulled the trigger again, the fusee went off, it did, and Jimmy O'Connor went under the bed." This unequal contest lasted for four long hours, and when the first blush of morning began to appear in the East, most of the chiefs were killed or wounded. The boastful Shawnee was transfixed in death, leaning against the gate which he had so valorously assaulted ; the White Owl's son and Unacate, or the White-man-killer, were mortally wounded, and the blood-thirsty John Watts was borne off on a litter, shot through both legs.

During this protracted fight Mrs. Buchanan aided the defenders by words and deeds, as if life or death depended upon the efforts which she was then making. She knew, and all knew, that if the assault could be repelled for four hours, relief would come from the neighboring posts. Foiled, discouraged, their leaders disabled, this formidable army of savage warriors precipitately retreated towards their country, bearing off most of their wounded, yet leaving many dead upon the field. This was the first formidable invasion of Cumberland Valley, and its tide was rolled back as much by the presence of mind and heroic firmness of Sarah Buchanan and Nancy Mulherrin, as by the rifles of their husbands and friends. The fame of this gallant defence went abroad, and the young wife of Major Buchanan was celebrated as the greatest heroine of the West. From 1780 to 1796, there was not a year in which her family had not been exposed to peril, in which of course she was a partaker.

In person Mrs. Buchanan was remarkably well formed, possessing great strength and activity. Her mind was active, her disposition sprightly, and al-

though one of the most fearless of women, her modesty
was such, that she seldom claimed that prominence
she deserved in the scenes described. Although she
never learned to read until after her marriage, she yet
found time, amidst the multifarious duties of her large
household, with no instructor but her husband, to
remedy the defects of her early education. She was
not a member of any church, but her conduct and conversation were always marked by unaffected respect
for religion and religious observances; she kept the
Sabbath and taught her children a regard for religious
duties. In some of the stories told of her youthful
exploits, she has been represented as an Amazon, fearing neither God nor man. Such, however, was not
her true character. Though born and reared in the
midst of a hardy frontier soldiery, she possessed a
native delicacy of mind, which always sought to soften
the asperities of life about her. When called upon, as
she often was, to detail the part she bore in " the times
that tried men's souls," she never failed to disclaim
any credit for herself, and always said that many
foolish stories had been told about her by gossipping
old ladies and garrulous old men, exhibiting her in a
character which she never displayed.

Mrs. Buchanan was the mother of thirteen children,
most of whom are yet living, and have acted their part
usefully and honorably in the affairs of life. She lived
to see also a number of her descendants—ending her
days at Buchanan's station, on the spot rendered
memorable by her intrepidity. Two gravestones on

the site of the old fort record the date of her death
Nov. 23d, 1831—and that of her husband, in 1832.

" Oh, Pilgrim Mothers! few the lyres
    Your praises to prolong;
Though fame embalms the pilgrim sires
    And trumpets them in song :—
Yet ye were to those hearts of oak
    The secret of their might;
Ye nerved the arm that hurled the stroke
    In labor or in fight.
Oh, Pilgrim Mothers! though ye lie
    Perchance in graves unknown,
A memory that cannot die
    Hath claimed you for its own."

XIX.

NANCY VAN ALSTINE.

NANCY, the daughter of Peter and Sarah Quack-inbush, was born in the vicinity of Canajoharie, about the year 1733. She was a descendant of one of the brothers Quackinbush who came from Holland some time in the seventeenth century, having purchased a tract of land, on which, as is supposed, a large portion of the business part of the city of New York was afterwards built. They were, however, deprived of their rights by some English adventurers whose shrewdness and knowledge of business enabled them to take advantage over the Hollanders, imperfectly acquainted with the language, and unaccustomed to business transactions. The title was found invalid, and the new settlers in New Amsterdam were compelled to resign their possessions to those who had no just claim upon them. After this the brothers separated, and the grandfather of the subject of this sketch removed to the wild but inviting region of the Mohawk Valley. Peter, the father of Nancy, was among the early settlers of this country, and did not escape the difficulties many of them were forced to encounter.

He pursued for many years the business of a trader with the Indians, and spent a large portion of his time in travelling to and from the aboriginal settlements— his line lying chiefly upon the Susquehanna. The Indians placed the utmost confidence in him, frequently applying to him for advice, and as it occasionally happened that he had a full supply of goods when other traders had disposed of all their stock—for he made a practice of providing himself with an extra supply of the most saleable articles—they imagined that he was peculiarly under the care of the good Spirit who gives abundance to those whom he favors. Their kind feelings towards their white brother who "always had something left for the Indian," disposed them to bestow on him some particular mark of regard, and after a meeting for consultation, they decided on giving him the name of *Otsego*, and christening the lake for him. The ceremony of naming both him and the lake was performed by pouring liquor upon his head as he knelt on the ground, a portion being afterwards poured into the water. It is probable that few are acquainted with this origin of the name of Otsego Lake; but the family tradition has been confirmed by the recollection of some who witnessed the occurrence.

The mother of Nancy belonged to the Wimple family, considered one of the most respectable Dutch families in the valley. The Brouks and Gansevorts were near connections, and for some time the daughter was an inmate of the family of John Brouk of Coxsackie, re-

ceiving while there all the instruction in the English
language she ever had. Schools were not common
among the Dutch settlers, on account of the distance
between their farms, and Nancy never enjoyed any
advantages of this kind; but possessing superior mental powers and a disposition to study, she acquired
what in those days was considered a good education.
She read Dutch with ease, and had her memory well
stored from the best of all books—the Bible. The
customs were simple among that primitive people, and
they had a natural dislike to innovation. English was
not spoken ; a Yankee was suspected and shunned, and
a general prejudice existed against strangers, which it
required a long acquaintance to overcome. In business
transactions, as verbal agreements were always held
sacred, and no writing was necessary among them, it
was but natural that they should dread being outwit-
ted by more crafty dealers. The women were of the
class described by a distinguished chronicler, who
" stayed at home, read the Bible, and wore pockets."
Miss Quackinbush was distinguished among them, not
only for remarkable beauty of person and a fine voice,
but for her intellectual superiority, her more cultivated
manners, and a certain pride of bearing common in
some of the more ancient families. She had the influence over all with whom she associated inseparable
from a strong cast of character, was looked up to by
all her youthful companions, and so generally admired
that she was for some years known through that region
as the belle of the Mohawk. To these attractive qual-

ities she joined great industry and ingenuity ; she gained the prize among all competitors in the knitting, spinning and weaving match, and moreover was perfect mistress of needlework in all its branches—an accomplishment of importance at that time, when all articles of male and female attire were of domestic manufacture. At the age of eighteen she was married to Martin J. Van Alstine, also a descendant of a Holland family who had settled in the valley of the Mohawk. It was probably an ancestor of his who was murdered by the Indians early in the French war—Eva, the wife of Jacob Van Alstine, who then resided in the valley.* While riding along the road, her little daughter in her arms, she stopped to open a swing gate, and was fired on and killed by the savages. The child was taken to Canada, returned after long captivity, and in 1843 was living, at the age of near a century, with her nephew, J. C. Van Alstine, at Auriesville, Montgomery County.

The young people, immediately on their marriage, removed to the Van Alstine family mansion in the neighborhood, which was their home for nearly thirty years. Their residence here was marked by much suffering from Indian hostility. The valley of the Mohawk, one of the richest agricultural districts in the country, and one of the most populous at the period of the Revolution, presented an inviting aspect to the plundering savages and the refugees who shared a precarious subsistence among them and in the wilds of

* History of Schoharie County.

Canada. Scarcely any other section was so frequently
invaded and overrun by the enemy. Month after
month during seven years its villages and settlements
were attacked or destroyed by the relentless foe, its
farms laid waste, and the inhabitants driven from their
homes, or killed and captured. The settlers in this
particular neighborhood were few, and were obliged to
band together for their mutual defence, forming parties
to serve as scouts through the country, for the travel-
ler from place to place was liable to attack in the
lonely forest, or to a bullet or arrow aimed from the
covert of rocks or bushes. Mr. Van Alstine was thus
compelled to be much from his home, where none but
females were left in his absence, except an old domestic, whose extreme fear of the savages prevented his
being of any service. Mrs. Van Alstine, however, had
a knowledge of the Indian language, which gave her
great advantages, and her natural sagacity and tact,
with her intimate acquaintance with their peculiarities
of character, enabled her on several occasions to protect her family. Her hospitality was always freely
extended to all who claimed it, although the entertainment of a savage was often not without risk from
others who might be lurking close at hand. Many
incidents might be mentioned illustrating the dangers
of this border life, but it is necessary to record merely
a few which concern the family of our heroine, and
exhibit her courage and firmness.

During the summer of 1778, the Indians and tories
being sufficiently employed in the destruction of

Wyoming and Cherry Valley, the Mohawk Valley remained unmolested, with the exception of a descent upon the German Flats. In the spring of 1779, Gen. Clinton moved up the Mohawk and encamped at Canajoharie, and in this summer also little mischief was done. But in the spring of 1780 the Indians again appeared, infuriated at the destruction of their villages, and eager to wreak vengeance on the unoffending inhabitants. In August, Brant, with an army of Indians and loyalists, burst upon the defenceless settlements, plundering, killing, burning and desolating the country; while in the autumn Sir John Johnson ravaged the north side of the river. Thus the destruction of the Mohawk settlements was almost complete, and if here and there a small one escaped, it afforded but a temporary shelter, being likely to be destroyed by the next storm that should sweep over the land.

While the enemy, stationed at Johnstown, were laying waste the country, parties continually going about to murder the inhabitants and burn their dwellings, the neighborhood in which Mrs. Van Alstine lived remained in comparative quiet, though the settlers trembled as each sun arose, lest his setting beams should fall on their ruined homes. Most of the men were absent, and when at length intelligence came that the destroyers were approaching, the people were almost distracted with terror. Mrs. Van Alstine called her neighbors together, endeavored to calm their fears, and advised them to make immediate arrangements for removing to an island belonging to her hus-

band near the opposite side of the river. She knew
that the spoilers would be in too great haste to make
any attempt to cross, and thought if some articles
were removed, they might be induced to suppose the
inhabitants gone to a greater distance. The seven
families in the neighborhood were in a few hours upon
the island, having taken with them many things necessary for their comfort during a short stay. Mrs. Van
Alstine remained herself to the last, then crossed in
the boat, helping to draw it far up on the beach.
Scarcely had they secreted themselves before they
heard the dreaded warwhoop, and descried the Indians
in the distance. It was not long before one and
another saw the homes they loved in flames. When
the savages came to Van Alstine's house, they were
about to fire that also, but the chief, interfering,
informed them that Sir John would not be pleased if
that house were burned—the owner having extended
civilities to the baronet before the commencement of
hostilities. " Let the old wolf keep his den," he said,
and the house was left unmolested. The talking of
the Indians could be distinctly heard from the island,
and Mrs. Van Alstine rejoiced that she was thus enabled
to give shelter to the houseless families who had fled
with her. The fugitives, however, did not deem it
prudent to leave their place of concealment for several
days, the smoke seen in different directions too plainly
indicating that the work of devastation was going on.
It was this company of Indians that destroyed the
family of Mr. Fonda.

The destitute families remained at Van Alstine's house till it was deemed prudent to rebuild their homes. Later in the following autumn an incident occurred which brought much trouble upon them. Three men from the neighborhood of Canajoharie, who had deserted the whig cause and joined the British, came back from Canada as spies, and were detected and apprehended. Their execution followed; two were shot, and one, a bold, adventurous fellow, named Harry Harr, was hung in Mr. Van Alstine's orchard. Their prolonged absence causing some uneasiness to their friends in Canada, some Indians were sent to reconnoitre and learn something of them. It happened that they arrived on the day of Harr's execution, which they witnessed from a neighboring hill. They returned immediately with the information, and a party was despatched—it is said by Brant—to revenge the death of the spies upon the inhabitants. Their continued shouts of "Aha, Harry Harr!" while engaged in pillaging and destroying, showed that such was their purpose. In their progress of devastation, they came to the house of Van Alstine, where no preparations had been made for defence, the family not expecting an attack, or not being aware of the near approach of the enemy. Mrs. Van Alstine was personally acquainted with Brant, and it may have been owing to this circumstance that the members of the family were not killed or carried away as prisoners. The Indians came upon them by surprise, entered the house without ceremony, and plundered and destroyed

everything in their way. Mrs. Van Alstine saw her
most valued articles, brought from Holland, broken
one after another, till the house was strewed with
fragments. As they passed a large mirror without
demolishing it, she hoped it might be saved; but presently two of the savages led in a colt from the stable,
and the glass being laid in the hall, compelled the
animal to walk over it. The beds which they could
not carry away they ripped open, shaking out the
feathers and taking the ticks with them. They also
took all the clothing. One young Indian, attracted
by the brilliancy of a pair of inlaid buckles on the
shoes of the aged grandmother seated in the corner,
rudely snatched them from her feet, tore off the
buckles, and flung the shoes in her face. Another
took her shawl from her neck, threatening to kill her
if resistance were offered. The eldest daughter, seeing
a young savage carrying off a basket containing a hat
and cap her father had brought her from Philadelphia,
and which she highly prized, followed him, snatched
her basket, and after a struggle succeeded in pushing
him down. She then fled to a pile of hemp and hid
herself, throwing the basket into it as far as she could.
The other Indians gathered round, and as the young
one rose clapped their hands, shouting " Brave girl!"
while he skulked away to escape their derision. During the struggle Mrs. Van Alstine had called to her
daughter to give up the contest; but she insisted that
her basket should not be taken. Having gone through
the house, the intruders went up to the kitchen cham-

ber, where a quantity of cream in large jars had been brought from the dairy, and threw the jars down stairs, covering the floor with their contents. They then broke the window glass throughout the house, and unsatisfied with the plunder they had collected, bribed a man servant by the promise of his clothes and a portion of the booty to show them where some articles had been hastily secreted. Mrs. Van Alstine had just finished cutting out winter clothing for her family— which consisted of her mother-in-law, her husband and twelve children, with two black servants—and had stowed it away in barrels. The servant treacherously disclosed the hiding place, and the clothing was soon added to the rest of the booty. Mrs. Van Alstine reproached the man for his perfidy, which she assured him would be punished, not rewarded by the savages, and her words were verified ; for after they had forced him to assist in securing their plunder, they bound him and put him in one of their wagons, telling him his treachery to the palefaces deserved no better treatment. The provisions having been carried away, the family subsisted on corn, which they pounded and made into cakes. They felt much the want of clothing, and Mrs. Van Alstine gathered the silk of milkweed, of which, mixed with flax, she spun and wove garments. The inclement season was now approaching, and they suffered severely from the want of window glass, as well as their bedding, woolen clothes, and the various articles, including cooking utensils, taken from them. Mrs. Van Alstine's most arduous labors could do little towards providing for so many destitute persons ; their neighbors were in no condition to help them, the roads were almost impassable, besides being infested by Indians, and their finest horses had been taken.   In this deplorable situation, she proposed to her husband to join with others who had been robbed in like manner, and make an attempt to recover their property from the Indian castle, eighteen or twenty miles distant, where it had been carried.   But the idea of such an enterprise against an enemy superior in numbers and well prepared for defence, was soon abandoned.   As the cold became more intolerable and the necessity for doing something more urgent, Mrs. Van Alstine, unable to witness longer the sufferings of those dependent on her, resolved to venture herself on the expedition.   Her husband and children endeavored to dissuade her, but firm for their sake, she left home, accompanied by her son, about sixteen years of age. The snow was deep and the roads in a wretched condition, yet she persevered through all difficulties, and by good fortune arrived at the castle at a time when the Indians were all absent on a hunting excursion, the women and children only being left at home.   She went to the principal house, where she supposed the most valuable articles must have been deposited, and on entering was met by the old squaw who had the superintendence, who demanded what she wanted.   She asked for food ; the squaw hesitated ; but on her visitor saying she had never turned an Indian away hungry, sullenly commenced preparations for a meal.

The matron saw ner bright copper tea-kettle, with other cooking utensils, brought forth for use. While the squaw was gone for water, she began a search for her property, and finding several articles gave them to her son to put into the sleigh. When the squaw, returning, asked by whose order she was taking those things, Mrs. Van Alstine replied, that they belonged to her; and seeing that the woman was not disposed to give them up peaceably, took from her pocket-book a paper, and handed it to the squaw, who she knew could not read. The woman asked whose name was affixed to the supposed order, and being told it was that of "Yankee Peter"—a man who had great influence among the savages, dared not refuse submission. By this stratagem Mrs. Van Alstine secured, without opposition, all the articles she could find belonging to her, and put them into the sleigh. She then asked where the horses were kept. The squaw refused to show her, but she went to the stable, and there found those belonging to her husband, in fine order—for the savages were careful of their best horses. The animals recognised their mistress, and greeted her by a simultaneous neighing. She bade her son cut the halters, and finding themselves at liberty they bounded off and went homeward at full speed. The mother and son now drove back as fast as possible, for she knew their fate would be sealed if the Indïans should return. They reached home late in the evening, and passed a sleepless night, dreading instant pursuit and a night attack from the irritated savages.

Soon after daylight the alarm was given that the
Indians were within view, and coming towards the
house, painted and in their war costume, and armed
with tomahawks and rifles.   Mr. Van Alstine saw no
course to escape their vengeance but to give up whatever they wished to take back ; but his intrepid wife
was determined on an effort, at least, to retain her
property.   As they came near she begged her husband
not to show himself—for she knew they would immediately fall upon him—but to leave the matter in her
hands.   The intruders took their course first to the
stable, and bidding all the rest remain within doors,
the matron went out alone, followed to the door by
her family, weeping and entreating her not to expose
herself.   Going to the stable, she inquired in the
Indian language what the men wanted.   The reply
was " our horses."   She said boldly—" They are ours ;
you came and took them without right ; they are ours,
and we mean to keep them."   The chief now came
forward threateningly, and approached the door.   Mrs.
Van Alstine placed herself against it, telling him she
would not give up the animals they had raised and were
attached to.   He succeeded in pulling her from the
door, and drew out the plug that fastened it, which
she snatched from his hand, pushing him away.   He
then stepped back and presented his rifle, threatening
to shoot her if she did not move ; but she kept her
position, opening her neckhandkerchief and bidding
him shoot if he dared.   It might be that the Indian
feared punishment from his allies for any such act of

violence, or that he was moved with admiration of her intrepidity ; he hesitated, looked at her for a moment, and then slowly dropped his gun, uttering in his native language expressions implying his conviction that the evil one must help her, and saying to his companions that she was a brave woman and they would not molest her. Giving a shout, by way of expressing their approbation, they departed from the premises. On their way they called at the house of Col. Frey, and related their adventure, saying that the white woman's courage had saved her and her property, and were there fifty such brave women as the wife of ' Big Tree,' the Indians would never have troubled the inhabitants of the Mohawk valley. She experienced afterwards the good effects of the impression made at this time.

It is probable some of these Indians were imbued with a portion of the humane disposition shown by Brant in his clemency to the conquered. In the spring a party of Canadian savages were sent to scour the country and collect provisions. Their orders were to take no prisoners, but they captured all who came in their way, murdering those who offered resistance. One of Mrs. Van Alstine's brothers was taken prisoner, and having repeatedly attempted to effect his escape, was sentenced by their council to be burned. He was bound to the stake and the faggots were piled around him, when an aged Indian who had not been present at the council interfered to save him, pleading that he had never harmed them, and had a wife and children, and pledging himself for his safe-keeping.   The victim was accordingly released, and being told to thank each Indian for his life, did so, and though he might have escaped afterwards, remained with his captors till the journey was accomplished—determined to fulfil the pledge given by his preserver.

It was not long after this occurrence that several Indians came upon some children left in the field while the men went to dinner, and took them prisoners, tomahawking a young man who rushed from an adjoining field to their assistance.   Two of these—six and eight years of age—were Mrs. Van Alstine's children.   The savages passed on towards the Susquehanna, plundering and destroying as they went. They were three weeks upon the journey, and the poor little captives suffered much from hunger and exposure to the night air, being in a deplorable condition by the time they returned to Canada.   On their arrival, according to custom, each prisoner was required to run the gauntlet, two Indian boys being stationed on either side, armed with clubs and sticks to beat him as he ran.   The eldest was cruelly bruised, and when the younger, pale and exhausted, was led forward, a squaw of the tribe, taking pity on the helpless child, said she would go in his place, or if that could not be permitted, would carry him.   She accordingly took him in her arms, and wrapping her blanket around him, got through with some severe blows.   The children were then washed and clothed by order of the chief, and supper was given them.   Their uncle—then also a prisoner—heard of the arrival of children from the Mohawk, and was permitted to visit them. The little creatures were sleeping soundly when aroused by a familiar voice, and joyfully exclaiming, " Uncle Quackinbush !" were clasped in his arms. In the following spring the captives were ransomed, and returned home in fine spirits.

In the year 1785 Mr. Van Alstine removed his family to the banks of the Susquehanna, eighteen miles below Cooperstown, where he had purchased a tract of land previous to the war. The comfortable house erected here had been burned by the Indians, and another had to be built before the owners could remove to their new home. There were at that time only three white families in the neighborhood, but several Indians were living near. Many incidents that occurred during their residence here are preserved in the family tradition, and illustrate life in the woods at this period. On one occasion an Indian whom Mr. Van Alstine had offended, came to his house with the intention of revenging himself. He was not at home, and the men were out at work, but his wife and family were within when the intruder entered. Mrs. Van Alstine saw his purpose in his countenance. When she inquired his business, he pointed to his rifle, saying, he meant " to show Big Tree which was the best man." She well knew that if her husband presented himself he would probably fall a victim unless she could reconcile the difficulty. With this view she commenced a conversation upon subjects in which she knew the savage would take an interest, and admiring his dress, asked permission to examine his rifle, which, after praising, she set down, and while managing to fix his attention on something else, poured water into the barrel. She then gave him back the weapon, and assuming a more earnest manner, spoke to him of the Good Spirit, his kindness to men, and their duty to be kind to each other. By her admirable tact she so far succeeded in pacifying him, that when her husband returned he was ready to extend to him the hand of reconciliation and fellowship. He partook of some refreshment, and before leaving informed them that one of their neighbors had lent him the rifle for his deadly purpose. They had for some time suspected this neighbor, who had coveted a piece of their land, of unkind feelings towards them because he could not obtain it, yet could scarcely believe him so depraved. The Indian, to confirm his story, offered to accompany Mrs. Van Alstine to the man's house, and although it was evening she went with him, made him repeat what he had said, and so convinced her neighbor of the wickedness of his conduct, that he was ever afterwards one of their best friends. Thus by her prudence and address she preserved, in all probability, the lives of her husband and family; for she learned afterwards that a number of savages had been concealed near, to rush upon them in case of danger to their companion.

At another time a young Indian came in and asked the loan of a drawing knife. As soon as he had it in his hand he walked up to the table, on which there was a loaf of bread, and unceremoniously cut several

slices from it. One of Mrs. Van Alstine's sons had a
deerskin in his hand, and indignantly struck the savage
with it. He turned and darted out of the door, giving
a loud whoop as he fled. The mother just then came
in, and hearing what had passed expressed her sorrow
and fears that there would be trouble, for she knew
the Indian character too well to suppose they would
allow the matter to rest. Her apprehensions were
soon realized by the approach of a party of savages,
headed by the brother of the youth who had been
struck. He entered alone, and inquired for the boy
who had given the blow. Mr. Van Alstine, starting
up in surprise, asked impatiently, "What the devilish
Indian wanted?" The savage, understanding the
expression applied to his appearance to be anything
but complimentary, uttered a sharp cry, and raising
his rifle, aimed at Van Alstine's breast. His wife
sprang forward in time to throw up the weapon, the
contents of which were discharged into the wall, and
pushing out the Indian, who stood just at the entrance,
she quickly closed the door. He was much enraged,
but she at length succeeded in persuading him to listen
to a calm account of the matter, and asked why the
quarrel of two lads should break their friendship. She
finally invited him to come in and settle the difficulty
in an amicable way. To his objection that they had
no rum, she answered—"But we have tea;" and at
length the party was called in, and a speech made by
the leader in favor of the "white squaw," after which
the tea was passed round. The Indian then took the

15*

grounds, and emptying them into a hole made in the ashes, declared that the enmity was buried forever. After this, whenever the family was molested, the ready tact of Mrs. Van Alstine, and her acquaintance with Indian nature, enabled her to prevent any serious difficulty. They had few advantages for religious worship, but whenever the weather would permit, the neighbors assembled at Van Alstine's house to hear the word preached. His wife, by her influence over the Indians, persuaded many of them to attend, and would interpret to them what was said by the minister. Often their rude hearts were touched, and they would weep bitterly while she went over the affecting narrative of our Redeemer's life and death, and explained the truths of the Gospel. Much good did she in this way, and in after years many a savage converted to Christianity blessed her as his benefactress.

Mrs. Van Alstine was the mother of fifteen children, having passed her fiftieth year when the youngest was born. Twelve of these were sons, and all lived to become useful members of society. Most of them are now deceased, but two of her daughters survive—Mrs. Wimple, who resides at Syracuse, and the youngest child, Mrs. Ellen McKnight, now living at Havana, in the State of New York. Mrs. Van Alstine died in 1831 at Nampsville, Madison County, having retained her mental faculties to the last. According to a wish expressed on her death-bed, her Dutch books were buried with her. She feared they might be regarded as rubbish, and knew not how much her descendants would have valued them.

XX.

ELEANOR WILSON.*

THE wives and mothers of Mechlenburg County, North Carolina, were called upon to bear more than their share of the toils and dangers of the Revolution. Among these was Eleanor, wife of Robert Wilson, of Steel Creek—a woman of singular energy of mind and devoted to the American cause. Her husband with three brothers and other kinsmen, settled in Mechlenburg about 1760, having removed from the Colony of Pennsylvania. These brothers were Scotch Presbyterians, arrayed by religious and natural prejudice, as well as early education, against tyranny in every form. At the time of the Declaration of Mechlenburg, May 20th, 1775, one of them—Zaccheus Wilson—representing all his kinsmen, signed that declaration, pledging himself and his extensive family connexions to its maintenance. This bold act of a county meeting was immediately published in the royal journals in Charleston, and copies were sent

---

* MILTON A. HAYNES, Esq., to whom I am indebted for this sketch, obtained the materials from different members of the family.

to the King of Great Britain by his Colonial governors, with letters representing the movement of Charlotte-town as a dangerous one, to be immediately suppressed. In this crisis there were not wanting citizens who shook their heads, and curling their lips in scorn, characterized the actors in this opening scene of the bloody drama of the Revolution as madmen, rebels and traitors, who were kindly admonished to look out for their necks. From the first to the last, Mrs. Wilson espoused the cause of liberty, exulting when-ever its defenders gained any triumph.

Animated by her enthusiasm, her husband and sons entered warmly into the contest. Her sons Robert and Joseph, in service under Col. Lytle with Lincoln at Charleston, were taken prisoners at the surrender of that city, but having given their parole, were allowed to return home. On the way one of their companions became so weak as to be unable to travel. Determined not to desert him, they carried him on their shoulders alternately, till he was able to go on as before. They had scarcely reached home when the British General issued his proclamation declaring the country subdued—withdrawing the paroles, and requir-ing every able-bodied militia man to join his standard. Refusing to fight against their country, and being no longer, as they believed, bound by their paroles, they immediately repaired to the standard of Sumter, and were with him in several battles. In that of Hanging Rock, Capt. David Reid, one of their kinsmen, was mortally wounded, and in great agony called for water, which young Robert brought in his hat. In the same action Joseph, a little in advance, was suddenly assaulted by a tory—a powerful man—whom he knew, but killed him after a severe struggle, carrying off his rifle, which is now in the possession of his son, David Wilson, of Maine County, Tennessee.

The elder Robert Wilson and his son John, having collected a supply of provisions and forage for Sumter's corps from the neighborhood of Steel Creek, were hastening to meet them at Fishing Creek, and arrived a short time after the surprise. The consequence was the capture of the two Wilsons, and the seizure of the supplies. The prisoners were hurried to the rear, after having been brutally threatened with hanging on the nearest tree, and by a forced march reached Camden next day, where they were added to a crowd of honorable captives, such as Andrew Jackson, Col. Isaacs, Gen. Rutherford and others, more than a hundred of whom were crowded into one jail.

Meanwhile Cornwallis, leaving Rawdon at Camden, advanced his army to rebellious Charlotte, to forage upon its farms and plantations, and to punish its inhabitants. Many scenes of rapine, house burnings and plunderings might be detailed in connection with his five weeks stay hereabouts. The whig inhabitants of Mechlenburg, Rowan and Iredell came up manfully to sustain their country in this crisis. Although a few of the wealthier ones hastened to Charlotte, and claimed and obtained the protection of the British General, these were in a proportion of scarcely one in a hundred. Unable to keep the open field, the republicans under Davie, Sumter, Davidson, Dickey, Brevard, Hall and Irwin, scattered through the forests and swamps, constantly falling in small parties upon the insolent dragoons of Tarleton and other troops sent out as scouts and on foraging excursions. It was a kind of guerilla warfare, boldly waged by the patriots of Mechlenburg, and feared by the British soldier, who always hated to be shot at from the thickets while he was quietly getting forage for his horse. Having already been rendered uneasy by the bold manner in which the rebels pounced upon his regulars, occasionally driving them within sight of his camp, Cornwallis, when he heard of the defeat of Ferguson at King's Mountain by a formidable body of patriots, fearing that so bold a party might attack his rear at Camden, concentrated his army, drew in his foraging parties, and on the 14th of October began his retrograde march towards Winnsboro'. During this march the British army halted for the night at Wilson's plantation near Steel Creek. The British General, with his staff, and the redoubtable Tarleton occupied the house of Mrs. Wilson, requiring her to provide for them as though they had been her friends. Although the soldiers were seizing every article in the way of provision on the place, Mrs. Wilson acted her part so well that the General decided in his own mind that she at least was not unfriendly to the Royal cause. Having drawn out in the conversation the principal items of her family history, and finding that he was occupying the house of a noted whig leader, the brother and father of more than a dozen active soldiers, who was, moreover, his prisoner in Camden jail, Lord Cornwallis artfully attempted to enlist her in the King's cause. He began by observing that he deeply regretted being compelled to wage a war in which many of its worst calamities fell upon woman. He was constrained to believe that in this instance, as well as many others, many worthy men who were at heart good subjects, had been seduced from their duty by the delusive promises of aspiring and unprincipled leaders. " Madam," he continued, " your husband and your son are my prisoners; the fortune of war may soon place others of your sons— perhaps all your kinsmen, in my power. Your sons are young, aspiring and brave. In a good cause, fighting for a generous and powerful king, such as George III., they might hope for rank, honor and wealth. If you could but induce your husband and sons to leave the rebels, and take up arms for their lawful sovereign, I would almost pledge myself that they shall have rank and consideration in the British army. If you, madam, will pledge yourself to induce them to do so, I will immediately order their discharge."

To this artful appeal Mrs. Wilson replied, that her husband and children were indeed dear to her, and that she had felt, as a woman must, the trials and troubles which the war had brought upon her. She felt proud of her sons, and would do anything she thought right to advance their real and permanent in-

terests ; but in this instance they had embarked in
the holy cause of liberty—had fought and struggled
for it five years, never faltering for a moment, while
others had fled from the contest and yielded up their
hopes at the first obstacle. " I have seven sons who
are now, or have been, bearing arms," she continued,
" —indeed my seventh son, Zaccheus, who is only
fifteen years old, I yesterday assisted to get ready to
go and join his brothers in Sumter's army. Now,
sooner than see one of my family turn back from the
glorious enterprise, I would take these boys, (pointing
to three or four small sons) and with them would myself enlist under Sumter's standard, and show my
husband and sons how to fight, and if necessary, to
die for their country !"

" Ah ! General !" interrupted the cold-hearted
Tarleton—" I think you've got into a hornet's nest !
Never mind, when we get to Camden, I'll take
good care that old Robin Wilson never comes back
again !"

On the next day's march a party of scouts captured
Zaccheus, who was found on the flank of the British
army with his gun, endeavoring to diminish the number of His Majesty's forces. He was immediately
taken to the head of the column, and catechised by
Cornwallis, who took the boy along with him on the
march, telling him he must act as his guide to the
Catawba, and show him the best ford. Arriving at
the river, the head of the army entered at the point
designated by the lad, but the soldiers had scarcely

gone half across before they found themselves in deep water—and drawn by a rapid current down the stream. Believing that this boy, on whom he had relied to show him the best ford, had purposely brought him to a deep one in order to embarrass his march, the General drew his sword, and flourishing it over him, swore he would cut his head off for his treachery. Zaccheus replied that he had the power to do so, as he had no arms, and was his prisoner; "but, sir," said he, "don't you think it would be a cowardly act for you to strike an unarmed boy with your sword? If I had but the half of your weapon, it would not be so cowardly; but then you know it would not be so safe!"

Struck by the lad's cool courage, the General became calmer—told him he was a fine fellow, and that he would not hurt a hair of his head. Having discovered that the ford was shallow enough by bearing up stream, the British army crossed over it safely and proceeded towards Winnsboro'. On this march Cornwallis dismissed Zaccheus, telling him to go home and take care of his mother, and to tell her to keep her boys at home. After he reached Winnsboro', Cornwallis despatched an order to Rawdon, to send Robin Wilson and his son John, with several others, to Charleston, carefully guarded. Accordingly in November, about the 20th, Wilson, his son and ten others set off under the escort of an officer and fifteen or twenty men. Below Camden, on the Charleston route, parties of British soldiers and trains of wagons were continually passing, so that the officer had no fear of the Americans, and never dreamed of the prisoners attempting an escape. Wilson formed plans and arranged everything several times, but owing to the presence of large parties of the enemy they could not be executed. At length, being near Fort Watson, they encamped before night, the prisoners being placed in the yard, and the guard in the portico and house. A sentinel was posted in the portico over the stacks of arms, and all hands went to providing for their evening repast.

Having bribed a soldier to buy some whiskey, for it had been a rainy day, the prisoners pretended to drink freely, and some of them seemingly more intoxicated than the rest, insisted upon treating the sentinel. Wilson followed him as if to prevent him from giving him the whiskey, it being a breach of military order. Watching a favorable opportunity he seized the sentinel's musket, and the drunken man, suddenly become sober, seized the sentinel. At this signal the prisoners rushed to the guns in the portico, while the guard, taking the alarm, rushed out of the house. In the scramble for arms the prisoners succeeded—drove the soldiers into the house at the point of the bayonet and the whole guard surrendered at discretion. Unable to take off their prisoners, Wilson made them all hold up their right hands and swear never again to bear arms against the cause of " liberty and the Continental Congress," and then told them that they might go to Charleston on parole ; but if he ever found a single mother's son of them in arms again, he would " hang him up to a tree like a dog!"

Scarcely were they rid of their prisoners before a party of British dragoons came in sight. As the only means of escape, they separated by twos and took to the woods. Some of them reached Marion's camp at Snow Island, and Wilson, with two or three others, arrived safely at Mechlenburg—a distance of over two hundred miles, through a country overrun by British troops.

The term of the services and imprisonment of the family, was not less than two years each, being in all near sixteen years. Several of the sons were officers; Aaron was a lieutenant at the battle of Stono, in June, 1779, and Robert was a captain in the Indian war towards the close of the Revolution.

Mrs. Wilson was the mother of eleven sons. She and her husband lived to a good old age at Steel Creek, and died about the same time, in 1810. It is estimated that their descendants, living in Tennessee and the West, will now number seven or eight hundred. About 1792, or in the two years following, Joseph, John, James, Aaron, Robert, Samuel, Zaccheus, Josiah, Moses and Thomas Wilson, removed with their families to the Cumberland Valley, near Bledsoe's Lick, and not long afterwards located themselves near Harpeth Lick, in the southeast corner of Williamson County. They lived to advanced ages, and with the exception of Josiah and Moses, have some time since been gathered to their fathers. They were generally inflexible Presbyterians—stern republicans and great haters of tories. Robert, the first man who crossed the Cumberland mountains with a wagon, married Jane, the daughter of William and Ellen McDowell, York District, South Carolina. The McDowells were of a brave family. Charles, Joseph and William were in the battle of King's Mountain; Ellen and her daughter Jane heard the firing from their house, and the mother immediately went to the scene of strife, where she remained several days, nursing and attending to the wounded soldiers. She was a woman of remarkable courage and energy. A party of marauders having taken some of her property during the absence of her husband, she followed them, assembling her friends on the way, and soon recovered the booty. Her husband had manufactured powder in a cave near his dwelling; but as he could not burn the charcoal there without detection, she burnt it by small quantities in her fire-place, and carried it to him. In this way part of the powder used at King's Mountain was procured. Young Robert Wilson was with McDowell at Hanging Rock, and it was in reward for his gallant conduct that he gave him his daughter Jane. In 1832, the mother, then near ninety years of age, removed to Clay County, Missouri. Her daughter, Mrs. Wilson, has lived at Harpeth Lick since 1819, when her husband died. She is eighty-seven years old, yet retains her mental faculties in remarkable vigor. She has one hundred and forty descendants, of whom the Rev. T. W. Haynes, of Charleston, S. C. is one, and also the writer of this notice.

XXI.

MARGARET MONCRIEFFE

THIS remarkable woman—whose history presents a warning, not an example—has been made the subject of a fanciful tale by W. L. Stone, entitled "The Language of Flowers"; and the story of her concealing the plan of an American fort in a painting of a group of flowers, is well known. Some of her early adventures are picturesque enough to need no aid from fiction. One of these has been furnished by a lady to whom the particulars were related by a relative who was an inmate of the family in which Miss Moncrieffe was for some time domesticated. The account is therefore reliable, confirmed as it is by a letter from an English officer, although the heroine herself makes no mention of the matter in her memoirs; an omission rather singular, since it may be supposed she would not neglect the opportunity afforded her for an appeal to British sympathy by the narration of an arrest and imprisonment suffered in the royal cause. According to this account :—Some time in the early part of the war, a gentleman named Wood was residing about seven miles from Peekskill. He was of American

birth, and a zealous whig ; but had married an English-
woman, whose associations and tastes were not such
as disposed her to be content with a republican state
of society.   Three grown daughters, and a son about
twelve years old, completed the family circle, which
was enlarged by the arrival of Miss Margaret Moncrieffe, a relation of Mrs. Wood, who came up from
New York to pay a visit, accompanied by her maid-
servant.   She was the daughter of Major Moncrieffe of
the British engineers, brigade-major to Lord Cornwallis.
There is an apparent inconsistency between Miss
Moncrieffe's own account of herself, with respect to her
age, and that of the lady who remembered her.   She
thought her at that time about twenty ; while the
autobiography states that she had not completed her
fifteenth year at the time of her marriage.   Perhaps
it suited her to represent herself as several years
younger than she was in reality ; or her mature de-
velopment of mind and person may have given the
impression that she was older—even supposing her
own statement to be correct.   The lady's recollection
was distinct as to her appearance and manners ; she
described her as surpassingly beautiful ; the loveliest
creature she had ever beheld.   Her hair was dark and
glossy, her eyes full of witchery, and her complexion
of a dazzling fairness, with a rich tint of rose on her
cheek.   She was an accomplished musician,—sang
charmingly, and played often on a stringed instrument,
the name of which the narrator did not remember.
In drawing and painting she was also skilled, and often

exercised her acquirements for the amusement of her
friends.   It was a rare thing in those simple days to
see a young female thus accomplished, and still more
rare to find one possessing such intellectual gifts united
to the varied attainments bestowed by education.   The
care lavished on the decoration of her person called
forth remarks from the curious—the interest of a
female population in matters of dress being proverbial
in all times.   The luggage she brought from the city
was unusually large in quantity, and more than could
conveniently be placed in the room occupied by her
Her wardrobe, thus extensive, was not composed of
ordinary materials ; her dresses were very costly—
"plenty good enough for the King's daughter"—as the
current saying went, yet not esteemed too rich for
setting forth the charms of the fair wearer.

Like many women of that day, both English and
American, Miss Moncrieffe was a capital equestrian.
Almost every day she rode out on horseback, sometimes alone, and sometimes with young Wood as an
escort.   She could manage the most spirited horse as
well as a rider on the course ; and the roads along the
river, and over the wooded hills in the vicinity, offered
a pleasant field for her favorite exercise.   The riding
habit she was accustomed to wear on these excursions
was the subject of much comment among the country
people.   They censured the eccentric girl for her defiance of " public opinion," accusing her of exhibiting
herself in " men's clothes."   To give some idea of the
equestrian style of that period it may be well to give

the description of this habit. The material was
of deep blue cloth. A very long skirt was set upon
a sort of coat or jacket, fitting close to the figure, and
edged with narrow gold lace. This coat was worn open
in front, and displayed a buff vest fashioned exactly
like a man's waistcoat, and decorated with plain but
brilliant buttons of the finest gold. The upper portion
of this vest stood open, exhibiting an immaculate shirt
bosom with neatly plaited ruffles, and a white lawn
neckhandkerchief, the ends of which were long and
garnished with lace. The hat was of white beaver,
three-cornered, and adorned with a rosette in front.
Small heed paid the fair horsewoman to the opinions
of the neighborhood, or to the circumstance that every
one who chanced to meet her enquired who it was that
wore a dress so conspicuous. She had probably no
unwillingness to become celebrated, confident in her
power of charming all whom curiosity might attract to
seek her acquaintance. The result might have been
anticipated; numbers heard of and were ardently desirous of knowing the beautiful and spirited girl, and
Mrs. Wood's house was thronged with company during
her stay. Among the visitors who came from far and
near to pay their respects, were generally a number of
young officers of the American army. It will not be
thought surprising that most of these speedily became
enslaved to the charms of Miss Moncrieffe, who de-
lighted in seeing how easily she could captivate, by
winning words and glances, the brave hearts that were
adamant to British allurements or threats. Her poli-

tical sentiments appear not to have been known. She
entered with apparently warm interest into the dis-
cussions she heard around the hearth and table of her
host, and pretended to sympathise with the feelings of
her admirers, expressing unbounded friendship for the
whig cause, and a generous indignation against the
oppressors of her native country. The young officers
who had been fascinated by her grace and beauty,
were enchanted to hear professions of patriotism from
such lips, and felt no restraint in conversing with her
upon the state and prospects of the country, the occurrences of the day, and the plans and movements by
which they expected to circumvent the enemy. Confi-
dential disclosures were made to her from time to time
by her visitors, and none imagined she could have
either inclination or opportunity to divulge the information she extracted, sometimes by teasing and per-
tinacious questioning.

One morning Miss Moncrieffe took her accustomed
ride, as she often preferred to do, without any companion. She had not rode far, when on passing a farm
house, the barking of a dog that suddenly sprang into
the road frightened her horse. The animal started
aside ; she was thrown to the ground, and so severely
stunned as to be entirely insensible. There were no
men about the house to render assistance ; but the women ran out, lifted her in their arms, carried her in and
laid her on the bed. While they were using all the
means in their power for her restoration, one of them
unbuttoned her vest to allow her to breathe more free-

ly. A letter dropped out, which was picked up and put on the table. It was not long before she began to recover consciousness; meanwhile the man who lived in the farm-house happened to come in, and was informed of the accident. In a few moments more Miss Moncrieffe was fully restored to her senses. Suddenly starting and seizing the open flaps of her vest, she sprang up, as if struck by a fearful thought. " Who unbuttoned my waistcoat? Where is the letter? Ah, I am lost—lost!" she exclaimed in tones that betrayed the utmost agitation and alarm. One of the women took up the letter, and was about to hand it to her quietly, when the man, suspecting from her strange behavior that something was wrong, sprang forward and seized it. Perceiving that the letter was directed to New York, he refused to give it up, though in extreme agitation she begged him to restore it; he felt convinced there was more in the affair than she was willing to admit, and her entreaties made him the more determined to have it sifted. There was no resource for the young lady, who found she had sustained no serious injury from her fall, but to adjust her dress and ride back to Mr. Wood's house. Fear of the consequences of detection now pointed out her course; no time was to be lost in returning to the city while she could do so with safety. She immediately commenced preparations by packing up her things. But before she could get ready to start, information of her proceedings had been carried to the proper quarter; a party of soldiers rode up and entered the house; the

officer announced to Miss Moncrieffe that she was their
prisoner, and she was conveyed under their escort
across the river to a public house, where a guard was
placed over her.

It was ascertained that the letter in question contained information respecting some intended movement
of the Continental forces.   It came out upon examination that the young lady had been in the habit regularly
of sending her British friends the information she
obtained from the young officers, who not suspecting
any sinister motive in the interest she evinced, confided
their plans to her.   When she wrote a letter, she concealed it beneath her vest, and in her solitary rides
contrived to drop the missive in a certain spot by the
road-side, previously agreed upon.   A man who waited,
hid among the bushes, came out directly, cautiously
picked up the letter, and conveyed it to another secret
agent some distance down the river, by whom it was
safely forwarded to its destination.   All this was
brought to light by the confession of the man himself.
He had a family in the neighborhood, and fearing discovery of his agency, judged it most prudent to throw
himself on the mercy of the Americans by a voluntary
confession, hoping to be let off as a reward for his
evidence against Miss Moncrieffe.   He was kept a long
time in custody, but there is no reason to believe he
ever received any other punishment.

The baggage of Miss Moncrieffe was examined, and
several papers relating to military affairs were found
in her trunks.   While she remained a prisoner, some

of the British officers appealed to the Americans in her behalf. Her countrymen were by no means disposed to deal harshly with a youthful female, especially one so beautiful, accomplished, and highly connected. Her trial was postponed from time to time; and it was finally decided to give her up to her friends. The crime for which a man would have suffered on the gibbet was pardoned to one of her sex and age, and she was escorted to a place agreed upon, adjoining the British lines, where she was delivered into the charge of those who undertook to conduct her in safety to her father. It was stipulated only that she should not again enter within the American lines.

The only notice of this occurrence in print which appears to be extant, is in a letter dated New York, August 17th, year not given, published in the " Universal Magazine" for February, 1781. It is as follows: " Without doubt it is generally known at home that Miss Moncrieffe, sister (daughter) to Major Moncrieffe of the Engineers, has been arrested by the rebels. She is still kept in durance at the house of one Elkins, in the region of Hudson's River, near to a place called Peakeskill. Information lately received from that point induces the belief that she is courteously treated, but is not permitted to go out of the house without the attendance of one of her keepers. The ridiculous charge whereon she was arrested does not deserve a minute's investigation, though we hear that Newman, the rebel lieutenant who was implicated with her, has been broken and sent home." At the end of the letter

Moncrieffe, demanding me, for he now considered me
as a prisoner."

The refusal to acquiesce in this demand she regarded
as proceeding from Washington's determination that
she should remain "a hostage for my father's good
behavior," or from a desire to win her father to the
American cause by influencing him through his
parental feelings. But the biographer of Burr sug-
gests a more probable theory for her detention and
change of residence. Burr lived at that time in Putnam's family, had ample opportunity to observe her
character, and could not but perceive that though
eccentric and volatile to indiscretion, she possessed
great tact and extraordinary mental powers. He came
to the conclusion that in spite of her youth, she was
extremely well calculated to play the spy, and might
even at that time be thus employed. His suspicions
were mentioned to Gen. Putnam, with a recommendation that she should be conveyed elsewhere as soon as
possible. In consequence of this she was removed to
Kingsbridge, where Gen. Mifflin commanded. Here,
she says, she was treated with the utmost tenderness;
the General's lady she describes as "a most accomplished, beautiful woman, a quakeress; and here my
heart received its first impression." The individual
for whom she acknowledges such unconquerable love
was undoubtedly Col. Burr, whose name, however, she
carefully avoids mentioning in her memoir. Her vows,
she avers, were plighted to him, and she communicated
his proposals by letter to Gen. Putnam, asserting her

determination to accept him for her husband. Putnam
in reply begged her to remember how obnoxious were
her lover's political opinions to her father, and that
" in his zeal for the cause of his country, he would
not hesitate to drench his sword in the blood of her
nearest relation, should he be opposed to him in battle."
The narrative continues—" Gen. Putnam, after this
discovery, appeared in all his visits to Kingsbridge
extremely reserved ; his eyes were constantly fixed on
me ; nor did he cease to make me the object of his
concern to Congress ; and after various applications,
he succeeded in obtaining leave for my departure ;
when, in order that I should go to Staten Island with
the respect due to my.sex and family, the barge
belonging to the Continental Congress was ordered,
with twelve oars, and a general officer together with
his suite was dispatched to see me safe across the bay
of New York. The day was so very tempestuous that
I was half drowned with the waves dashing against
me. When we came within hail of the Eagle man-
of-war, which was Lord Howe's ship, a flag of truce
was sent to meet us ; the officer dispatched on this
occasion was Lieut. Brown. Gen. Knox told him that
he had received orders to see me safe to head-quarters.
Lieut. Brown replied—' It was impossible, as no person from the enemy could approach nearer the English
fleet ;' but added, ' that if I would place myself under
his protection, he certainly would attend me thither.'
I then entered the barge."—" We first rowed along-
side the Eagle, and Mr. Brown afterwards conveyed

me to head-quarters.   When my name was announced,
the British Commander-in-Chief sent Col. Sheriff with
an invitation from Sir William Howe to dinner, which
was necessarily accepted.   When introduced, I cannot
describe the emotion I felt, so sudden was the transi-
tion in a few hours."—"It was some relief to be placed
at table next the wife of Major Montresor, who had
known me from my infancy.   Owing to this circumstance I recovered a degree of confidence ; but being
unfortunately asked, agreeably to military etiquette, for
a toast, I gave 'Gen. Putnam.'   Col. Sheriff said, in
a low voice, 'You must not give him here ;' when Sir
William Howe complaisantly replied—'Oh, by all
means ; if he be the lady's sweetheart, I can have no
objection to drink his health.'   This involved me in a
new dilemma—I wished myself a thousand miles
distant—and to divert the attention of the company,
I gave to the General a letter that I had been commissioned to deliver from Gen. Putnam.   He then
informed me that my father was with Lord Percy,
and obligingly said 'that a carriage should be provided
to convey me to him ;' gallantly adding, 'amongst so
many gentlemen a beautiful young lady certainly could
not want a *cicisbeo* to conduct her.'   Knowing Col.
Small from childhood, I asked him to render me that
service, to which he consented.   Lord Percy then lived
nine miles distant from head-quarters, and when we
arrived at his house, my father was walking with him
on the lawn."   His lordship ordered one of his own
apartments to be prepared for the daughter, and she

remained here till the royal army quitted Staten Island.

As a proof of his esteem for Moncrieffe, Lord Cornwallis requested permission to adopt his eldest son, to whom he gave his name. The successes of the Royalists restored to him his property in New York. When they were once more established in their home, the Major invited the widow of a British paymaster-general to reside in his house, on account of his daughter, his public situation obliging him to be continually absent from home. It must have been somewhere about this period that the visit was paid to the house of Mr. Wood. Miss Moncrieffe, by her own account, had a great number of admirers, but thought not of marrying any of them, least of all the person who finally obtained her hand. Mr. Coghlan, an Irish officer, who fell in love with her at an assembly, gained her father's confidence, and the poor girl, besieged by her brother's entreaties, as well as the commands of her parent, yielded after an unsuccessful appeal to the generosity of her suitor. " In consequence," she says, " of these fatal persuasions, I was married to Mr. John Coghlan on the 28th February, 1777, at New York, by special license, granted by Sir William Tryon, who was then civil governor of the province." A dismal omen succeeded the wedding. Dr. Auchmuty, then Rector of Trinity Church, who performed the ceremony, on the same evening complained of indisposition, and three days afterwards was no more. It was the last marriage at which he officiated.

A few months after these ill-starred nuptials, Mr.

Coghlan was ordered with his regiment to Philadelphia,
whither he repaired, leaving his wife on Long Island
with her father. She was afterwards with her husband in New York, and in February, 1778, they sailed
for Cork. From this period the history of Mrs.
Coghlan offers only repulsive and painful details.
Being treated by her husband with neglect and brutality, she fled from him, performing a fatiguing
journey on foot, alone and utterly destitute ; and
probably urged at first by the desperation of misery,
plunged into the abyss of vice, from which there is no
recovery to the world's good opinion.

From 1780 to 1795, she made much noise in the
courtly and fashionable circles of Great Britain and
France, being a theme of conversation among lords,
dukes and members of parliament. Her extravagance
appears to have been excessive, and she was alternately
revelling in wealth and sunk in poverty, in all vicissitudes bearing within her the sting of self-reproach and
the sense of deserved degradation. Her father, from
whom her misconduct separated her, settled in New
York after the peace, where he died in 1791. Mrs.
Coghlan was relieved by her brother when suffering
from poverty and debt ; and two of her mother's sisters
pitied and aided her. Her memoir, in which the unhappy writer frequently appeals to the compassion of
her readers, was penned and published in the hope of
raising funds. She lived long, and died in obscurity,—
a sad example of the worthlessness of great endowments
when unaccompanied by the strength of principle which
can preserve amidst temptation.

XXII.

MARY MURRAY.

THE important service rendered to the American cause by Mrs. Murray, who saved Gen. Putnam and his troops from a surprise by the British, has been mentioned.* One of her descendants has communicated a few additional particulars concerning her. Her maiden name was Mary Lindley, and she was of a Quaker family. She was born in Pennsylvania, and resided in that colony for some years after her marriage to Robert Murray. Her eldest son, Lindley—so extensively known for his work on the grammar of the English language—was born at the town of Snetara, near Lancaster. In 1753 she removed with her family to the city of New York, where Murray became ere long one of the wealthiest and most respected merchants. He had joined the society of Friends from a persuasion of the truth of their creed and approbation of their customs, and though he was one of the four or five gentlemen who first rode in their coaches, he had a dislike to everything like luxury or ostentation, always terming his carriage his 'leather convenience.' Mrs. Murray is remembered in the family tradition as

* See Vol. II., p. 294.

a person of great dignity and stateliness of deportment. Her disposition is described by a tribute to her
memory in the memoirs of her son, Lindley Murray :
" My mother was a woman of amiable disposition, and
remarkable for mildness, humanity and liberality of
sentiment. She was indeed a faithful and affectionate
wife, a tender mother, and a kind mistress. I recollect
with emotions of affection and gratitude her unwearied
solicitude for my health and happiness."

About the year 1764 Mr. Murray removed his family
to England and remained there, on account of his
health, till 1775. He was descended of a noble Scottish family, whose younger branches, like many other
scions of nobility, had found themselves obliged, in
impoverished and troublous times, to seek their fortune
in the new world. It was natural, therefore, that he
should retain their prejudices, and he continued disposed to loyalism during his life, while his wife, as the
anecdote recorded of her testifies, joined with all her
sympathies in the contest for liberty in her native land.
The scene of her detention of the British officers was
' The Grange,' a small country seat at Murray Hill,
some time since removed to make way for the improvements of the growing city.

Mrs. Murray died Dec. 25th, 1782, (O. S.) Many
of her descendants are now living in New York: those
of her son, John Murray, and her daughters, Beulah—
Mrs. Martin Hoffman—and Susannah—the wife of a
British officer—Col. Gilbert Colden Willett, a grandson
of the English Lieutenant-Governor Colden.

A few miscellaneous notices will further illustrate our subject.

The distinguished author of "Revolutionary Incidents of Long Island" has kindly furnished me with the following anecdotes of its women:

Dr. Z. Platt, imprisoned in New York, was restored to liberty through the personal application of his daughter Dorothea to Sir Henry Clinton.—Col. Smith was thrown into the Provost, and his daughter Hannah, in her excursions and labors to procure his release, caught a cold that brought on incurable deafness.—When the house of Hendrick Onderdonk was robbed by British soldiers, his wife resolutely went after them about the house, telling them not to enter such a room, as her daughters slept there. They picked up some rolls of fine goods and hurried away, Mrs. Onderdonk following, and pulling away now and then a piece, till they were out of the house.—When a robber grasped the throat of Martin Schenck, to make him say where his treasures were hid, his wife caught up a bellows and so belabored the soldier that he let go his hold, and her husband escaped.—When a foraging officer demanded of the wife of Jotham Townsend the keys of her corn-crib, and on her refusal drew his sword, she flourished an oven peel—for she was preparing to bake bread—at the representative of the Crown, and asked scornfully if he drew his sword upon women. The disconcerted officer smiled and was soon out of sight.—When the house of John Burtis was attacked by a gang of whale-boatmen, his wife measured out and handed the charges of powder to those that fired, and the party was driven off.— "Molly Pitcher" was the name of the heroic wife of the gunner who was killed at the battle of Monmouth.*

When Gen. Woodhull was brought wounded and bleeding to Mrs. Hinchman's Inn, and laid on her best bed, he begged her not to leave him alone with his enemies. "Don't be uneasy, General," said the patriotic hostess, "I will not leave you ; I do not expect to go to bed to-night." The next morning Woodhull, with his head and arm bandaged, was taken westward, and left with a guard under the horse-shed at Howard's Inn. His wife went out, invited the weak and fainting General to partake of some refreshment, and gave him some bread and butter, with smoked beef and wine sangaree. When the guard asked if she had nothing for them, she replied, "I *give* to prisoners; you can *buy*." The wife of Gen. Woodhull was an intelligent and most excellent woman. Her maiden name was Ruth Floyd. She was the daughter of Nicoll Floyd, and the sister of Gen. William Floyd, one of the signers of the Declaration of Independence. She was born at Brookhaven, Long Island, in February, 1732, married Gen. Woodhull in 1761, and lived to about the age of ninety. Her only child who lived to maturity was Elizabeth, born in 1762. She married Henry Nicoll, and afterwards became the third wife of Gen. John Smith, U. S. Senator from Long Island. Her daughter Sarah married the Hon. John

* See vol. ii., p. 124.

L. Lawrence—The sister of Gen. Woodhull displayed patriotic zeal worthy of such a connection. Her name too was Ruth; she was the daughter of Nathaniel Woodhull, born at Brookhaven, December, 1740, and married in 1760 to Judge William Smith, of the Tangier family, who was also a native of Brookhaven. He was a member of the Provincial Convention which met in May, 1775, and of the Convention that framed the first State constitution in 1777; remaining in public service until the close of the war. When Major Benjamin Tallmadge was on his march across Long Island,* he met Mrs. Smith at a place called Middle Island, where she was then staying, her husband being in the Provincial Congress, and informed her that he was going to her house for the purpose of capturing the force in possession of Fort St. George. He added that he might be under the necessity of burning the dwelling-house, or otherwise destroying the buildings, to dislodge the occupants. Mrs. Smith received his intelligence in the same spirit exhibited by the heroine of Fort Motte. She begged Major Tallmadge to have no hesitation in destroying the property should he deem it necessary to do so; the loss being nothing in her estimation compared with success in the object of his mission.

A young girl named Lena Hewlett had received favorably the advances of a Highlander against the

* See Revol. Incidents of Long Island, vol. ii. p. 96, for the details of the march. The particulars respecting the wife and sister of Gen. Woodhull were communicated by Mr. Thompson.

wishes of her friends. She was missing when the soldiers marched away; her father pursued and overtook the regiment, and when at his request the men were drawn up in line, his daughter was discovered in the guise of a Highlander, being detected by the whiteness of her skin.——The wife of John Rapalje, a noted loyalist, who lived at Brooklyn Ferry when the American army first came there in the spring of 1776, persisted in drinking the prohibited tea, and took great satisfaction in showing to her friends a cannon ball lodged in the wall a few feet over her tea-table. It had been sent by some of the lawless whig militia into her house, at her usual tea time, as a token of their disapprobation. When General Washington, a few months later, was preparing with the utmost secresy for his famous night retreat from Long Island, Mrs. Rapalje suspected what was going on, and in revenge for the insult she had received, sent her negro slave to inform the British general of the intended movement. The negro fell in with a Hessian guard, who could not understand the importance of his errand, and detained him until the next morning. He arrived, in consequence, at headquarters just in time to be too late; the American army, with nearly all their baggage was safely across the river! On so trifling an incident, at that time, hung the safety of the army, and perhaps the destiny of the infant republic!

I am indebted also to H. Onderdonk, Jr. who has so ably depicted the condition of Long Island in his "Revolutionary Incidents," for the following anecdote:

The late Rev. Thomas Andros, of Berkley, Mass., when a young man enlisted on board a privateer, but was soon after captured by the British and put on board the Jersey prison ship. Thence he managed to escape in the fall of 1781, and wandered to the east end of Long Island. He gratefully acknowledges the protection he received from different females. "I came," he says in his Journal, "to a respectable dwelling-house and entered it. Among the inmates were a decent woman and a tailor. To the woman I expressed my want of something to nourish my feeble frame, telling her if she would give me a morsel, it would be a mere act of charity. She made no objection, asked no questions, but promptly furnished me with the dish of light food I desired. Expressing my obligations to her, I rose to depart. But going round through another room, she met me in the front entry, placed a hat on my head, put an apple pie in my hand, and said, "you will want this before you get through the woods." I opened my mouth to give vent to the grateful feelings with which my heart was filled. But she would not tarry to hear a word, and instantly vanished. The mystery of her conduct I suppose was this: she was satisfied that I had escaped from prison, and if she granted me any succor, knowing me to be such, it might cost her family the confiscation of their estate. She did not therefore wish to ask me any questions or hear me explain who I was in the hearing of the tailor, who might turn informer. This mark of kindness was more than I could well bear, and as I

went on the tears flowed copiously !   The recollection
of her humanity and pity revives in my breast even
now the same feeling of gratitude.

" Some time after, in Suffolk County, being repulsed
from one dwelling I entered another, and informed the
mistress of the house of my wants. By the cheerfulness and good-nature depicted in her countenance and
first movements, I knew my suit was granted, and I
had nothing more to say than to apprise her I was
penniless.   In a few moments she placed on the table
a bowl of bread and milk, a dried bluefish roasted,
and a mug of cider, and said, ' sit down and eat.'

"It was now growing dark, so I went but a short
distance further, entered a house and begged the privilege of lodging by the fire. My request was granted.
There was no one in the house but the man and his
wife. They appeared to be cordial friends to each
other—it was indeed one of the few happy matches.
Before it became late in the evening the man took his
Bible and read a chapter. He then arose and offered
up his grateful acknowledgments and supplications to
God through the Mediator. I now began to think I
had got into a safe and hospitable retreat. They had
before made many inquiries such as indicated that
they felt tenderly and took an interest in my welfare.
I now confessed my situation to them. All was
silence. It took some time to recover themselves from
a flood of tears. At last the kind woman said, ' Let
us go and bake his clothes.' No sooner said than the
man seized a brand of fire and threw it into the oven.

The woman provided a clean suit of clothes to supply the place of mine till they had purified them by fire. The work done, a clean bed was laid down on which I was to rest, and rest I did as in a new world ; for I had got rid of a swarm of cannibals who were eating me up alive ! In the morning I took my leave of this dear family with a gratitude that for fifty years has suffered no abatement."

Mary Knight, the sister of Gen. Isaac Worrell, died not long since in Philadelphia. A New Jersey journal dated July, 1849, pays her the following tribute :

"The deceased was one of those devoted women who aided to relieve the horrible sufferings of Washington's army at Valley Forge—cooking and carrying provisions to them alone, through the depth of winter, even passing through the outposts of the British army in the disguise of a market woman. And when Washington was compelled to retreat before a superior force, she concealed her brother, Gen. Worrell, (when the British set a price on his head,) in a cider hogshead in the cellar for three days, and fed him through the bunghole; the house being ransacked four different times by the troops in search of him, without success. She was over ninety years of age at the time of her death."

The ladies of Charleston dressed in *green*, wearing green feathers and ribbons, when the successes of Gen. Greene afforded the opportunity of retaliating the provocations of their invaders.

On the passage of the American army through Scotch

Plains, New Jersey, after the taking of Fort Washington, and severe losses, the soldiers were in great destitution, being without tents, blankets, shoes, or provisions, and under the utmost depression of spirits. The young wife of Mr. Osborn, who resided in the village, exerted herself with patriotic zeal to supply their wants, and gave for that purpose everything eatable or wearable that her house afforded. In the following year her husband went to join the continental army, and she encouraged him to encounter the hardships and dangers of military life. Her maiden name was Mary Darby, and she was married to John B. Osborn in 1774, at the age of nineteen. Intelligent, amiable, and pious, as well as patriotic, she lived with him seventy-four years, and died peacefully only two weeks before he was called from this world. Her brother, Hon. Ezra Darby, was a member of Congress.

The anecdote of Miss Susan Livingston's presence of mind in preserving her father's papers, when the house was entered by a party of British from New York, on the 28th February, 1779, has been mentioned.* But one or two circumstances connected with the occurrence, communicated by herself in after years to a friend, have never been made public. Governor Livingston, informed of the approaching invasion, left home at an early hour to escape capture, having confided his valuable papers to the care of his daughter. She had them placed in a carriage-box, and taken to a room in an upper story. When the enemy was advancing, Miss

* See Vol. II., p. 115.

Livingston stepped from the window of this apartment upon the roof of a piazza to look at the red-coats. A horseman in front of the detachment rode hastily up, and begged that she would retire; for there was danger of some of his soldiers mistaking her for a man and firing upon her. The young lady attempted to climb in at the window, but found it impracticable, though it had been easy enough to get out. The horseman, seeing her difficulty, instantly sprang from his horse, went into the house, and up stairs into the chamber, and leaping out upon the roof lifted Miss Livingston through the window. She asked to whom was she indebted for the courtesy;—the reply was, "Lord Cathcart." She then, with admirable presence of mind, appealed to him as a gentleman for the protection of the box, which, she said, contained her private property; promising, if that could be secured, to open her father's library to the soldiers. A guard was accordingly placed over the box.

Sarah, the sister of Governor William Livingston, and wife of Major General the Earl of Stirling, was the daughter of Philip Livingston, second proprietor of the Manor, and was born at his residence in Albany in 1722. She was brought up in the communion of the Dutch Reformed Church, of which she continued a devout member till her death at the age of eighty-two. Possessed naturally of a strong mind, she preserved her mental faculties unimpaired to the last, and found in her religious faith consolation for the reverses of fortune she had experienced in her later

years. Of the mere competency left for her support
she always appropriated a proportionally large part to
charitable uses.

Catherine, the daughter of Mr. Cooper, a member of
the Assembly from Rockland County, New York, was
the wife of Michael Cornelison, who was taken prisoner
in his own house at Nyack, carried to New York, and
thrown into the Provost, in 1777. His wife went
alone to the city to visit him and carry provisions,
leaving six children at home. She was detained there
four months, stayed at a cousin's house, and every day
took her husband his meals, which he shared with
other prisoners. Her daughter, with another female, a
relation and neighbor, came with their horses and
wagon loaded with provisions, which she sent over from
Hoboken, not venturing to cross. The same day the
mother procured a pass to leave the city, and returned
to Nyack, her husband being released on his parole.
The house of Mr. Miles, by Rockland Lake, was robbed,
his daughters turned out of bed, and the feather beds
set on fire. The money had been concealed in the
spring under the sand; but the horses were taken from
the stable, and the meat from the smoke-house. Miles
was conveyed in the night to Slaughter's landing, and
thence to the vessel.

Experience Bozarth lived in the southwest part of
Greene County, Pennsylvania. In March, 1779, two
or three families of the vicinity, afraid to remain at
home, were gathered at her house. One day some of
the children came in with news that the red men were

17

there.   One of the men in the house went to the door, received a shot, and fell back, while an Indian rushed over him into the house.   The other man engaged in a scuffle with the savage, and having thrown him on the bed, called for a knife.   Unable to find one, Mrs. Bozarth seized the axe, with which she killed the Indian.   A second now entered and shot the white man on the bed ; she turned and struck him several times ; he cried out, and other savages who were slaughtering the children, rushed to the house.   Mrs Bozarth clove the head of one as he appeared at the door ; another drew out the wounded savage, and then, assisted by the man who had been first shot, she fastened the door, and succeeded in keeping out the besiegers until a party arrived for their relief.

A young couple who lived in Union County in the same State, James Thompson and Margaret his wife, were captured by the Indians and taken up the Susquehanna.   James communicated to Margaret his intention to escape, and being urged to go without her, fled while they were gathering sticks for a fire, and found the canoe.   Margaret was taken to Montreal where she was given to an old squaw, and required to work for the maintenance of both.   Being advised to be lazy, and she would be sold to the whites, she pretended incorrigible stupidity, and when sent to hoe corn, would cut up the grain and dress some worthless weed.   Weary of teaching one so dull and awkward, the squaw at length sold her at Montreal to a cousin of hers, in whose family she lived till her return home after the war.

In a manuscript volume of poems by Elizabeth
Ferguson, copied by her for her friend Mrs. Richard
Stockton, is the following note : " When the writer was
in London, on the 18th of March, 1765, Dr. Fother-
gill, her friend and physician, called to pay her a visit.
' Betsy,' said he, ' yesterday you were made a slave
of.' ' No, sir, I am a slave to no man; my heart is
my own !' (for, girl-like, she thought some little rail-
lery on the subject of matrimony was meant.) He
replied—' No, no ; *heart* has nothing to do with it !
you and all your country people were yesterday enslaved ; for on that day the bill passed the House for
the American Stamp Act.' "

In a note to an ode to " The Litchfield Willow,"
Mrs. Ferguson states that a basket of willow osiers
brought from England, was kept in a damp cellar in
the house of Dr. Franklin, and that in the spring germs
shot out from the woven sprigs. Franklin gave it to
Mrs. Deborah Norris, who planted the sprigs in her
garden in Chestnut street. From this almost all the
willows in Pennsylvania are lineally descended.

THE following letter from MRS. WARREN to MRS.
ADAMS,—at Braintree, has never been given to the
public.

WATERTOWN, 17th April, 1776.

If my dear friend required only a very long letter to make it
agreeable, I could easily gratify her, but I know there must be
many more requisites to make it pleasing to her taste. If you
measure by lines I can at once comply :—if by sentiment, I fear I

shall fall short.   But as curiosity seems to be awake witn respect
to the company I keep, and the manner of spending my time, I
will endeavor to gratify you.   I arrived at my lodgings before
dinner the day I left you,—found an obliging family,—and in the
main, an agreeable set of lodgers.   The next morning I took a ride
to Cambridge, and waited on Mrs. Washington at eleven o'clock,
where I was received with that politeness and respect shown in a
first interview among the well bred, and with the ease and cordial-
ity of friendship of a much earlier date.   If you wish to hear more
of this lady's character, I will tell you.   I think the complacency
of her manners speaks at once the benevolence of her heart, and
her affability, candor and gentleness, qualify her to soften the
hours of private life, or to sweeten the cares of the Hero, and
smooth the rugged paths of War.   I did not dine with her, though
much urged.   She desired me to name an early hour in the morning, when she would send her chariot and accompany me to see
the deserted lines of the enemy, and the ruins of Charlestown.   A
melancholy sight!   The last evinces the barbarity of the foe, and
leaves a deep impression of the sufferings of that unhappy town.
Mr. Custis is the only son of the lady above described,—
a sensible, modest, agreeable young man.   His lady, a daughter of
Col. Calvert of Maryland, appears to be of an engaging disposition,
but of so extremely delicate a constitution, that it deprives her as
well as her friends of part of the pleasure which I am sure would
result from her conversation did she enjoy a more perfect share of
health.   She is pretty, genteel, easy and agreeable, but a kind of
languor about her prevents her being sociable as some ladies.   Yet
it is evident it is not owing to a want of that vivacity which renders youth agreeable, but to a want of health which a little clouds
her spirits.

    This family, which consists of about eight or nine, was prevented
dining with us the Tuesday following by an alarm from Newport,
but called and took leave of us the next day, when I own I felt
that kind of pain which arises from affection when the object of
esteem is separated perhaps forever.   After this I kept house a

week, amusing myself with my book, my work, and sometimes a letter to an absent friend.

My next visit was to Mrs. Morgan, but as you are acquainted with her I shall not be particular with regard to her person or manners. With the Doctor she dined with us last Saturday in company with Gen. Putnam's lady. She is what is commonly called a very good kind of woman, and commands esteem without the graces of politeness, the brilliancy of wit, or the merit of peculiar understanding above the rest of her sex, yet to be valued for an honest, unornamented, plain-hearted friendship, discovered in her deportment at the first acquaintance.

I have sent forward my letter to Mr. Adams, but I suppose I should have no answer unless stimulated by you ; therefore when you write again, you will not forget

Your affectionate MARCIA.

P. S.—I am very glad Colonel Quincy's family are well,—to whom my regards.

APPENDIX.

~~~~~~~~~~

SURPRISE OF GENERAL SUMTER.

AFTER the fall of Charleston, May 12th, 1780, the British overran the State, establishing posts at Georgetown, Camden, Rocky
Mount, Ninety-Six and Augusta, with others on the line from
those to Charleston, to serve as places for rest, or to keep open theiı
communication. The province was thus to all appearance conquered, the people generally having submitted; but a few resolute
spirits scattered over the country could not be subdued by the
severest measures. The 'outlyers' gathered under the command
of Pickens and Williams, did service, while in the upper country
the battles described were fought, and Marion harassed the enemy
from the recesses of his swamps. This was the state of the war
during May, June, July and August; the patriots endeavoring to
supply their lack of numbers by laborious service and rapid
marches. The news of the approach of Gates gave a new impulse
to their zeal, and brought recruits to the standard of Sumter, enabling him to commence an aggressive warfare. By August 13th
Gen. Gates rested at Clermont, thirteen miles from Camden. The
mistake he committed in sending four hundred regulars to aid
Sumter in the taking of Carey Fort, was productive of a train of
disasters. Had he, instead, ordered Sumter with his riflemen to
join him, he might have advanced on Camden, and fought the battle before aid arrived from Georgetown; or had he still delayed and

commenced the night march when he did, such an addition to his force, and of such men, might have turned his defeat into a splendid victory. Sumter's attack on the convoy and Carey Fort was crowned with success, and with his three hundred prisoners and forty-four wagons loaded with munitions of war, he hastened to join Gen. Gates, on the way receiving the news of his defeat. Encumbered with prisoners and baggage wagons—many of the regulars and country militia being on foot—his march on the retreat was slow, though kept up during the nights of the 16th and 17th August. It was not more than forty miles above Camden that he pitched his camp on the ill-fated morning of the 18th. (See KATHARINE STEEL, page 101.)

A strong guard could have disputed the passage from Fishing Creek up the valley, for half a mile from the place where the road passed on the ridge. The enemy could only have kept the road in file, and a few discharges of artillery would have demolished them. Had they taken the open field lying a few hundred yards from the camp, they must have passed in column over parts of the ground —the ravines narrowing one pass into a mere strip of land. Gen. Sumter had occupied this very ground on the night following his attack on Rocky Mount, having chosen it as a stronghold in expectation that the British, reinforced from Hanging Rock, would attack him. They did, in fact, march for this purpose, but the creek was too much swollen by the heavy rains to be crossed. This strong military position was guarded by the Catawba on the east, and the creek on the west, with ravines in front and rear, and on either hand a narrow strip of ground affording the only space for occupation; while at the place of encampment the ground was so spread out that he could have used his whole force, or if driven from that position could have taken a similar one at almost every hnndred yards distance on the ridge road for miles up the river. Its great natural advantages, therefore, justified his selection. When his army halted and struck their tents, the guard. being mounted, repaired to their posts, Major Crowford of the Waxhaws being the officer in command. The men in camp who had no duty to do, and were not too hungry, were soon fast asleep in their tents, having had no rest for two nights. Some were engaged in slaughtering beeves, and every few moments the crack of a rifle might be heard, while those awake would call out "Beef!" to one another. The sentinels posted down the road towards the ford of the creek, were marching up and down the line appointed, while others of the guard made for the river, desirous of a bath, as the weather was oppressively warm, and intending to be back at the station in time to take their turn. It is said that Major Crowford gave them permission to go; in any case, it is likely that these forest hunters, unaccustomed to military discipline, would have exercised their own discretion. Just as the army halted, Sarah Featherston, a young woman of a tory family, passed the road. Many of Sumter's men gave her the credit of having informed Tarleton of their situation, and some thought she had guided the British up the creek to what was called McKown's ford. This, however, she did not do, for they came up the road from the stream. The sentinels did their duty, delivering their fire in turn; but there was no guard to oppose the advance of the enemy. Each dragoon had a foot soldier mounted behind him, and these dismounted near the camp. In front, a short distance from the tents, Mrs. Pray, of Fairfield District, was seated upon a log feeding her two children. Her husband had gone into North Carolina after Gates' defeat, to join his force, and she having to leave home because her neighbors were loyalists, thought it safest to travel with the army. She had with her a negro boy, and two horses. As she sat upon the log, the British dragoons charged past her, and she would have been run over had not the log been large and furnished with branches, so that they were obliged to pass round it. She sat still, her eyes fixed on the terrible spectacle, and saw the defenceless or slumbering men shot down or cut to pieces, till she turned sickening from the scene of massacre. She saw a few of the regulars rallying behind the wagons, and returning the fire, and presently the bullets whistling near brought her to her recollection. Slipping down from the log, she pulled the children after her, and kept them close by her side till the firing ceased. When the British left the ground they took her servant and horses, and she was left with her children, alone with the dead and wounded. Next day she went with the little ones, who were crying for bread, to the house of Nat Rives, a tory living in the neighborhood, to beg some food for them. He coolly told her there was the peach orchard, and she might take what she wanted ; it was good enough for a rebel. This Rives afterwards accompanied Mrs. Johnston to the ground. When the British made their onset on the camp, Mrs. Pray's brother, John Starke, mounted his horse and made for the river. Plunging in, he reached an island, and spurred his horse from a high bank into deep water, rising in a few moments and effecting thus his escape to the opposite shore. The dragoons had pursued several of the men into the river, and were shooting and stabbing them. Starke, indignant at the sight, rose from his saddle to call the attention of the enemy, and made them a gesture of defiance. They were nearer than he had calculated, and their fire wounded him severely in the thigh. Some of the whigs who had escaped across the river procured a cart and carried him to his mother's house, where he lay helpless a long time, exposed to ill usage from the tories, whom in after life he could never forgive.

At the time of the surprise, it is supposed that between one and two hundred young men were bathing in the river. The dragoons, pursuing those who fled, came in among them, and an indiscriminate slaughter ensued. One William Reeves had his hair cut with a bullet, and was so stunned he would have been drowned, had not George Weir dragged him upon a rock. John Nesbit, Richard Wright, and Stephen White were making for the opposite bank, when White called out that he was shot. His companions dragged him to a rock, and then hid themselves till the British had left the river. When they came back they could find nothing of White, nor was it ever known what became of him. Many of the soldiers stood on the east bank of the river with no covering from the burning sun. Some of them went to the house of McMeans, whose wife gave them all her husband's clothes, and even exhausted her own wardrobe, so that more than one of the survivors of that disastrous day went home in petticoats! Ben Rowan, " the

17*

boxer of the army," heard the firing of the sentinels in the direction of the creek, but supposed it to be the killing of beeves a little further from the camp. The men had just brought in some of the meat, and were cooking before the tents. Ben, on his way to the next tent, had in his hand a piece of buckskin, of which he meant to have a pair of moccasins made for his blistered feet. He was startled by the enemy's broadside, and seeing in an instant that all was lost, ran for safety to the place where the three hundred prisoners were under guard. They were shouting for joy and flinging up their hats, when with his Herculean strength he forced himself a pathway through and over them. Just as he got through them, he saw a loose horse grazing, and flung himself upon the animal without saddle or bridle, slapping first with one hand and then with the other to direct his course. The horse went off at a brisk pace through the woods, and Ben made good his escape, to be an actor in every subsequent battle of the South. Joel McClemore, as he ran through the camp, picked up a rifle, not knowing if it were loaded or not; he was presently pursued by a dragoon, and after dodging from tree to tree for some time, got near the fence and succeeded in crossing it. It then occurred to him that the open field was not so safe as the woods in case of continued pursuit, and turning round, he said to the dragoon in his Virginia vernacular, "I'll eat fire if you cross that fence but I'll shoot you !" The dragoon put spurs to his horse, and as he leaped Joel drew trigger at a venture. The gun went off, and the man fell, while the horse leaped the fence. Joel lost no time in mounting, and thus escaped with a fine horse, holster and pistols. William Nesbit was in his tent asleep at the first alarm, but taking a horse from one of the wagons, escaped up the river, and was with the foremost at McDonald's ford. On another part of the field, the brave Capt. Pagan was rallying his men, among whom were the brothers Gill; he was shot and fell down the hill, while his company scattered. Archibald Gill, though but a stripling, showed so much indignation at what he witnessed at this defeat, that he was afterwards called " mad Archy." A few regulars who contended for a time behind the wagons against overpowering numbers, were forced to yield. Gen. Sumter was saved in the manner already mentioned. Near the spot where James Johnston was wounded after killing one of the British dragoons, John Reynolds shot another, and secured his horse. Everywhere up the river and creek the woods were full of men flying for their lives, while some who escaped butchery were driven back to the camp by the troopers.

The prisoners were placed under a strong guard, having to do without dinner as well as breakfast, with the prospect of the gibbet before many who had taken British protection, when they should reach Camden. Among these were Col. Thomas Taylor (distinguished afterwards in the war) and his brother, Capt. John Taylor. Tarleton remained master of the field of slaughter, for it could not be called a battle. By his order the wagons for which they could not find horses were collected together and consumed, with such articles as could not conveniently be taken away. Long before sunset the British commenced their return march towards Camden, leaving the dead unburied and the wounded who could not be removed, to perish. The march was continued several hours after dark. Thomas Taylor advised those among the prisoners who expected no mercy to effect their escape, and showed them how this was to be done. The guard could not long keep on the edge of the road, but must march in the front and rear of the prisoners; they were to get as near the centre as they could, drop off on the side, and lie down till they were passed. Many escaped in this way. It was near midnight when Tarleton halted to encamp on the bank of Wateree creek. While the men were reposing, Col. Taylor watched his opportunity, and proposed to his brother and a Mr. Lake to attempt escape by jumping down a steep bank fifteen or twenty feet in height, sliding gently into the water, and swimming down the stream. The feat was accomplished, though it was very dark and in leaping down they fell one over the other. Col. Taylor profited by the lesson of this surprise at the Fishdam, Nov. 7th, when the same corps of Tarleton, under Major Wemyss, attempted to steal a march on Sumter's army at dead of night, and were repulsed with such loss.

The scattered men of Sumter's army with one accord made their way to Charlotte, as if that destination had been previously appointed. Those who went home stayed only long enough to procure such articles of clothing as they had lost, and went on. They might be seen the next day upon every road leading towards Charlotte. Sumter himself went on the same night, and Capt. Steel, as already mentioned, returned to the battle ground.

Capt. Berry, who with some of his men had escaped after the defeat of Gen. Gates, on the night of the 17th wandered up the river as far as George Wade's house. Wade, who came home in the night, gave him three hundred pounds of flour for his soldiers, and informed him that Gen. Sumter would be on the other side of the river the next morning. Berry crossed the next day with his command, and had not been an hour in camp before the surprise took place, in which he was captured; thus leaving one disastrous field to meet misfortune in another.